The Bondage of the Will

The Bondage of the Will

Martin Luther

Sovereign Grace Publishers, Inc.
P.O. Box 4998
Lafayette, IN 47903

ISBN 1-878442-51-1

*Printed In the United States of America
By Lightning Source, Inc.*

CONTENTS

PREFACE

BY
THE TRANSLATOR

The Translator has long had it in meditation, to present the British Church with an English version of a choice Selection from the Works of that great Reformer, MARTIN LUTHER: and in November last, he issued Proposals for such a publication. He considers it however necessary to state, that this Treatise on the BONDAGE OF THE WILL, formed no part of his design when those Proposals were sent forth. But receiving, subsequently, an application from several Friends to undertake the present Translation, he was induced not only to accede to their request, but also to acquiesce in the propriety of their suggestion, that this work should precede those mentioned in the Proposals. The unqualified encomium bestowed upon it by a Divine so eminent as the late Reverend AUGUSTUS MONTAGUE TOPLADY, who considered it a masterpiece of polemical composition, had justly impressed the minds of those friends with a correct idea of the value of the Treatise; and it was their earnest desire that the plain sentiments and forcible arguments of Luther upon the important subject which it contained, should be presented to the Church, unembellished by any superfluous ornament, and unaltered from the original, except as to their appearance in an English version. In short, they wished to see a correct and faithful Translation of LUTHER ON THE BONDAGE OF THE WILL–*without note or comment!* In this wish, the Translator fully concurred: and having received and accepted the application, he sat down to the work immediately: which was, on Monday, December 23rd, 1822.

As it respects the character of the version itself–the Translator, after much consideration of the eminence of his Author as a standard authority in the Church of God, and the importance of deviating from the original text in any shape whatever, at last decided upon translating according to the following principle; to which, it is his design strictly to adhere in every future translation with which he may present the public–to deliver FAITHFULLY the MIND of LUTHER; retaining LITERALLY, as much of his own WORDING, PHRASEOLOGY, and EXPRESSION, as could be admitted into the English version. –With what degree of fidelity he has adhered to this principle in the present work, the public are left to decide.

The addition of the following few remarks shall suffice for observation.

1. The Work is translated from Melancthon's Edition, which he published immediately after Luther's death.

2. The division-heads of the Treatise, which are not distinctively expressed in the original, are so expressed in the Translation, to facilitate the Reader's view of the whole work and all its parts. The Heads are these–Introduction, Preface, Exordium, Discussion part the First, part the Second, part the Third, and Conclusion.

3. The subdividing Sections of the matter, which, in the original, are distinguished by a very large capital at the commencement, are, in the Translation, for typographical reasons, distinguished by Sections I, II, III, IV, &c.

4. The Quotations from the Diatribe, are, in the Translation, preceded and followed by a dash and inverted commas: but with this distinction–where Erasmus' own words are quoted in the original, the commas are double; but single, where the substance of his sentiments only is quoted. The reader will observe, however, that this distinction was not adopted till after the first three sheets were printed: which will account for all the quotations, in those sheets, being preceded and followed by double commas. Though it is presumed, there will be no difficulty in discovering which are Erasmus' own words, and which are his sentiments in substance only.

5. The portions of Scripture adduced by Luther, are, in some instances, translated from his own words, and not given according to our English version. This particular was

attended to, in those few places where Luther's reading varies a little from our version, as being more consistent with a correct Translation of the author, but not with any view to favour the introduction of inovated and diverse readings of the Word of God.

With these few and brief preliminary observations, the Translator presents this profound Treatise of the immortal Luther on the Bondage of the Will to the Public. And he trusts he has a sincere desire, that his own labour may prove to be, in every respect, a faithful Translation: and that the work itself may be found, under the Divine blessing, to be—an invaluable acquisition to the Church—"A sharp threshing instrument having teeth" for the exposure of subtlety and error—a banner in defence of the truth—and a means of edification and establishment to all those, who are willing to come to the light to have their deeds made manifest, and to be taught according to the oracles of God!

HENRY COLE.

London, March, 1823.

INTRODUCTION.

*Martin Luther, to the venerable D. Erasmus of
Rotterdam, wishing Grace and Peace in Christ.*

That I have been so long answering your DIATRIBE on FREE-WILL, venerable Erasmus, has happened contrary to the expectation of all, and contrary to my own custom also. For hitherto, I have not only appeared to embrace willingly opportunities of this kind for writing, but even to seek them of my own accord. Some one may, perhaps, wonder at this new and unusual thing, this forbearance or fear, in Luther, who could not be roused up by so many boasting taunts, and letters of adversaries, congratulating Erasmus on his victory, and singing to him the song of Triumph—What that Maccabee, that obstinate assertor, then, has at last found an Antagonist a match for him, against whom he dares not open his mouth!

But so far from accusing them, I myself openly concede to you, which I never did to any one before:—that you not only by far surpass me in the powers of eloquence, and in genius, (which we all concede to you as your desert, and the more so, as I am but a barbarian and do all things barbarously,) but that you have damped my spirit and impetus, and rendered me languid before the battle; and that by two means. First, by art: because, that is, you conduct this discussion with a most specious and uniform modesty; by which you have met and prevented me from being incensed against you. And next, because, on so great a subject, you say nothing but what has been said before: therefore, you say less about, and attribute more unto "Free-will," than the Sophists have hitherto said and attributed: (of which I shall speak more fully hereafter.) So that it seems even superfluous to reply to these your arguments, which have been indeed often refuted by me; but trodden down, and trampled under foot, by the incontrovertible Book of Philip Melancthon "Concerning Theological Questions:" a book, in my judgment, worthy not only of being immortalized, but of being included in the ecclesiastical canon: in comparison of which, your Book is, in my estimation, so mean and vile, that I greatly feel for you for having defiled your most beautiful and ingenious language with such vile trash; and I feel an indignation against the matter also, that such unworthy stuff should be borne about in ornaments of eloquence so rare; which is as if rubbish, or dung, should be carried in vessels of gold and silver. And this you yourself seem to have felt, who were so unwilling to undertake this work of writing; because your conscience told you, that you would of necessity have to try the point with all the powers of eloquence; and that, after all, you would not be able so to blind me by your colouring, but that I should, having torn off the deceptions of language, discover the real dregs beneath. For, although I am rude in speech, yet, by the grace of God, I am not rude in understanding. And, with Paul, I dare arrogate to myself understanding, and with confidence derogate it from you; although I willingly, and deservedly, arrogate eloquence and genius to you, and derogate it from myself.

Wherefore, I thought thus—If there be any who have not drank more deeply into, and more firmly held my doctrines, which are supported by such weighty Scriptures, than to be moved by these light and trivial arguments of Erasmus, though so highly ornamented, they are not worthy of being healed by my answer. Because, for such men, nothing could be spoken or written of enough, even though it should be in many thousands of volumes a thousand times repeated: for it is as if one should plough the seashore, and sow seed in the sand, or attempt to fill a cask, full of holes, with water. For, as to those who have drank into the teaching of the Spirit in my books, to them, enough and an abundance has been administered, and they at once contemn your writings. But, as to those who read without the Spirit, it is no wonder if they be driven to and fro, like a reed, with every wind. To such, God would not have said enough, even if all his creatures should be converted into tongues. Therefore it would, perhaps, have been wisdom, to have left these offended at your book, along with those who glory in you and decree to you the triumph.

Hence, it was not from a multitude of engagements, nor from the difficulty of the undertaking, nor from the greatness of your eloquence, nor from a fear of yourself; but from mere irksomeness, indignation, and contempt, or (so to speak) from my judgment of your Diatribe, that my impetus to answer you was damped. Not to observe, in the mean time, that, being ever like yourself, you take the most diligent care to be on every occasion slippery and pliant of speech; and while you wish to appear to assert nothing, and yet, at the same time, to assert something, more cautious than Ulysses, you seem to be steering your course between Scylla and Charybdis. To meet men of such a sort, what, I would ask, can be brought forward or composed, unless any one knew how to catch Proteus himself? But what I may be able to do in this matter, and what profit your art will be to you, I will, Christ cooperating with me, hereafter shew.

This my reply to you, therefore, is not wholly without cause. My brethren in Christ press me to it, setting before me the expectation of all; seeing that the authority of Erasmus is not to be despised, and the truth of the Christian doctrine is endangered in the hearts of many. And indeed, I felt a persuasion in my own mind, that my silence would not be altogether right, and that I was deceived by the prudence or malice of the flesh, and not sufficiently mindful of my office, in which I am a debtor, both to the wise and to the unwise; and especially, since I was called to it by the entreaties of so many brethren.

For although our cause is such, that it requires more than the external teacher, and, beside him that planteth and him that watereth outwardly, has need of the Spirit of God to give the increase, and, as a living Teacher, to teach us inwardly living things, (all which I was led to consider;) yet, since that Spirit is free, and bloweth, not where we will, but where He willeth, it was needful to observe that rule of Paul, "Be instant in season, and out of season." (2 Tim. iv. 2.) For we know not at what hour the Lord cometh. Be it, therefore, that those who have not yet felt the teaching of the Spirit in my writings, have been overthrown by that Diatribe—perhaps their hour was not yet come.

And who knows but that God may even condescend to visit you, my friend Erasmus, by me His poor weak vessel; and that I may (which from my heart I desire of the Father of mercies through Jesus Christ our Lord) come unto you by this Book in a happy hour, and gain over a dearest brother. For although you think and write wrong concerning "Free-will," yet no small thanks are due unto you from me, in that you have rendered my own sentiments far more strongly confirmed, from my seeing the cause of "Free-will" handled by all the powers of such and so great talents, and so far from being bettered, left worse than it was before: which leaves an evident proof, that "Free-will" is a downright lie; and that, like the woman in the gospel, the more it is taken in hand by physicians, the worse it is made. Therefore the greater thanks will be rendered to you by me, if you by me gain more information, as I have gained by you more confirmation. But each is the gift of God, and not the work of our own endeavours. Wherefore, prayer must be made unto God, that He would open the mouth in me, and the heart in you and in all; that He would be the Teacher in the midst of us, who may in us speak and hear.

But from you, my friend Erasmus, suffer me to obtain the grant of this request; that, as I in these matters bear with your ignorance, so you in return, would bear with my want of eloquent utterance. God giveth not all things to each, nor can we each do all things. Or, as Paul saith, "there are diversities of gifts, but the same Spirit." (1 Cor. xii. 4.) It remains, therefore, that these gifts render a mutual service; that the one, with his gift, sustain the burden and what is lacking in the other; so shall we fulfil the law of Christ (Gal. vi. 2.)

ERASMUS' PREFACE REVIEWED.

Sect. I.—First of all, I would just touch upon some of the heads of your PREFACE; in which, you somewhat disparage our cause and adorn your own. In the first place, I would notice your censuring in me, in all your former books, an obstinacy of assertion; and saying, in this book,—"that you are so far from delighting in assertions, that you would rather at once go over to the sentiments of the sceptics, if the inviolable authority of the Holy Scriptures, and the decrees of the church, would permit you: to which authorities you willingly submit yourself in all things, whether you follow what they prescribe, or follow it not."—These are the principles that please you.

I consider, (as in courtesy bound,) that these things are asserted by you from a benevolent mind, as being a lover of peace. But if any one else had asserted them, I should, perhaps, have attacked him in my accustomed manner. But, however, I must not even allow you, though so very good in your intentions, to err in this opinion. For not to delight in assertions, is not the character of the Christian mind: nay, he must delight in assertions, or he is not a Christian. But, (that we may not be mistaken in terms) by *assertion*, I mean a constant adhering, affirming, confessing, defending, and invincibly persevering. Nor do I believe the term signifies any thing else, either among the Latins or as it is used by us at this day.

And moreover, I speak concerning the asserting of those things, which are delivered to us from above in the Holy Scriptures. Were it not so, we should want neither Erasmus nor any other instructor to teach us, that, in things doubtful, useless, or unnecessary; assertions, contentions, and strivings, would be not only absurd, but impious: and Paul condemns such in more places than one. Nor do you, I believe, speak of these things, unless, as a ridiculous orator, you wish to take up one subject, and go on with another, as the Roman Emperor did with his Turbot; or, with the madness of a wicked writer, you wish to contend, that the article concerning "Free-will" is doubtful, or not necessary.

Be sceptics and academics far from us Christians; but be there with us assertors twofold more determined than the stoics themselves. How often does the apostle Paul require that assurance of faith; that is, that most certain, and most firm assertion of Conscience, calling it (Rom. x. 10), confession, "With the mouth confession is made unto salvation? " And Christ also saith, "Whosoever confesseth Me before men, him will I confess before My Father." (Matt. x. 32) Peter commands us to "give a reason of the hope" that is in us. (1 Pet. iii. 15.) But why should I dwell upon this; nothing is more known and more general among Christians than assertions. Take away assertions, and you take away Christianity.

Nay, the Holy Spirit is given unto them from heaven, that He may glorify Christ, and confess Him even unto death; unless this be not to assert—to die for confession and assertion. In a word, the Spirit so asserts, that He comes upon the whole world and reproves them of sin (John xvi. 8), thus, as it were, provoking to battle. And Paul enjoins Timothy to reprove, and to be instant out of season. (2 Tim. iv. 2) But how ludicrous to me would be that reprover, who should neither really believe that himself, of which he reproved, nor constantly assert it! —Why I would send him to Anticyra, to be cured.

But I am the greatest fool, who thus lose words and time upon that, which is clearer than the sun. What Christian would bear that assertions should be contemned? This would be at once to deny all piety and religion together; or to assert, that religion, piety, and every doctrine, is nothing at all. Why therefore do you too say, that you do not delight in assertions, and that you prefer such a mind to any other?

But you would have it understood that you have said nothing here concerning confessing Christ, and His doctrines.—I receive the admonition. And, in courtesy to you, I give up my right and custom, and refrain from judging of your heart, reserving that for another time, or for others. In the mean time, I admonish you to correct your tongue, and your pen, and to refrain henceforth from using such expressions. For, how upright and honest soever your heart may be, your words, which are the index of the heart, are not so. For, if you think the matter of "Free-will" is not necessary to be known, nor at all concerned with Christ, you speak honestly, but think wickedly: but, if you think it is necessary, you speak wickedly, and think rightly. And if so, then there is no room for you to complain and exaggerate so much concerning useless assertions and contentions:

for what have they to do with the nature of the cause?

ERASMUS' SCEPTICISM.

Sect. II.—But what will you say to these your declarations, when, be it remembered, they are not confined to "Free-will" only, but apply to all doctrines in general throughout the world—that, "if it were permitted you, by the inviolable authority of the sacred Writings and decrees of the church, you would go over to the sentiments of the Sceptics? "—

What an all-changeable Proteus is there in these expressions, "inviolable authority" and "decrees of the church! " As though you could have so very great a reverence for the Scriptures and the church, when at the same time you signify, that you wish you had the liberty of being a Sceptic! What Christian would talk in this way? But if you say this in reference to useless and doubtful doctrines, what news is there in what you say? Who, in such things, would not wish for the liberty of the sceptical profession? Nay, what Christian is there who does not actually use this liberty freely, and condemn all those who are drawn away with, and captivated by every opinion? Unless you consider all Christians to be such (as the term is generally understood) whose doctrines are useless, and for which they quarrel like fools, and contend by assertions. But if you speak of necessary things, what declaration more impious can any one make, than that he wishes for the liberty of asserting nothing in such matters? Whereas, the Christian will rather say this—I am so averse to the sentiments of the Sceptics, that wherever I am not hindered by the infirmity of the flesh, I will not only steadily adhere to the Sacred Writings every where, and in all parts of them, and assert them, but I wish also to be as certain as possible in things that are not necessary, and that lie without the Scripture: for what is more miserable than uncertainty.

What shall we say to these things also, where you add—"To which authorities I submit my opinion in all things; whether I follow what they enjoin, or follow it not."—

What say you, Erasmus? Is it not enough that you submit your opinion to the Scriptures? Do you submit it to the decrees of the church also? What can the church decree, that is not decreed in the Scriptures? If it can, where then remains the liberty and power of judging those who make the decrees? As Paul, 1 Cor. xiv., teaches, "Let others judge." Are you not pleased that there should be any one to judge the decrees of the church, which, nevertheless, Paul enjoins? What new kind of religion and humility is this, that, by our own example, you would take away from us the power of judging the decrees of men, and give it unto men without judgment? Where does the Scripture of God command us to do this?

Moreover, what Christian would so commit the injunctions of the Scripture and of the church to the winds,—as to say "whether I follow them, or follow them not? " You submit yourself, and yet care not at all whether you follow them or not. But let that Christian be anathema, who is not certain in, and does not follow, that which is enjoined him. For how will he believe that which he does not follow? —Do you here, then mean to say, that *following* is understanding a thing certainly, and not doubting of it at all in a sceptical manner? If you do, what is there in any creature which any one can follow, if following be understanding, and seeing and knowing perfectly? And if this be the case, then it is impossible that any one should, at the same time, follow some things, and not follow others: whereas, by following one certain thing, God, he follows all things; that is, in Him, whom whoso followeth not, never followeth any part of His creature.

In a word, these declarations of yours amount to this—that, with you, it matters not what is believed by any one, any where, if the peace of the world be but undisturbed; and if every one be but allowed, when his life, his reputation, or his interest is at stake, to do as he did, who said, "If they affirm, I affirm, if they deny, I deny:" and to look upon the Christian doctrines as nothing better than the opinions of philosophers and men: and that it is the greatest of folly to quarrel about, contend for, and assert them, as nothing can arise therefrom but contention, and the disturbance of the public peace: "that what is above us, does not concern us." This, I say, is what your declarations amount to.—Thus, to put an end to our fightings, you come in as an intermediate peace-maker, that you may cause each side to suspend arms, and persuade us to cease from drawing swords about things so absurd and useless.

What I should cut at here, I believe, my friend Erasmus, you know very well. But, as I said before, I will not openly express myself. In the mean time, I excuse your very good intention of heart; but do you go no further; fear the Spirit of God, who searcheth the reins and the heart, and who is not deceived by artfully contrived expressions. I have, upon this occasion, expressed myself thus, that henceforth you may cease to accuse our cause of pertinacity or obstinacy. For, by so doing, you only evince that you hug in your heart a Lucian, or some other of the swinish tribe of the Epicureans; who, because he does not believe there is a God himself, secretly laughs at all those who do believe and confess it. Allow *us* to be assertors, and to study and delight in assertions: and do you favour your Sceptics and Academics until Christ shall have called you also. The Holy Spirit is not a Sceptic, nor are what He has written on our hearts doubts or opinions, but assertions more certain, and more firm, than life itself and all human experience.

Sect. III.—Now I come to the next head, which is connected with this; where you make a "distinction between the Christian doctrines," and pretend that "some are necessary, and some not necessary." You say, that "some are abstruse, and some quite clear." Thus you merely sport the sayings of others, or else exercise yourself, as it were, in a rhetorical figure. And you bring forward, in support of this opinion, that passage of Paul, Rom. xi. 33, "O the depth of the riches both of the wisdom and goodness of God! " And also that of Isaiah xl. 13, "Who hath holpen the Spirit of the Lord, or who hath been His counsellor? "

You could easily say these things, seeing that, you either knew not that you were writing to Luther, but for the world at large, or did not think that you were writing against Luther: whom, however, I hope you allow to have some acquaintance with, and judgment in, the Sacred Writings. But, if you do not allow it, then, behold, I will also twist things thus. This is the distinction which I make, that I also may act a little the rhetorician and logician—God, and the Scripture of God, are two things; no less so than God, and the Creature of God. That there are in God many hidden things which we know not, no one doubts: as He himself saith concerning the last day: "Of that day knoweth no man but the Father." (Matt. xxiv. 36.) And (Acts i. 7.) "It is not yours to know the times and seasons." And again, "I know whom I have chosen," (John xiii. 18.) And Paul, "The Lord knoweth them that are His," (2 Tim. ii. 19.). And the like.

But, that there are in the Scriptures some things abstruse, and that all things are not quite plain, is a report spread abroad by the impious Sophists; by whose mouth you speak here, Erasmus. But they never have produced, nor ever can produce, one article whereby to prove this their madness. And it is with such scare-crows that Satan has frightened away men from reading the Sacred Writings, and has rendered the Holy Scripture contemptible, that he might cause his poisons of philosophy to prevail in the church. This indeed I confess, that there are many *places* in the Scriptures obscure and abstruse; not from the majesty of the things, but from our ignorance of certain terms and grammatical particulars; but which do not prevent a knowledge of all the *things* in the Scriptures. For what *thing* of more importance can remain hidden in the Scriptures, now that the seals are broken, the stone rolled from the door of the sepulchre, and that greatest of all mysteries brought to light, Christ made man: that God is Trinity and Unity: that Christ suffered for us, and will reign to all eternity? Are not these things known and proclaimed even in our streets? *Take Christ out of the Scriptures, and what will you find remaining in them?*

All the *things*, therefore, contained in the Scriptures, are made manifest, although some *places*, from the words not being understood, are yet obscure. But to know that all *things* in the Scriptures are set in the clearest light, and then, because a few words are obscure, to report that the *things* are obscure, is absurd and impious. *And, if the words are obscure in one place, yet they are clear in another.* But, however, the same *thing*, which has been most openly declared to the whole world, is both spoken of in the Scriptures in plain words, and also still lies hidden in obscure words. Now, therefore, it matters not if the *thing* be in the light, whether any certain representations of it be in obscurity or not, if, in the mean while, many other representations of the same thing be in the light. For who would say that the public fountain is not in the light, because those who are in some dark narrow lane do not see it, when all those who are in the open market place can see it plainly?

Sect. IV.—What you adduce, therefore, about the darkness of the Corycian cavern, amounts to nothing; matters are not so in the Scriptures. For those things which are of the greatest majesty, and the most abstruse mysteries, are no longer in the dark corner, but before the very doors, nay, brought forth and manifested openly. For Christ has opened our understanding to understand the Scriptures, Luke xxiv. 45. And the Gospel is preached to every creature. (Mark xvi. 15, Col. 1, 23.) "Their sound is gone out into all the earth." (Psalm xix. 4.) And "All things that are written, are written for our instruction." (Rom. xv. 4.) And again, "All Scripture is inspired from above, and is profitable for instruction." (2 Tim. iii. 16.)

Therefore come forward, you and all the Sophists together, and produce any one mystery which is still abstruse in the Scriptures. But, if many things still remain abstruse to many, this does not arise from obscurity in the Scriptures, but from their own blindness or want of understanding, who do not go the way to see the all-perfect clearness of the truth. As Paul saith concerning the Jews, 2 Cor. iii. 15. "The veil still remains upon their heart." And again, "If our gospel be hid it is hid to them that are lost, whose heart the god of this world hath blinded." (2 Cor. iv. 3-4). With the same rashness any one may cover his own eyes, or go from the light into the dark and hide himself, and then blame the day and the sun for being obscure. Let, therefore, wretched men cease to impute, with blasphemous perverseness, the darkness and obscurity of their own heart to the all-clear Scriptures of God.

You, therefore, when you adduce Paul, saying, "His judgments are incomprehensible," seem to make the pronoun *His (ejus)* refer to Scripture *(Scriptura)*. Whereas Paul does not say, The judgments of the Scripture are incomprehensible, but the judgments of God. So also Isaiah xl. 13, does not say, Who has known the mind of the Scripture, but who has known "the mind of the Lord?" Although Paul asserts that the mind of the Lord is known to Christians: but it is in those things which are freely given unto us: as he saith also in the same place, 1 Cor. ii. 10, 16. You see, therefore, how sleepily you have looked over these places of the Scripture: and you cite them just as aptly as you cite nearly all the passages in defence of "Free-will."

In like manner, your examples which you subjoin, not without suspicion and bitterness, are nothing at all to the purpose. Such are those concerning the distinction of Persons: the union of the Divine and human natures: the unpardonable sin: the ambiguity attached to which, you say, has never been cleared up.—If you mean the questions of Sophists that have been agitated upon those subjects, well. But what has the all-innocent Scripture done to you, that you impute the abuse of the most wicked of men to its purity? The Scripture simply confesses the Trinity of God, the humanity of Christ, and the unpardonable sin. There is nothing here of obscurity or ambiguity. But *how* these things are the Scripture does not say, nor is it necessary to be known. The Sophists employ their dreams here; attack and condemn them, and acquit the Scripture.—But, if you mean the reality of the matter, I say again, attack not the Scriptures, but the Arians, and those to whom the Gospel is hid, that, through the working of Satan, they might not see the all-manifest testimonies concerning the Trinity of the Godhead, and the humanity of Christ.

But to be brief. The *clearness* of the Scripture is twofold; even as the *obscurity* is twofold also. The one is *external*, placed in the ministry of the word; the other *internal*, placed in the understanding of the heart. If you speak of the internal clearness, no man sees one iota in the Scriptures, but he that hath the Spirit of God. All have a darkened heart; so that, even if they know how to speak of, and set forth, all things in the Scripture, yet, they cannot feel them, nor know them: nor do they believe that they are the creatures of God, nor any thing else: according to that of Psalm xiv. 1. "The fool hath said in his heart, God is nothing." For the Spirit is required to understand the whole of the Scripture and every part of it. If you speak of the external clearness, nothing whatever is left obscure or ambiguous; but all things that are in the Scriptures, are by the Word brought forth into the clearest light, and proclaimed to the whole world.

Sect. V.–But this is still more intolerable,–Your enumerating this subject of "Free-will" among those things that are "useless, and not necessary;" and drawing up for us, instead of it, a "Form" of those things which you consider "necessary unto Christian piety." Such a form as, certainly, any Jew, or any Gentile utterly ignorant of Christ, might draw up. For of Christ you make no mention in one iota. As though you thought, that there may be Christian piety without Christ, if God be but worshipped with all the powers as being by nature most merciful.

What shall I say here, Erasmus? To me, you breathe out nothing but Lucian, and draw in the gorging surfeit of Epicurus. If you consider this subject "not necessary" to Christians, away, I pray you, out of the field; I have nothing to do with you. I consider it necessary.

If, as you say, it be "irreligious," if it be "curious," if it be "superfluous," to know, whether or not God foreknows any thing by contingency; whether our own will does any thing in those things which pertain unto eternal salvation, or is only passive under the work of grace; whether or not we do, what we do of good or evil, from necessity, or rather from being passive; what then, I ask, is religious; what is grave; what is useful to be known? All this, Erasmus, is to no purpose whatever. And it is difficult to attribute this to your ignorance, because you are now old, have been conversant with Christians, and have long studied the Sacred Writings; therefore you leave no room for my excusing you, or having a good thought concerning you.

And yet the Papists pardon and put up with these enormities in you: and on this account, because you are writing against Luther: otherwise, if Luther were not in the case, they would tear you in pieces tooth and nail. Plato is a friend; Socrates is a friend; but Truth is to be honoured above all. For, granting that you have but little understanding in the Scriptures and in Christian piety, surely even an enemy to Christians ought to know what Christians consider useful and necessary, and what they do not. Whereas you, a theologian, a teacher of Christians, and about to draw up for them a "Form" of Christianity, not only in your sceptical manner doubt of what is necessary and useful to them, but go away into the directly opposite, and, contrary to your own principles, by an unheard of assertion, declare it to be your judgment, that those things are "not necessary:" whereas, if they be not necessary, and certainly known, there can remain neither God, nor Christ, nor Gospel, nor Faith, nor any thing else, even of Judaism, much less of Christianity! In the name of the Immortal God, Erasmus, what an occasion, yea, what a field do you open for acting and speaking against you! What could you write well or correctly concerning "Free-will," who confess, by these your declarations, so great an ignorance of the Scripture and of Godliness? But I draw in my sails: nor will I here deal with you in my words (for that perhaps I shall do hereafter) but in your own.

Sect. VI.–The "Form" of Christianity set forth by you, among other things, has this–"That we should strive with all our powers, have recourse to the remedy of repentance, and in all ways try to gain the mercy of God; without which, neither human will, not endeavour, is effectual." Also, "that no one should despair of pardon from a God by nature most merciful."—

These statements of yours are without Christ, without the Spirit, and more cold than ice: so that, the beauty of your eloquence is really deformed by them. Perhaps a fear of the Popes and those tyrants, extorted them from you their miserable vassal, lest you should appear to them a perfect atheist. But what they assert is this—That there is ability in us; that there is a striving with all our powers; that there is mercy in God; that there are ways of gaining that mercy; that there is a God, by nature just, and most merciful, &c.—But if a man does not know what these powers are; what they can do, or in what they are to be passive; what their efficacy, or what their inefficacy is; what can such an one do? What will you set him about doing?

"It is irreligious, curious, and superfluous, (you say) to wish to know, whether our own will does any thing in those things which pertain unto eternal savlation, or whether it is wholly passive under the work of grace."—But here, you say the contrary: that it is Christian piety to "strive with all the powers;" and that, "without the mercy of God the will is ineffective."

Here you plainly assert, that the will does something in those things which pertain unto eternal salvation, when you speak of it as striving: and again, you assert that it is passive, when you say, that without the mercy of God it is ineffective. Though, at the same time, you do not define how far that doing, and being passive, is to be understood: thus, designedly keeping us in ignorance how far the mercy of God extends, and how far our own will extends; what our own will is to do, in that which you enjoin, and what the mercy of God is to do. Thus, that prudence of yours, carries you along; by which, you are resolved to hold with neither side, and to escape safely through Scylla and Charybdis; in order that, when you come into the open sea, and find yourself overwhelmed and confounded by the waves, you may have it in your power, to assert all that you now deny, and deny all that you now assert.

THE NECESSITY OF KNOWING GOD AND HIS POWER

Sect. VII.—But I will set your theology before your eyes by a few similitudes.—What if any one, intending to compose a poem, or an oration, should never think about, nor inquire into his abilities, what he could do, and what he could not do, nor what the subject undertaken required; and should utterly disregard that precept of Horace, "What the shoulders can sustain, and what they must sink under;" but should precipitately dash upon the undertaking and think thus—I must strive to get the work done; to inquire whether the learning I have, the eloquence I have, the force of genius I have, be equal to it, is curious and superfluous:—Or, if any one, desiring to have a plentiful crop from his land, should not be so curious as to take the superfluous care of examining the nature of the soil, (as Virgil curiously and in vain teaches in his Georgics,) but should rush on at once, thinking of nothing but the work, and plough the seashore, and cast in the seed wherever the soil was turned up, whether sand or mud:—Or if any one, about to make war, and desiring a glorious victory, or intending to render any other service to the state, should not be so curious as to deliberate upon what it was in his power to do; whether the treasury could furnish money, whether the soldiers were fit, whether any opportunity offered; and should pay no regard whatever to that of the historian, "Before you act, there must be deliberation, and when you have deliberated, speedy execution;" but should rush forward with his eyes blinded, and his ears stopped, only exclaiming war! war! and should be determined on the undertaking:—What, I ask you, Erasmus, would you think of such poets, such husbandmen, such generals, and such heads of affairs? I will add also that of the Gospel—If any one going to build a tower, sits not down first and counts the cost, whether he has enough to finish it,—What does Christ say of such an one? (Luke xiv. 28-32).

Thus you also enjoin us works only. But you forbid us to examine, weigh, and know, first, our ability, what we can do, and what we cannot do, as being curious, superfluous, and irreligious. Thus, while with your over-cautious prudence you pretend to detest temerity, and make a show of sobriety, you go so far, that you even teach the greatest of all temerity. For, although the Sophists are rash and mad in reality while they pursue their curious inquiries, yet their sin is less enormous than yours; for you even teach and enjoin men to be mad, and to rush on with temerity. And to make your madness still greater, you persuade us, that this temerity is the most exalted and Christian piety, sobriety, religious gravity, and even salvation. And you assert, that if we exercise it not, we are irreligious, curious, and vain: although you are so great an enemy to assertions. Thus, in steering clear of Charybdis, you have, with excellent grace, escaped Scylla also. But into this state you are driven by your confidence in your own talents. You believe, that you can by your eloquence, so impose upon the understandings of all, that no one shall discover the design which you secretly hug in your heart, and what you aim at in all those your pliant writings. But God is not mocked, (Gal. vi. 7,) upon whom it is not safe to run.

Moreover, had you enjoined us this temerity in composing poems, in preparing for fruits, in conducting wars or other undertakings, or in building houses; although it would have been intolerable, especially in so great a man, yet you might have been deserving of some pardon, at least from Christians, for they pay no regard to these temporal things. But, when you enjoin Christians themselves to become rash workers, and charge them not to be curious about what they can do and what they cannot do, in obtaining eternal salvation; this, evidently, and in reality, is the sin unpardonable. For while they know not what or how much they can do, they will not know what to do; and if they know not what to do, they cannot repent when they do wrong: and impenitence is the unpardonable sin: and to this, does that moderate and sceptical theology of yours lead us.

Therefore, it is not irreligious, curious, or superfluous, but essentially wholesome and necessary, for a Christian to know, whether or not the will does any thing in those things which pertain unto Salvation. Nay, let me tell you, this is the very hinge upon which our discussion turns. It is the very heart of our subject. For our object is this: to inquire what "Free-will" can do, in what it is passive, and how it stands with reference to the grace of God. *If we know nothing of these things, we shall know nothing whatever of Christian matters, and shall be far behind all people upon the earth.* He that does not feel this, let him confess that he is no Christian. And he that despises and laughs at it, let him know that he is the Christian's greatest enemy. For, if I know not how much I can do myself, how far my ability extends, and what I can do God-wards; I shall be equally uncertain and ignorant how much God is to do, how far His ability is to extend, and what He is to do toward me: whereas it is "God that worketh all in all." (1 Cor. xii. 6.) But if I know not the distinction between our working and the power of God, I know not God Himself. And if I know not God, I cannot worship Him, praise Him, give Him thanks, nor serve Him; for I shall not know how much I ought to ascribe unto myself, and how much unto God. It is necessary, therefore, to hold the most certain distinction, between the power of God and our power, the working of God and our working, if we would live in His fear.

Hence you see, this point, forms another part of the whole sum of Christianity; on which depends, and in which is at stake, the knowledge of ourselves, and the knowledge and glory of God. Wherefore, friend Erasmus, your calling the knowledge of this point irreligious, curious, and vain, is not to be borne in you. We owe much to you, but we owe all to the fear of God. Nay you yourself see, that all our good is to be ascribed unto God, and you assert that in your Form of Christianity: and in asserting this, you certainly, at the same time assert also, that the mercy of God alone does all things, and that our own will does nothing, but is rather acted upon: and so it must be, otherwise the whole is not ascribed unto God. And yet, immediately afterwards, you say, that to assert these things, and to know them, is irreligious, impious, and vain. But at this rate a mind, which is unstable in itself, and unsettled and inexperienced in the things of godliness, cannot but talk.

Sect. VIII.—Another part of the sum of Christianity is, to know, whether God foreknows any thing by contingency, or whether we do all things from necessity. This part also you make to be irreligious, curious, and vain, as all the wicked do: the devils and the damned also, make it detestable and execrable. And you shew your wisdom in keeping yourself clear from such questions, wherever you can do it. But however, you are but a very poor rhetorician and theologian, if you pretend to speak of "Free-will" without these essential parts of it. I will therefore act as a whetstone, and though no rhetorician myself, will tell a famed rhetorician what he ought to do—If, then, Quintilian, purposing to write on Oratory, should say, "In my judgment, all that superfluous nonsense about invention, arrangement, elocution, memory, pronunciation, need not be mentioned; it is enough to know, that Oratory, is the art of speaking well"—would you not laugh at such a writer? But you act exactly like this: for pretending to write on "Free-will," you first throw aside, and cast away, the grand substance and all the parts of the subject on which you undertake to write. Whereas, it is impossible that you should know what "Free-will" is, unless you know what the human will does, and what God does or foreknows.

Do not your rhetoricians teach, that he who undertakes to speak upon any subject, ought first to show, whether the thing exist; and then, what it is, what its parts are, what is contrary to it, connected with it, and like unto it, &c.? But you rob that miserable subject in itself, "Free-will," of all these things: and define no one question concerning it, except this first, viz., whether it exist: and even this with such arguments as we shall presently see: and so worthless a book on "Free-will" I never saw, excepting the elegance of the language. The Sophists, in reality, at least argue upon this point better than you, though those of them who have attempted the subject of "Free-will," are no rhetoricians; for they define all the questions connected with it: whether it exists, what it does, and how it stands with reference to, &c.: although they do not effect what they attempt. In this book, therefore, I will push you, and the Sophists together, until you shall define to me the power of "Free-will," and what it can do: and I hope I shall so push you, (Christ willing) as to make you heartily repent that you ever published your Diatribe.

THE SOVEREIGNTY OF GOD.

Sect. IX.—This, therefore, is also essentially necessary and wholesome for Christians to know: *that God foreknows nothing by contingency, but that He foresees, purposes, and does all things according to His immutable, eternal, and infallible will.* By this thunderbolt, "Free-will" is thrown prostrate, and utterly dashed to pieces. Those, therefore, who would assert "Free-will", must either deny this thunderbolt, or pretend not to see it, or push it from them. But, however, before I establish this point by any arguments of my own, and by the authority of Scripture, I will first set it forth in your words.

Are you not then the person, friend Erasmus, who just now asserted, that God is by nature just, and by nature most merciful? If this be true, does it not follow that He is *immutably* just and merciful? That, as His nature is not changed to all eternity, so neither His justice nor His mercy? And what is said concerning His justice and His mercy, must be said also concerning His knowledge, His wisdom, His goodness, His will; and His other Attributes. If therefore these things are asserted religiously, piously, and wholesomely concerning God, as you say yourself, what has come to you, that, contrary to your own self, you now assert, that it is irreligious, curious, and vain, to say, that God foreknows of necessity? You openly declare that the immutable *will* of God is to be known, but you forbid the knowledge of His immutable *prescience.* Do you believe that He foreknows against His will, or that He wills in ignorance? If then, He foreknows, willing, His will is eternal and immovable, because His nature is so: and, if He wills, foreknowing, His knowledge is eternal and immovable, because His nature is so.

From which it follows unalterably, that all things which we do, although they may appear to us to be done mutably and contingently, and even may be done thus contingently by us, are yet, in reality, done necessarily and immutably, with respect to the will of God. For the will of God is effective and cannot be hindered; because the very power of God is natural to Him, and His wisdom is such that He cannot be deceived. And as His will cannot be hindered, the work itself cannot be hindered from being done in the place, at the time, in the measure, and by whom He foresees and wills. If the will of God were such, that, when the *work* was done, the *work* remained but the *will* ceased, (as is the case with the *will* of men, which, when the house is built which they wished to build, ceases to *will*, as though it ended by death) then, indeed, it might be said, that things are done by contingency and mutability. But here, the case is the contrary; the *work ceases,* and the *will remains.* So far is it from possibility, that the doing of the work or its remaining, can be said to be from contingency or mutability. But, (that we may not be deceived in terms) *being done by contingency*, does not, in the Latin language, signify that the work itself which is done is contingent, but that it is done according to a contingent and mutable will—such a will as is not to be found in God! Moreover, a work cannot be called contingent, unless it be done by us unawares, by contingency, and, as it were, by chance; that is, by our will or hand catching at it, as presented by chance, we thinking nothing of it, nor willing any thing about it before.

Sect. X.—I could wish, indeed, that we were furnished with some better term for this discussion, than this commonly used term, *necessity,* which cannot rightly be used, either with reference to the human will, or the divine. It is of a signification too harsh and ill-suited for this subject, forcing upon the mind an idea of compulsion, and that which is altogether contrary to *will*; whereas, the subject which we are discussing, does not require such an idea: for Will, whether divine or human, does what it does, be it good or evil, not by any compulsion, but by mere willingness or desire, as it were, totally free. The will of God, nevertheless, which rules over our mutable will, is immutable and infallible; as Boëtius sings, "Immovable Thyself, Thou movement giv'st to all." And our own will, especially our corrupt will, cannot of itself do good; therefore, where the term fails to express the idea required, the understanding of the reader must make up the deficiency, knowing what is wished to be expressed—the immutable will of God, and the impotency of our depraved will; or, as some have expressed it, the *necessity of immutability*, though neither is that sufficiently grammatical, or sufficiently theological.

Upon this point, the Sophists have now laboured hard for many years, and being at last conquered, have been compelled to retreat. All things take place from the *necessity of the consequence*, (say they) but not from the *necessity of the thing consequent.* What nothingness this amounts to, I will not take the trouble to show. By the *necessity of the consequence*, (to give a general idea of it) they mean this—If God wills any thing, that same thing must, of necessity, be done; but it is not necessary that the thing done should be necessary: for God alone is necessary; all other things cannot be so, if it is God that wills. Therefore, (say they) the action of God is necessary, where He wills, but the act itself is not necessary; that is, (they mean) it has not *essential necessity.* But what do they effect by this playing upon words? Only this, that the act itself is not necessary, that is, it has not essential necessity. This is no more than saying, the act is not God Himself. This, nevertheless, remains certain, that if the action of God is necessary, or if there is a necessity of the consequence, every thing takes place of necessity, how much soever the act be not necessary; that is, be not God Himself, or have not essential necessity. For, if I be not made of necessity, it is of little moment with me, whether my existence and being be mutable or not, if, nevertheless, I, that contingent and mutable being, who am not the necessary God, am made.

Wherefore, there ridiculous play upon words, that all things take place from *the necessity of the consequence,* but not from *the necessity of the thing consequent*, amounts to nothing more than this—all things take place of necessity, but all the things that do take place are not God Himself. But what need was there to tell us this? As though there were any fear of our asserting, that the things done were God Himself, or possessed divine or necessary nature. This asserted truth, therefore, stands and remains invincible—that all things take place according to the immutable will of God! which they call the necessity of the consequence. Nor is there here any obscurity or ambiguity. In Isaiah He saith, "My counsel shall stand, and My will shall be done." (Isa. xlvi. 10.) And what schoolboy does not understand the meaning of these expressions, "Counsel," "will," "shall be done," "shall stand? "

Sect. XI.—But why should these things be abstruse to us Christians, so that it should be considered irreligious, curious, and vain, to discuss and know them, when heathen poets, and the very commonalty, have them in their mouths in the most frequent use? How often does Virgil alone make mention of Fate? "All things stand fixed by law immutable." Again, "Fixed is the day of every man." Again, "If the Fates summon you." And again, "If thou shalt break the binding chain of Fate." All this poet aims at, is to show, that in the destruction of Troy, and in raising the Roman empire, Fate did more than all the devoted efforts of men. In a word, he makes even their immortal gods subject to Fate. To this, even Jupiter and Juno must, of necessity, yield. Hence they made the three Parcae immutable, implacable, and irrevocable in decree.

Those men of wisdom knew that which the event itself, with experience, proves; that no man's own counsels ever succeeded, but that the event happened to all contrary to what they thought. Virgil's Hector says, "Could Troy have stood by human arm, it should have stood by mine." Hence that common saying was on every one's tongue, "God's will be done." Again, "If God will, we will do it." Again, "Such was the will of God." "Such was the will of those above." "Such was your will," says Virgil. Whence we may see, that the knowledge of predestination and of the prescience of God, was no less left in the world than the notion of the divinity itself. And those who wished to appear wise, went in their disputations so far, that, their hearts being darkened, they became fools," (Rom. i. 21-22,) and denied, or pretended not to know, those things which their poets, and the commonalty, and even their own consciences, held to be universally known, most certain, and most true.

Sect. XII.—I observe further, not only how true these things are (concerning which I shall speak more at large hereafter out of the Scriptures), but also how religious, pious, and necessary it is to know them; for if these things be not known there can be neither faith, nor any worship of God: nay, not to know them, is to be in reality ignorant of God, with which ignorance salvation, it is well known, cannot consist. For if you doubt, or disdain to know that God foreknows and wills all things, not contingently, but necessarily and immutably, how can you believe confidently, trust to, and depend upon His promises? For when He promises, it is necessary that you should be certain that He knows, is able, and willing to perform what He promises; otherwise, you will neither hold Him true nor faithful; which is unbelief, the greatest of wickedness, and a denying of the Most High God!

And how can you be certain and secure, unless you are persuaded that He knows and wills certainly, infallibly, immutably, and necessarily, and will perform what He promises? Nor ought we to be certain only that God wills necessarily and immutably, and will perform, but also to glory in the same; as Paul, (Rom. iii. 4,) "Let God be true, but every man a liar." And again, "For the word of God is not without effect." (Rom. ix. 6.) And in another place, "The foundation of God standeth sure, having this seal, the Lord knoweth them that are His." (2 Tim. ii. 19.) And, "Which God, that cannot lie, promised before the world began." (Titus i. 2.) And, "He that cometh, must believe that God is, and that He is a rewarder of them that hope in Him." (Heb. xi. 6.)

If, therefore, we are taught, and if we believe, that we ought not to know the necessary prescience of God, and the necessity of the things that are to take place,

Christian faith is utterly destroyed, and the promises of God and the whole Gospel entirely fall to the ground; for the greatest and only consolation of Christians in their adversities, is the knowing that God lies not, but does all things immutably, and that His will cannot be resisted, changed, or hindered.

Sect. XIII.—Do you now, then, only observe, friend Erasmus, to what that most moderate, and most peace-loving theology of yours would lead us. You call us off, and forbid our endeavouring to know the prescience of God, and the necessity that lies on men and things, and counsel us to leave such things, and to avoid and disregard them; and in so doing, you at the same time teach us your rash sentiments; that we should seek after an ignorance of God, (which comes upon us of its own accord, and is engendered in us), disregard faith, leave the promises of God, and account the consolations of the Spirit, and the assurances of conscience, nothing at all! Such counsel scarcely any Epicure himself would give!

Moreover, not content with this, you call him who should desire to know such things, irreligious, curious, and vain; but him who should disregard them, religious, pious, and sober. What else do these words imply, than that Christians are irreligious, curious, and vain? And that Christianity is a thing of nought, vain, foolish, and plainly impious? Here again, therefore, while you wish by all means to deter us from temerity, running, as fools always do, directly into the contrary, you teach nothing but the greatest temerity, impiety, and perdition. Do you not see, then, that in this part, your book is so impious, blasphemous, and sacrilegious, that its like is not any where to be found.

I do not, as I have observed before, speak of your heart; nor can I think that you are so lost, that from your heart, you wish these things to be taught and practised. But I would shew you what enormities that man must be compelled unknowingly to broach, who undertakes to support a bad cause. And moreover, what it is to run against divine things and truths, when, in mere compliance with others and against our own conscience, we assume a strange character and act upon a strange stage. It is neither a game nor a jest, to undertake to teach the sacred truths and godliness: for it is very easy here to meet with that fall which James speaks of, "He that offendeth in one point is guilty of all." (James ii. 10.) For when we begin to be, in the least degree, disposed to trifle, and not to hold the sacred truths in due reverence, we are soon involved in impieties, and overwhelmed with blasphemies: as it has happened to you here, Erasmus—May the Lord pardon, and have mercy upon you!

That the Sophists have given birth to such numbers of reasoning questions upon these subjects, and have intermingled with them many unprofitable things, many of which you mention, I know and confess, as well as you: and I have inveighed against them much more than you have. But you act with imprudence and rashness, when you liken the purity of the sacred truths unto the profane and foolish questions of the impious, and mingle and confound it with them. "They have defiled the gold with dung, and changed the good colour," (Lam. iv. 1., as Jeremiah saith.) But the gold is not to be compared unto, and cast away with the dung; as you do it. The gold must be wrested from them, and the pure Scripture separated from their dregs and filth; which it has ever been my aim to do, that the divine truths may be looked upon in one light, and the trifles of these men in another. But it ought not to be considered of any service to us, that nothing has been effected by these questions, but their causing us to favour them less with the whole current of our approbation, if, nevertheless, we still desire to be wiser than we ought. The question with us is not, how much the Sophists have effected by their reasonings, but how we may become good men, and Christians. Nor ought you to impute it to the Christian doctrine that the impious do evil. That is nothing to the purpose: you may speak of that somewhere else, and spare your paper here.

Sect. XIV.—Under your third head, you attempt to make us some of those very modest and quiet Epicureans. With a different kind of advice indeed, but no better than that, with which the two forementioned particulars are brought forward:—"Some things (you say) are of that nature, that, although they are true in themselves, and might be known, yet it would not be prudent to prostitute them to the ears of every one."—

Here again, according to your custom, you mingle and confound every thing, to bring the sacred things down to a level with the profane, without making any distinction whatever: again falling into the contempt of, and doing an injury to God. As I have said before, those things which are either found in the sacred Writings, or may be proved by them, are not only plain, but wholesome; and therefore may be, nay, ought to be, spread abroad, learnt, and known. So that your saying, that they ought not to be prostituted to the ears of every one, is false: if, that is, you speak of those things which are in the Scripture: but if you speak of any other things, they are nothing to me, and nothing to the purpose: you lose time and paper in saying any thing about them.

Moreover, you know that I agree not with the Sophists in any thing: you may therefore spare me, and not bring me in at all as connected with their abuse of the truth. You had, in this book of yours, to speak against me. I know where the Sophists are wrong, nor do I want you for my instructor, and they have been sufficiently inveighed against by me: this, therefore, I wish to be observed once for all, whenever you shall bring me in with the Sophists, and disparage my side of the subject by their madness. For you do me an injury; and that you know very well.

Sect. XV.—Now let us see your reasons for giving this advice—'you think, that, although it may be true, that God, from His nature, is in a beetle's hole, or even in a sink, (which you have too much holy reverence to say yourself, and blame the Sophists for talking in such a way) no less than in Heaven, yet it would be unreasonable to discuss such a subject before the multitude.'—

First of all, let them talk thus, who can talk thus. We do not here argue concerning what are facts in men, but concerning justice and law: not that we may live, but that we may live as we ought. Who among us lives and acts rightly? But justice and the doctrine of law are not therefore condemned: but rather they condemn us. You fetch from afar these irrelevant things, and scrape together many such from all quarters, because you cannot get over this one point, the prescience of God: and since you cannot overthrow it in any way, you want, in the mean time, to tire out the reader with a multiplicity of empty observation. But of this, no more. Let us return to the point.

What then is your intention, in observing that there are some things which ought not to be spoken of openly? Do you mean to enumerate the subject of "Free-will" among those things? If you do, the whole that I have just said concerning the necessity of knowing what "Free-will" is, will turn round upon you. Moreover, if so, why do you not keep to your own principles, and have nothing to do with your Diatribe? But, if you do well in discussing "Free-will," why do you speak against such discussion? and if it is a bad subject, why do you make it worse? But if you do not enumerate it among those things, then, you leave your subject-point; and like an orator of words only, talk about those irrelevant things that have nothing to do with the subject.

Sect. XVI.—Nor are you right in the use of this example; nor in condemning the discussion of this subject before the multitude, as useless—that God is in a beetle's hole and even in a sink! For your thoughts concerning God are too human. I confess indeed, that there are certain fantastical preachers, who, not from any religion, or fear of God, but from a desire of vain-glory, or from a thirst after some novelty, or from impatience of silence, prate and trifle in the lightest manner. But such please neither God nor men, although they assert that God is in the Heaven of Heavens. But when there are grave and pious preachers, who teach in modest, pure, and sound words; they, without any danger, nay, unto much profit, speak on such a subject before the multitude.

Is it not the duty of us all to teach, that the Son of God was in the womb of the Virgin, and proceeded forth from her belly? And in what does the human belly differ from any other unclean place? Who, moreover, may not describe it in filthy and shameless terms? But such persons we justly condemn; because, there are numberless pure words, in which we speak of that necessary subject, even with decency and grace. The body also of Christ Himself was human, like ours. Than which body, what is more filthy? But shall we, therefore, not say what Paul saith, that God dwelt in it bodily? (Col. ii. 9.) What is more unclean than death? What more horrible than hell? Yet the prophet glorieth that God was with him in death, and left him not, in hell. (Ps. xvi. 10, Ps. cxxxix. 8.)

The pious mind, therefore, is not shocked at hearing that God was in death and in hell: each of which is more horrible, and more loathsome, than either a hole or a sink. Nay, since the Scripture testifies that God is every where, and fills all things, such a mind, not only says that He is in those places, but will, of necessity, learn and know that He is there. Unless we are to suppose, that if I should at any time be taken and cast into a prison, or a sink, (which has happened to many saints,) I could not there call upon God, or believe that He was present with me, until I should come into some ornamented church. If you teach us that we are thus to trifle concerning God, and if you are thus offended at the places of His essential presence, by and by you will not even allow that He dwells with us in Heaven. Whereas, "the Heaven of Heavens cannot contain Him," (1 Kings viii. 27.); or, they are not worthy. But, as I said before, you, according to your custom, thus maliciously point your sting at our cause, that you may disparage and render it hateful, because you find it stands against you insuperable and invincible.

Sect. XVII.—In the remaining example concerning confession and satisfaction, it is wonderful to observe with what dexterous prudence you proceed. Throughout the whole, according to your custom, you move along on the tiptoe of caution, lest you should seem, neither plainly to condemn my sentiments, nor to oppose the tyranny of the Popes: a path which you found to be by no means safe. Therefore, throwing off, in this matter, both God and conscience, (for what are these things to Erasmus? What has he to do with them? What profit are they to him?) you rush upon the external bugbear, and attack the commonalty.

—'That they, from their depravity, abuse the preaching of a free confession and of satisfaction, to an occasion of the flesh. But, nevertheless, (you say) by the necessity of confessing, they are, in a measure, restrained.'—

O memorable and excellent speech! Is this teaching theology? To bind souls by laws, and, (as Ezekiel saith, xiii. 18,) to hunt them to death, which are not bound by God! Why, by this speech you bring upon us the universal tyranny of the laws of the Popes, as useful and wholesome; because, that by them also the depravity of the commonalty is restrained.

But I will not inveigh against this place as it deserves. I will descant upon it thus briefly—A good theologian teaches, that the commonalty are to be restrained by the external power of the sword, where they do evil: as Paul teaches. (Rom. xiii. 1-4.) But their consciences are not to be fettered by false laws, that they might be tormented with sins where God wills there should be no sins at all. For consciences are bound by the law of God only. So that, that intermediate tyranny of Popes, which falsely terrifies and murders the souls within, and vainly wearies the bodies without is to be taken entirely out of the way. Because, although it binds to confession and other things, outwardly, yet the mind is not, by these things restrained, but exasperated the more into the hatred both of God and men. And in vain does it butcher the body by external things, making nothing but hypocrites.—So that tyrants, with laws of this kind, are nothing else but ravening wolves, robbers, and plunderers of souls. And yet you, an excellent counseller of souls, recommend these to us again: that is, you are an advocate for these most barbarous soul-murderers, who fill the world with hypocrites, and with such as blaspheme God and hate Him in their hearts, in order that they may restrain them a little from outward sin. As though there were no other way of restraining, which makes no hypocrites, and is wrought without any destroying of consciences.

Sect. XVIII.—Here you produce similitudes (in which you aim at appearing to abound, and to use very appropriately); that is,—'that there are diseases, which may be borne with less evil than they can be cured: as the leprosy, &c.' You add, moreover, the example of Paul, who makes a distinction between those things that are lawful, and those that are not expedient. "It is lawful (you say) to speak the truth; but, before every one, at all times, and in every way, it is not expedient."—

How copious an orator! And yet you understand nothing of what you are saying. In a word, you treat this discussion, as though it were some matter between you and me only, about the recovering of some money that was at stake, or some other trivial thing, the loss of which, as being of much less consideration than the general peace of the community, ought not so to concern any one, but that he may yield, act, and suffer upon the occasion, in any way that may prevent the necessity of the whole world being thrown into a tumult. Wherein, you plainly evince, that this peace and tranquillity of the flesh, are, with you, a matter of far greater consideration than faith, than conscience, than salvation, than the Word of God, than the glory of Christ, than God Himself! Wherefore, let me tell you this; and I entreat you to let it sink deep into your mind—I am, in this discussion, seeking an object solemn and essential; nay, such, and so great, that it ought to be maintained and defended through death itself; and that, although the whole world should not only be thrown into tumult and set in arms thereby, but even if it should be hurled into chaos and reduced to nothing.—If you cannot receive this, or if you are not affected by it, do you mind your own business, and allow us to receive it and to be affected by it, to whom it is given of God.

For, by the grace of God, I am not so great a fool or madman, as to have desired to sustain and defend this cause so long, with so much fortitude and so much firmness, (which you call obstinacy) in the face of so many dangers of my life, so much hatred, so many traps laid for me; in a word, in the face of the fury of men and devils—I have not done this for money, for that I neither have nor desire; nor for vain-glory, for that, if I wished, I could not obtain in a world so enraged against me, nor for the life for my body, for that cannot be made sure of for an hour.—Do you think, then, that you only have a heart that is moved by these tumults? Yet, I am not made of stone, nor was I born from the Marpesian rocks. But since it cannot be otherwise, I choose rather to be battered in temporal tumult, happy in the grace of God, for God's word's sake, which is to be maintained with a mind incorrupt and invincible, than to be ground to powder in eternal tumult, under the wrath of God and torments intolerable! May Christ grant, what I desire and hope, that your heart may not be such—but certainly your words imply, that, with Epicurus, you consider the Word of God and a future life, to be mere fables. For, in your instructions, you would have us, for the sake of the Popes, the heads, and the peace of the community, to put off, upon an occasion, and depart from the all-certain word of God: whereas, if we put off that, we put off God, faith, salvation and all Christianity together. How far different from this is the instruction of Christ: that, we should rather despise the whole world!

Sect. XIX.—But you say these things, because you either do not read or do not observe, that such is most constantly the case with the word of God, that because of it, the world is thrown into tumult. And that Christ openly declares: "I came not (says He) to send peace but a sword." (Matt. x. 34.) And in Luke, "I came to send fire upon the earth." (Luke xii. 49.) And Paul, (2 Cor. vi. 5,) "In tumults," &c. And the Prophet, in the Second Psalm, abundantly testifies the same: declaring 'that the nations are in tumult, the people roaring, the kings rising up, and the princes conspiring against the Lord and against His Christ.' As though He had said, multitude, height, wealth, power, wisdom, righteousness, and whatever is great in the world, sets itself against the word of God.

Look into the Acts of the Apostles, and see what happened in the world on account of the word of Paul only (to say nothing of the other apostles): how he alone throws both the Gentiles and Jews into commotion: or, as the enemies themselves express it, "turns the world upside down." (Acts xvii. 6.) Under Elijah, the kingdom of Israel was thrown into commotion: as king Ahab complains. (1 Kings xviii. 17.) What tumult was there under the other prophets, while they are all either killed at once or stoned to death; while Israel is taken captive into Assyria, and Judah also to Babylon! Was all this peace? The world and its god (2 Cor. iv. 4,) cannot and will not bear the Word of the true God: and the true God cannot and will not keep silence. While, therefore, these two Gods are at war with each other, what can there be else in the whole world, but tumult?

Therefore, to wish to silence these tumults, is nothing else, than to wish to hinder the Word of God, and to take it out of the way! For the Word of God, wherever it comes, comes to change and to renew the world. And even heathen writers testify, that changes of things cannot take place, without commotion and tumult, nor even without blood. It therefore belongs to Christians, to expect and endure these things, with a stayed mind: as Christ says, "When ye shall hear of wars and rumours of wars, be not dismayed, for these things must first come to pass, but the end is not yet." (Matt. xxiv. 6.) And as to myself, if I did not see these tumults, I should say the Word of God was not in the world. But now, when I do see them, I rejoice from my heart, and fear them not: being surely persuaded, that the kingdom of the Pope, with all his followers, will fall to the ground: for it is especially against this, that the Word of God, which now runs, is directed.

I see indeed, my friend Erasmus, that you complain in many books of these tumults, and of the loss of peace and concord; and you attempt many means whereby to afford a remedy, and (as I am inclined to believe) with a good intention. But this gouty foot laughs at your doctoring hands. For here, in truth, as you say, you sail against the tide; nay, you put out fire with straw. Cease from complaining, cease from doctoring; this tumult proceeds, and is carried on, from above, and will not cease until it shall make all the adversaries of the word as the dirt of the streets. Though I am sorry that I find it necessary to teach you, so great a theologian, these things, like a disciple, when you ought to be a teacher of others.

Your excellent sentiment, then, that some diseases may be borne with less evil than they can be cured applies here: which sentiment you do not appositely use. Rather call these tumults, commotions, perturbations, seditions, discords, wars, and all other things of the same kind with which the world is shaken and tossed to and fro on account of the Word of God,—the diseases. These things, I say, as they are temporal, are borne with less evil than inveterate and evil habits; by which all souls must be destroyed if they be not changed by the word of God: which being taken away, eternal good, God, Christ, and the Spirit, must be taken away with it.

But how much better is it to lose the whole world, than to lose God the Creator of the world, who can create innumerable worlds again, and is better than infinite worlds? For what are temporal things when compared with eternal? This leprosy of temporal things, therefore, is rather to be borne, than that every soul should be destroyed and eternally damned, and the world kept in peace, and preserved from these tumults, by their blood and perdition: whereas, one soul cannot be redeemed with the price of the whole world.

You certainly have command of elegant and excellent similitudes, and sentiments: but, when you are engaged in sacred discussions, you apply them childishly, nay, pervertedly: for you crawl upon the ground, and enter in thought into nothing above what is human. Whereas, those things which God works, are neither puerile, civil, nor human, but divine; and they exceed human capacity. Thus, you do not see, that these tumults and divisions increase throughout the world, according to the counsel, and by the operation of God; and therefore, you fear lest heaven should tumble about our ears. But I, by the grace of God, see these things clearly; because, I see other tumults greater than these that will arise in the age to come; in comparison of which, these appear but as the whispering of a breath of air, or the murmuring of a gentle brook.

Sect. XX.—But, the doctrine concerning the liberty of confession and satisfaction, you either deny, or know not that there is the Word of God.—And here arises another inquiry. But we know, and are persuaded, that there is a Word of God, in which the Christian liberty is asserted, that we might not suffer ourselves to be ensnared into bondage by human traditions and laws. This I have abundantly shewn elsewhere. But if you wish to enter the lists, I am prepared to discuss the point with you, and to fight it out. Though upon these subjects I have books extant not a few.

But,—"the laws of the Popes (you say,) may at the same time be borne with and observed, in charity; if perchance thus, eternal salvation by the word of God, and the peace of the world, may together consist, without tumult."—

I have said before, that cannot be. The prince of this world will not allow the Pope and his high-priests, and their laws to be observed in liberty, but his design is, to entangle and bind consciences. This the true God will not bear. Therefore, the Word of God, and the traditions of men, are opposed to each other with implacable discord; no less so, than God Himself and Satan; who each destroy the works and overthrow the doctrines of the other, as regal kings each destroying the kingdom of the other. "He that is not with Me (saith Christ) is against Me." (Luke xi. 23.)

And as to—"a fear, that many who are depravedly inclined, will abuse this liberty"—

This must be considered among those tumults, as a part of that temporal leprosy which is to be borne, and of that evil which is to be endured. But these are not to be considered of so much consequence, as that, for the sake of restraining their abuse, the Word of God should be taken out of the way. For if all cannot be saved, yet some are saved; for whose sake the Word of God is sent; and these, on that account, love it the more fervently, and assent to it the more solemnly. For, what evils did not impious men commit before when there was no word? Nay, what good did they do? Was not the world always drowned in war, fraud, violence, discord, and every kind of iniquity? For if Micah (vii. 4) compares the best among them to a thorn hedge, what to you suppose he would call the rest?

But now the Gospel is come, men begin to impute unto it, that the world is evil. Whereas, the truth is, that by the good Gospel, it is more manifest how evil it was, while, without the Gospel, it did all its works in darkness. Thus also the illiterate attribute it to learning, that, by its flourishing, their ignorance becomes known. This is the return we make for the word of life and salvation! —And what fear must we suppose there was among the Jews, when the Gospel freed all from the law of Moses? What occasion did not this great liberty seem to give to evil men? But yet, the Gospel was not, on that account, taken away; but the impious were left, and it was preached to the pious, that they might not use their liberty to an occasion of the flesh. (Gal. v. 13.)

Sect. XXI.—Nor is this part of your advice, or your remedy, to any purpose, where you say—"It is lawful to speak the truth; but it is not expedient, either before every one, or at all times, or in every manner." And ridiculously enough, you adduce Paul, where he says, "All things are lawful for me, but all things are not expedient."—(1 Cor. vi. 12.)

But Paul does not there speak of teaching doctrine or the truth; as you would confound his words, and twist them which way you please. On the contrary, he will have the truth spoken every where, at all times, and in every manner. So that he even rejoices that Christ is preached even through envy and strife. Nay, he declares in plain words, that he rejoices, let Christ be preached in any way. (Phil. i. 15-18.)

Paul is speaking of facts, and the use of doctrine: that is, of those, who, seeking their own, had no consideration of the hurt and offence given to the weak. Truth and doctrine, are to be preached always, openly, and firmly, and are never to be dissembled or concealed; for there is no offence in them; they are the staff of uprightness.—And who gave you the power, or committed to you the right, of confining the Christian doctrine to persons, places, times, and causes, when Christ wills it to be proclaimed, and to reign freely, throughout the world? For Paul saith, "the Word of God is not bound," (2 Tim. ii. 9,) but Erasmus bounds the word. Nor did God give us the word that it should be had with respect of places, persons, or times: for Christ saith, "Go ye out into the whole world": He does not say, as Erasmus does,—go to this place and not to that. Again, "Preach the Gospel to every creature." (Mark xvi. 15.): He does not say—preach it to some and not to others. In a word, you enjoin, in the administration of the Word of God, a respect of persons, a respect of places, a respect of customs, and a respect of times: whereas, the one and especial part of the glory of the word consists in this,—that, as Paul saith, there is, with it, no respect of persons; and that God is no respecter of persons. You see therefore, again, how rashly you run against the Word of God, as though you preferred far before it, your own counsel and cogitations.

Hence, if we should demand of you that you would determine for us, the times in which, the persons to whom, and the manner in which, the truth is to be spoken, when would you come to an end? The world would sooner compute the termination of time and its own end, than you would settle upon any one certain rule. In the meantime, where would remain the duty of teaching? Where that of teaching the soul? And how could you, who know nothing of the nature of persons, times, and manner, determine upon any rule at all? And even if you should know them perfectly, yet you could not know the hearts of men. Unless, with you, the manner, the time, and the person be this:—teaching the truth so, that the Pope be not indignant, Caesar be not enraged, and that many be not offended and made worse! But what kind of counsel this is, you have seen above.—I have thus rhetorically figured away in these vain words, lest you should appear to have said nothing at all.

How much better is it for us wretched men to ascribe unto God, who knoweth the hearts of all men, the glory of determining the manner in which, the persons to whom, and the times in which the truth is to be spoken! For He knows what is to be spoken to each, and when, and how it is to be spoken. He then, determines that His Gospel which is necessary unto all, should be confined to no place, no time; but that it should be preached unto all, at all times and in all places. And I have already proved, that those things which are handed down to us in the Scriptures, are such, that they are quite plain and wholesome, and of necessity to be proclaimed abroad; even as you yourself determined in your Paraclesis was right to be done; and that, with much more wisdom than you advise now. But let those who would not that souls should be redeemed, such as the Pope and his adherents—let it be left to them to bind the Word of God, and hinder men from life and the kingdom of heaven, that they might neither enter in themselves nor suffer others to enter:—to whose fury you, Erasmus, by this advice of yours, are perniciously subservient.

Sect. XXII.—Of the same stamp with this, is that prudence of yours also, with which you next give it as your advice—'that, if any thing were settled upon, in the councils, that was wrong, it ought not to be openly confessed: lest, a handle should be thereby afforded, for contemning the authority of the fathers.'—

This, indeed, is just what the Pope wished you to say! And he hears it with greater pleasure than the Gospel itself, and will be a most ungrateful wretch, if he do not honour you in return, with a cardinal's cap together with all the revenues belonging to it. But in the mean time, friend Erasmus, what will the souls do that shall be bound and murdered by that iniquitous statute? Is that nothing to you? But however, you always think, or pretend to think, that human statutes can be observed together with the Word of God, without peril. If they could, I would at once go over to this your sentiment.

But if you are yet in ignorance, I tell you again, that human statutes cannot be observed together with the Word of God: because, the former bind consciences, the latter looses them. They are directly opposed to each other, as water to fire. Unless, indeed, they could be observed in liberty; that is, not to bind the conscience. But this the Pope wills not, nor can he will it, unless he wishes his kingdom to be destroyed and brought to an end: for that stands only in ensnaring and binding those consciences, which the Gospel pronounces free. The authority of the fathers, therefore, is to be accounted nought: and those statutes which have been wrongly enacted, (as all have been that are not according to the Word of God) are to be rent in sunder and cast away: for Christ is better than the authority of the fathers. In a word, if it be concerning the Word of God that you think thus, you think impiously; if it be concerning other things, your verbose disputing about your sentiment is nothing to me: I am disputing concerning the Word of God!

Sect. XXIII.—In the last part of your Preface, where you deter us from this kind of doctrine, you think your victory is almost gained.

"What (you say) can be more useless than that this paradox should be proclaimed openly to the world—that whatever is done by us, is not done by Free-will, but from mere necessity. And that of Augustine also—that God works in us both good and evil: that He rewards His good works in us, and punishes His evil works in us." (You are mightily copious here in giving, or rather, in expostulating concerning a reason.) "What a flood-gate of iniquity (you say) would these things, publicly proclaimed, open unto men! What bad man would amend his life! Who would believe that he was loved of God! Who would war against his flesh! "

I wonder, that in so great vehemency, and contending zeal, you did not remember our main subject, and say—where then would be found "Free-will."

My friend, Erasmus! here, again, I also say, if you consider that these paradoxes are the inventions of men, why do you contend against them? Why are you so enraged? Against whom do you rail? Is there any man in the world, at this day, who has inveighed more vehemently against the doctrines of men, than Luther! This admonition of yours, therefore, is nothing to me! But if you believe that those paradoxes are the words of God, where is your countenance, where is your shame, where is, I will not say your modesty, but that fear of, and that reverence which is due to the true God, when you say, that nothing is more useless to be proclaimed than that Word of God! What! shall your Creator, come to learn of you His creature, what is useful, and what not useful to be preached? What! did that foolish and unwise God, know not what is necessary to be taught, until you His instructor prescribed to Him the measure, according to which He should be wise, and according to which He should command? What! did He not know before you told Him, that that which you infer would be the consequence of this His paradox? If, therefore, God willed that such things should be spoken of and proclaimed abroad, without regarding what would follow,—who art thou that forbiddest it?

The apostle Paul, in his Epistle to the Romans, discourses on these same things, not "in a corner," but in public and before the whole world, and that with a freely open mouth, nay in the harshest terms, saying, "whom He will He hardeneth." (Rom. ix. 18.) And again, "God, willing to shew forth His wrath," &c. (Rom. ix. 22.) What is more severe, that is to the flesh, than that word of Christ: "Many are called but few chosen? " (Matt. xxii. 14.) And again, "I know whom I have chosen? " (John xiii. 18.) According to your judgment then, all these things are such, that nothing can be more uselessly spoken; because that by these things, impious men may fall into desperation, hatred, and blasphemy.

Here then, I see, you suppose that the truth and the utility of the Scripture are to be weighed and judged of according to the opinion of men, nay, of men the most impious; so that, what pleases them or seems bearable, should be deemed true, divine, and wholesome: and what has the contrary effect upon them, should at once be deemed useless, false, and pernicious. What else do you mean by all this, than that the words of God should depend on, stand on, and fall by, the will and authority of men? Whereas the Scripture, on the contrary saith, that all things stand and fall by the will and authority of God: and in a word, that "all the earth keeps silence before the face of the Lord." (Hab. ii. 20.) He who could talk as you do, must imagine that the living God is nothing but a kind of trifling and inconsiderate pettifogger declaiming on a certain rostrum, whose words you may if you be disposed, interpret, understand, and refute as you please, because He merely spoke, as He saw a set of impious men to be moved and affected.

Here you plainly discover, how much your advice above,—'that the majesty of the judgments of God should be reverenced,'—was from your heart! There, when we were speaking of the doctrines of the Scripture only, where there was no need of reverencing things abstruse and hidden, because there were no such doctrines, you awed us, in the most religious terms, with the darkness of the Corycian cavern, lest we should rush forward with too much curiosity; so that, by the awe, you well nigh frightened us from reading the Scriptures altogether; (to the reading of which Christ and His apostles urge and persuade us, as well as you do yourself elsewhere.) But here, where we are come not to the doctrines of the Scripture, nor to the Corycian cavern only, but to the very, and greatly to be reverenced secrets of the divine Majesty, viz., why He works thus? —here, as they say, you burst open all bars and rush in; all but, openly blaspheming! What indignation against God do you not discover, because you cannot see His reason why, and His design in this His counsel! Why do you not here frame, as an excuse, obscurity and ambiguity? Why do you not restrain yourself, and deter others from prying into these things which God wills should be hidden from us, and which He has not delivered to us in the Scriptures? It is here the hand is to be laid upon the mouth, it is here we are to reverence what lies hidden, to adore the secret counsels of the divine Majesty, and to exclaim with Paul, "Who art thou, O man, that contendest with God? " (Rom. ix. 20.)

Sect. XXIV.—"Who (you say) will endeavour to amend his life? "—I answer, No man! no man can! For your self-amenders without the Spirit, God regardeth not, for they are hypocrites. But the Elect, and those that fear God, will be amended by the Holy Spirit; the rest will perish unamended. Nor does Augustine say, that the works of *none*, nor that the works *of all* are crowned, but the works *of some.* Therefore, there will be *some,* who shall amend their lives.

"Who will believe (you say) that he is loved of God? "—I answer, no man will believe it! No man can! But the Elect shall believe it; the rest shall perish without believing it, filled with indignation and blaspheming, as you here describe them. Therefore, there will be *some* who shall believe it.

And as to your saying that—"by these doctrines the flood-gate of inquity is thrown open unto men"—be it so. They pertain to that leprosy of evil to be borne, spoken of before. Nevertheless, by the same doctrines, there is thrown open to the Elect and to them that fear God, a gate unto righteousness,—an entrance into heaven—a way unto God! But if, according to your advice, we should refrain from these doctrines, and should hide from men this Word of God, so that each, deluded by a false persuasion of salvation, should never learn to fear God, and should never be humbled, in order that through this fear he might come to grace and love; then, indeed, we should shut up your flood-gate to purpose! For in the room of it, we should throw open to ourselves and to all, wide gates, nay, yawning chasms and sweeping tides, not only unto iniquity, but unto the depths of hell! Thus, we should not enter into Heaven ourselves, and them that were entering in we should hinder.

—"What utility therefore (you say) is there in, or necessity for proclaiming such things openly, when so many evils seem likely to proceed therefrom? "—

I answer. It were enough to say—God has willed that they should be proclaimed openly: but the reason of the divine will is not to be inquired into, but simply to be adored, and the glory to be given unto God: who, since He alone is just and wise, doth evil to no one, and can do nothing rashly or inconsiderately, although it may appear far otherwise unto us. With this answer those that fear God are content. But that, from the abundance of answering matter which I have, I may say a little more than this, which might suffice;—there are two causes which require such things to be preached. The first is, the humbling of our pride, and the knowledge of the grace of God. The second is,

Christian faith itself.

First, God has promised certainly His grace to the humbled: that is, to the self-deploring and despairing. But a man cannot be thoroughly humbled, until he comes to know that his salvation is utterly beyond his own powers, counsel, endeavors, will, and works, and absolutely depending on the will, counsel, pleasure, and work of another, that is, of God only. For if, as long as he has any persuasion that he can do even the least thing himself towards his own salvation, he retain a confidence, in himself and do not utterly despair in himself, so long he is not humbled before God; but he proposes to himself some place, some time, or some work, whereby he may at length attain unto salvation. But he who hesitates not to depend wholly upon the good-will of God, he totally despairs in himself, chooses nothing for himself, but waits for God to work in him; and such an one, is the nearest unto grace, that he might be saved.

These things, therefore, are openly proclaimed for the sake of the Elect: that, being by these means humbled and brought down to nothing, they might be saved. The rest resist this humiliation; nay, they condemn the teaching of self-desperation; they wish to have left a little something that they may do themselves. These secretly remain proud, and adversaries to the grace of God. This, I say, is one reason:—that those who fear God, being humbled, might know, call upon, and receive the grace of God.

The other reason is—that faith is, in *things not seen.* Therefore, that there might be room for faith, it is necessary that all those things which are believed should be hidden. But they are not hidden more deeply, than under the contrary of sight, sense, and experience. Thus, when God makes alive, He does it by killing; when He justifies, He does it by bringing in guilty: when He exalts to Heaven, He does it by bringing down to hell: as the Scripture saith, "The Lord killeth and maketh alive, He bringeth down to the grave and raiseth up," (1 Sam. ii. 6.); concerning which, there is no need that I should here speak more at large, for those who read my writings, are well acquainted with these things.—Thus He conceals His eternal mercy and loving-kindness behind His eternal wrath: His righteousness, behind apparent iniquity.

This is the highest degree of faith—to believe that He is merciful, who saves so few and damns so many; to believe Him just, who according to His own will, makes us necessarily damnable, that He may seem, as Erasmus says, 'to delight in the torments of the miserable, and to be an object of hatred rather than of love.' If, therefore, I could by any means comprehend how that same God can be merciful and just, who carries the appearance of so much wrath and iniquity, there would be no need of faith. But now, since that cannot be comprehended, there is room for exercising faith, while such things are preached and openly proclaimed: in the same manner as, while God kills, the faith of life is exercised in death. Suffice it to have said thus much upon your PREFACE.

In this way, we shall more rightly consult for the benefit of those who dispute upon these paradoxes, than according to your way: whereby, you wish to indulge their impiety by silence, and a refraining from saying any thing: which is to no profit whatever. For if you believe, or even suppose these things to be true, (seeing they are paradoxes of no small moment,) such is the insatiable desire of mortals to search into secret things, and the more so the more we desire to keep them secret, that, by this admonition of yours, you will absolutely make them public; for all will now much more desire to know whether these paradoxes be true or not: thus they will, by your contending zeal, be so roused to inquiry, that not one of us ever afforded such a handle for making them known, as you yourself have done by this over-religious and zealous admonition. You would have acted much more prudently, had you said nothing at all about being cautious in mentioning these paradoxes, if you wished to see your desire accomplished. But, since you do not directly deny that they are true, your aim is frustrated: they cannot be concealed: for, by their appearance of truth, they will draw all men to search into them. Therefore, either deny that they are true altogether, or else hold your own tongue first, if you wish others to hold theirs.

Sect. XXV.—As to the other paradox you mention,—that, 'whatever is done by us, is not done by Free-will, but from mere necessity'—

Let us briefly consider this, lest we should suffer any thing most perniciously spoken, to pass by unnoticed. Here then, I observe, that if it be proved that our salvation is apart from our own strength and counsel, and depends on the working of God alone, (which I hope I shall clearly prove hereafter, in the course of this discussion,) does it not evidently follow, that when God is not present with us to work in us, every thing that we do is evil, and that we of necessity do those things which are of no avail unto salvation? For if it is not we ourselves, but God only, that works salvation in us, it must follow, whether or no, that we do nothing unto salvation *before* the working of God in us.

But, by *necessity*, I do not mean *compulsion;* but (as they term it) the *necessity of immutability,* not of *compulsion:* that is, a man void of the Spirit of God, does not evil against his will as by violence, or as if he were taken by the neck and forced to it, in the same way as a thief or cut-throat is dragged to punishment against his will; but he does it spontaneously, and with a desirous willingness. And this willingness and desire of doing evil he cannot, by his own power, leave off, restrain, or change; but it goes on still desiring and craving. And even if he should be compelled by force to do any thing *outwardly* to the contrary, yet the craving will *within* remains averse to, and rises in indignation against that which forces or resists it. But it would not rise in indignation, if it were changed, and made willing to yield to a constraining power. This is what we mean by the necessity of immutability:—that the will cannot change itself, nor give itself another bent; but rather the more it is resisted, the more it is irritated to crave; as is manifest from its indignation. This would not be the case if it were free, or had a "Free-will." Ask experience, how hardened against all persuasion they are, whose inclinations are fixed upon any one thing. For if they yield at all they yield through force, or through something attended with greater advantage; they never yield willingly. And if their inclinations be not thus fixed, they let all things pass and go on just as they will.

But again, on the other hand, when God works in us, the *will,* being changed and sweetly breathed on by the Spirit of God, desires and acts, not from *compulsion,* but *responsively,* from pure willingness, inclination, and accord; so that it cannot be turned another way by any thing contrary, nor be compelled or overcome even by the gates of hell; but it still goes on to desire, crave after, and love that which is good; even as before, it desired, craved after, and loved that which was evil. This, again, experience proves. How invincible and unshaken are holy men, when, by violence and other oppressions, they are only compelled and irritated the more to crave after good! Even as fire, is rather fanned into flames than extinguished, by the wind. So that neither is there here any willingness, or "Free-will," to turn itself into another direction, or to desire any thing else, while the influence of the Spirit and grace of God remain in the man.

In a word, if we be under the god of this world, without the operation and Spirit of God, we are led captives by him at his will, as Paul saith. (2 Tim. ii. 26.) So that, we cannot will any thing but that which he wills. For he is that "strong man armed," who so keepeth his palace, that those whom he holds captive are kept in peace, that they might not cause any motion or feeling against him; otherwise, the kingdom of Satan, being divided against itself, could not stand; whereas, Christ affirms it does stand. And all this we do willingly and desiringly, according to the nature of *will:* for if it were forced, it would be no longer *will:* For compulsion is (so to speak) *unwillingness.* But if the "stronger than he" come and overcome him, and take us as His spoils, then, through the Spirit, we are His servants and captives (which is the royal liberty) that we may desire and do, willingly, what He wills.

Thus the human will is, as it were, a beast between the two. If God sit thereon, it wills and goes where God will: as the Psalm saith, "I am become as it were a beast before thee, and I am continually with thee." (Ps. lxxiii. 22-23.) If Satan sit thereon, it wills and goes as Satan will. Nor is it in the power of its own will to choose, to which rider it will run, nor which it will seek; but the riders themselves contend, which shall have and hold it.

Sect. XXVI.—And now, what if I prove from your own words, on which you assert the freedom of the will, that there is no such thing as "Free-will" at all! What if I should make it manifest that you unknowingly deny that, which, with so much policy, you labour to affirm. And if I do not this, actually, I vow that I will consider all that I advance in this book against you, revoked; and all that your Diatribe advances against me, and aims at establishing, confirmed.

You make the power of "Free-will" to be—'that certain small degree of power, which, without the grace of God, is utterly ineffective.'

Do you not acknowledge this? —Now then, I ask and demand of you, if the grace of God be wanting, or, if it be taken away from that certain small degree of power, what can it do of itself? 'It is ineffective (you say) and can do nothing of good.' Therefore, it cannot do what God or His grace wills. And why? because we have now separated the grace of God from it; and what the grace of God does not, is not good. And hence it follows, that "Free-will," without the grace of God is, absolutely, not FREE; but, immutably, the servant and bond-slave of evil; because, it cannot turn itself unto good. This being determined, I will allow you to make the power of "Free-will," not only a certain small degree of power, but to make it evangelical if you will, or, if you can, to make it divine: provided that, you add to it this doleful appendage—that, without the grace of God, it is ineffective. Because, then you will at once take from it all power: for, what is ineffective power, but plainly, no power at all?

Therefore, to say, that the will is FREE, and that it has indeed power, but that it is ineffective, is what the Sophists call 'a direct contrariety.' As if one should say, "Free-will" is that which is not free. Or as if one should term fire cold, and earth hot. For if fire had the power of heat, yea of the heat of hell, yet, if it did not burn or scorch, but were cold and produced cold, I should not call it fire, much less should I term it hot; unless, indeed, you were to mean an imaginary fire, or fire represented in a picture.—But if we call the power of "Free-will" that, by which a man is fitted to be caught by the Spirit, or to be touched by the grace of God, as one created unto eternal life or eternal death, may be said to be; this power, that is, fitness, or, (as the Sophists term it) 'disposition-quality,' and 'passive aptitude,' this I also confess. And who does not know, that this is not in trees or beasts? For, (as they say) Heaven was not made for geese.

Therefore, it stands confirmed, even by your own testimony, that we do all things from necessity, not from "Free-will:" seeing that, the power of "Free-will" is nothing, and neither does, nor can do good, without grace. Unless you wish efficacy to bear a new signification, and to be understood as meaning *perfection:* that is, that "Free-will" can, indeed, will and begin, but cannot perfect: which I do not believe: and upon this I shall speak more at large hereafter.

It now then follows, that Free-will is plainly a divine term, and can be applicable to none but the divine Majesty only: for He alone "doth, (as the Psalm sings) what He will in Heaven and earth." (Ps. cxxxv. 6.) Whereas, if it be ascribed unto men, it is not more properly ascribed, than the divinity of God Himself would be ascribed unto them: which would be the greatest of all sacrilege. Wherefore, it becomes Theologians to refrain from the use of this term altogether, whenever they wish to speak of human ability, and to leave it to be applied to God only. And moreover, to take this same term out of the mouths and speech of men; and thus to assert, as it were, for their God, that which belongs to His own sacred and holy Name.

But if they must, whether or no, give some power to men, let them teach, that it is to be called by some other term than "Free-will"; especially since we know and clearly see, that the people are miserably deceived and seduced by that term, taking and understanding it to signify something far different from that which Theologians mean and understand by it, in their discussions. For the term, "Free-will," is by far too grand, copious, and full: by which, the people imagine is signified (as the force and nature of the term requires) that power, which can freely turn itself as it will, and such a power as is under the influence of, and subject to no one. Whereas, if they knew that it was quite otherwise, and that by that term scarcely the least spark or degree of power was signified, and that, utterly ineffective of itself, being the servant and bond-slave of the devil, it would not be at all surprising if they should stone us as mockers and deceivers, who said one thing and meant something quite different; nay, who left it uncertain and unintelligible what we meant. For "he who speaks sophistically (the wise man saith) is hated," and especially if he does so in things pertaining to godliness, where eternal salvation is at stake.

Since, therefore, we have lost the signification of so grand a term and the thing signified by it, or rather, never had them at all, (which the Pelagians may heartily wish had been the case, being themselves illuded by this term,) why do we so tenaciously hold an empty word, to the peril and mockery of the believing people? There is no more wisdom in so doing, than there is in kings and potentates retaining, or claiming and boasting of, empty titles of kingdoms and countries, when they are at the same time mere beggars, and any thing but the possessors of those kingdoms and countries. But however, this is bearable, since they deceive and mock no one thereby, but only feed themselves on vanity without any profit. But here, is a peril of salvation, and the most destructive mockery.

Who would not laugh at, or rather hold up to hatred, that most untimely innovator of terms, who, contrary to all established use, should attempt to introduce such a mode of speaking, as by the term 'beggar,' to have understood, 'wealthy;' not because such an one has any wealth himself, but because some king may, perchance, give him his wealth? And what if such an one should really do this, not by any figure of speech, as by periphrasis or irony, but in plain serious meaning? In the same way, speaking of one 'sick unto death,' he may wish to be understood as meaning, one in 'perfect health:' giving this as his reason, because the one may give the other his health. So also, he may, by 'illiterate idiot,' mean 'most learned;' because some other may perchance give him his learning. Of precisely the same nature is this:—man has a "Free-will:" for this reason, if perchance God should give him His. By this abuse of the manner of speaking, any one may boast that he has any thing: that He is the Lord of heaven and earth—if perchance God should give this unto him. But this is not the way in which Theologians should proceed, this is the way of stage-players and public informers. Our words ought to be proper words, pure and sober; and, as Paul saith, "sound speech that cannot be condemned." (Titus ii. 7-8.)

But, if we do not like to leave out this term altogether, (which would be most safe, and also most religious) we may, nevertheless, with a good conscience teach, that it be used so far as to allow man a "Free-will," not in respect of those which are above him, but in respect only of those things which are below him: that is, he may be allowed to know, that he has, as to his goods and possessions, the right of using, acting, and omitting, according to his "Free-will;" although, at the same time, that same "Free-will" is overruled by the Free-will of God alone, just as He pleases: but that, God-ward, or in things which pertain unto salvation or damnation, he has no "Free-will," but is a captive, slave, and servant, either to the will of God, or to the will of Satan.

Sect. XXVII.—These observations have I made upon the heads of your PREFACE, which, indeed, themselves, may more properly be said to embrace the whole subject, than the following body of the book. But however, the whole of these observations in reply, might have been summed up and made in this one short compendious answer to you.—Your Preface complains, either of the Words of God, or of the words of men. If of the words of men, the whole is written in vain; if of the Words of God, the whole is impious. Wherefore, it would have saved much trouble, if it had been plainly mentioned, whether we were disputing concerning the Words of God, or the words of men. But this, perhaps, will be handled in the EXORDIUM which follows, or in the body of the discussion itself.

But the hints which you have thrown together in the conclusion of your Preface, have no weight whatever.

—Such as, your calling my doctrines 'fables, and useless:' and saying, 'that Christ crucified should rather be preached, after the example of Paul: that wisdom is to be taught among them that are perfect: that the language of Scripture is attempered to the various capacities of hearers: and your therefore thinking, that it should be left to the prudence and charity of the teacher, to teach that which may be profitable to his neighbour'—

All this you advance senselessly, and away from the purpose. For rather do we teach any thing but Christ crucified. But Christ crucified, brings all these things along with Himself, and that 'wisdom also among them that are perfect:' for there is no other wisdom to be taught among Christians, than that which is 'hidden in a mystery:' and this belongs to the 'perfect,' and not to the sons of the Jewish and legal generation, who, without faith, glory in their works, as Paul, 1 Cor. ii., seems to think! Unless by preaching Christ crucified, you mean nothing else but calling out these words—Christ is crucified!

And as to your observing—'that, God is represented as being angry, in a fury, hating, grieving, pitying, repenting, neither of which, nevertheless, ever takes place in Him'—

This is only purposely stumbling on plain ground. For these things neither render the Scriptures obscure, nor necessary to be attempered to the various capacities of hearers. Except that, many like to make obscurities where there are none. For these things are no more than grammatical particulars, and certain figures of speech, with which even school-boys are acquainted. But we, in this disputation, are contending, not about grammatical figures, but about doctrines of truth.

EXORDIUM.

Sect. XXVIII.—At your entrance, then, upon the disputation, you promise—'that you will go according to the Canonical Scriptures: and that, because Luther is swayed by the authority of no other writer whatever'—

Very well! I receive your promise! But however, you do not make the promise on this account, because you judge that these same writers are of no service to your subject; but that you might not enter upon a field of labour in vain. For you do not, I know, quite approve of this audacity of mine, or, by what other term soever you choose to designate this my mode of discussion.

For you say—'so great a number of the most learned men, approved by the consent of so many ages, has no little weight with you. Among whom were, some of the most extensively acquainted with the sacred writings, and also some of the most holy martyrs, many renowned for miracles, together with the more recent theologians, and so many colleges, councils, bishops, and popes: so that, in a word, on your side of the balance are (you say) learning, genius, multitude, greatness, highness, fortitude, sanctity, miracles, and what not! —But that, on my side, are only a Wycliffe and a Laurentius Valla (although Augustine also, whom you pass by, is wholly on my side), who in comparison with the others, are of no weight whatever; that Luther, therefore, stands alone, a private individual, an upstart, with his followers, in whom there is neither that learning nor that genius, nor multitude, nor magnitude, nor sanctity, nor miracles. For they have not ability enough (you say) to cure a lame horse. They make a show of Scripture, indeed; concerning which, however, they are as much in doubt as those on the other side of the question. They boast of the Spirit also, which however, they never show forth.'—And many other things, which, from the length of your tongue, you are able to enumerate in great profusion. But these things have no effect upon us, for we say to you, as the wolf did to the nightingale, which he devoured, *"You are Sound, and that's all!"*—"They say (you observe,) and upon this only, they would have us believe them."

I confess, my friend Erasmus, that you may well be swayed by all these. These had such weight with me for upwards of ten years, that I think no other mortal was ever so much under their sway. And I myself thought it incredible that this Troy of ours, which had for so long a time, and through so many wars stood invincible, could ever be taken. And I call God for a record upon my soul, that I should have continued so, and have been under the same influence even unto this day, had not an urging conscience and an evidence of things, forced me into a different path. And you may easily imagine that my heart was not of stone; and that, if it had been of stone, it would at least have been softened in struggling against so many tides, and being dashed to and fro by so many waves, when I was daring that, which, if I accomplished, I saw that the whole authority of those whom you have just enumerated, would be poured down upon my head like an overwhelming flood.

But this is not a time for setting forth a history of my own life or works; nor have I undertaken this discussion for the purpose of commending myself, but that I might exalt the grace of God. What I am, and with what spirit and design I have been led to these things, I leave to Him who knows, that all this is carrying on according to His own Free-will, not according to mine: though even the world itself ought to have found that out already. And certainly, by this Exordium of yours, you throw me into a very offensive situation, out of which, unless I speak in favour of myself, and to the disparagement of so many fathers, I shall not easily extricate myself. But I will do it in a few words.—According to your own judgment of me, then, I stand apart from all such learning, talents, multitude, authority, and every thing else of the kind.

Now, if I were to demand of you these three things, What is the Manifestation of the Spirit? What are Miracles? What is Sanctification? as far as I have known you from your letters and books, you would appear so great a novice and ignoramus, that you would not be able to give three syllables of explanation. Or, if I should put it to you closely, and demand of you, which one among all those of whom you boast, you could to a certainty bring forth, either as being or having been a saint, or as having possessed the Spirit, or as having wrought miracles, I apprehend you would have hot work of it, and all in vain. You bring forth many things that have been handed about in common use and in public sermons; but you do not credit, how much of their weight and authority they lose, when they are brought to the judgment of conscience. There is an old proverb, "Many were accounted saints on earth, whose souls are now in hell! "

Sect. XXIX.—But we will grant you, if you please, that they were all saints, that they all had the Spirit, that they all wrought miracles (which, however, you do not require.) But tell me this—was any one of them made a saint, did any one of them receive the Spirit or work miracles, in the name, or by virtue of "Free-will," or to confirm the doctrine of "Free-will"? Far be such a thought (you will say,) but in the name, and by virtue of Jesus Christ, and for the confirmation of the doctrine of Christ, all these things were done. Why then do you bring forward the sanctity, the spirit, and the miracles of these, in confirmation of the doctrine of "Free-will," for which they were not wrought and given?

Their miracles, Spirit, and sanctity, therefore, belong to us who preach Jesus Christ, and not the ability and works of men. And now, what wonder if those who were thus holy, spiritual, and wonderful for miracles, were sometimes under the influence of the flesh, and spoke and wrought according to the flesh; since that happened, not once only, to the very apostles under Christ Himself. For you do not deny, but assert, that "Free-will" does not belong to the Spirit, or to Christ, but is human; so that, the Spirit who is promised to glorify Christ, cannot preach "Free will." If, therefore, the fathers have at any time preached "Free-will," they have certainly spoken from the flesh, (seeing they were men,) not from the Spirit of God; much less did they work miracles for its confirmation. Wherefore, your allegation concerning the sanctity, the Spirit, and the miracles of the fathers is nothing to the purpose, because "Free-will" is not proved thereby, but the doctrine of Jesus Christ against the doctrine of "Free-will."

But come, shew forth still, you that are on the side of "Free-will," and assert that a doctrine of this kind is true, that is, that it proceeds from the Spirit of God—shew forth still, I say, the Spirit, still work miracles, still evidence sanctity. Certainly you who make the assertion owe this to us, who deny these things. The Spirit, sanctity, and miracles ought not to be demanded of us who maintain the negative, but from you who assert in the affirmative. The negative proposes nothing, is nothing, and is bound to prove nothing, nor ought to be proved: it is the affirmative that ought to be proved. You assert the power of "Free-will" and the human cause: but no miracle was ever seen or heard of, as proceeding from God, in support of a doctrine of the human cause, only in support of the doctrines of the divine cause. And we are commanded to receive no doctrine whatever, that is not first proved by signs from on high. (Deut. xviii. 15-22.) Nay, the Scripture calls man "vanity," and "a lie:" which is nothing less than saying, that all human things are vanities and lies. Come forward then! come forward! I say, and prove, that your doctrine, proceeding from human vanity and a lie, is true. Where is now your shewing forth the Spirit! Where is your sanctity! Where are your miracles! I see your talents, your erudition, and your authority; but those things God has given alike unto all the world!

But however, we will not compel you to work great miracles, nor "to cure a lame horse," lest you should plead, as an excuse, the carnality of the age. Although God is wont to confirm His doctrines by miracles, without any respect to the carnality of the age: nor is He at all moved, either by the merits or demerits of a carnal age, but by pure mercy and grace, and a love of souls which are to be confirmed, by solid truth, unto their glory. But we give you the choice of working any miracles, as small an one as you please.

But come! I, in order to irritate your Baal into action, insult, and challenge you to create even one frog, in the name, and by virtue of "Free-will;" of which, the Gentile and impious Magi in Egypt, could create many. I will not put you to the task of creating lice; which, neither could they produce. But I will descend a little lower yet. Take even one flea, or louse, (for you tempt and deride our God by your 'curing of the lame horse,') and if, after you have combined all the powers, and concentrated all the efforts both of your god and your advocates, you can, in the name and by virtue of "Free-will," kill it, you shall be victors; your cause shall be established; and we also will immediately come over and adore that god of yours, that wonderful killer of the louse. Not that I deny, that you could even remove mountains; but it is one thing to say, that a certain thing was done by "Free-will," and another to prove it.

And, what I have said concerning miracles, I say also concerning sanctity.—If you can, out of such a series of ages, men, and all the things which you have mentioned, shew forth one work, (if it be but the lifting a straw from the earth,) or one word, (if it be but the syllable MY,) or one thought of "Free-will," (if it be but the faintest sigh,) by which men applied themselves unto grace, or by which they have merited the Spirit, or by which they have obtained pardon, or by which they have prevailed with God even in the smallest degree, (I say nothing about being sanctified thereby,) again, I say, you shall be victors, and we vanquished; and that, as I repeat, in the name and by virtue of "Free-will."

For what things soever are wrought in men by the power of divine creation, are supported by Scripture testimonies in abundance. And certainly, you ought to produce the same: unless you would appear such ridiculous teachers, as to spread abroad throughout the world, with so much arrogance and authority, doctrines concerning that, of which you cannot produce one proof. For such doctrines will be called mere dreams, which are followed by nothing: than which, nothing can be more disgraceful to men of so many ages, so great, so learned, so holy, and so miraculous! And if this be the case, we shall rank even the stoics before you: for although they took upon them to describe such a wise man as they never saw, yet they did attempt to set forth some part of the character. But you cannot set forth any thing whatever, not even the shadow of your doctrine.

The same also I observe concerning the Spirit. If you can produce one out of all the assertors of "Free-will," who ever had a strength of mind and affection, even in the smallest degree, so as, in the name and by virtue of "Free-will," to be able to disregard one farthing, or to be willing to be without one farthing, or to bear one word or sign of injury, (I do not speak of the stoical contempt of riches, life, and fame,) again, the palm of victory shall be yours, and we, as the vanquished, will willingly pass under the spear. And these proofs you, who with such trumpeting mouths sound forth the power of "Free-will," are bound to produce before us. Or else, again, you will appear to be striving to give establishment to a nothing: or to be acting like him, who sat to see a play in an empty theatre.

Sect. XXX.—But I will easily prove to you the contrary of all this:—that such holy men as you boast of, whenever they approach God, either to pray or to do, approach Him, utterly forgetful of their own "Free-will" and despairing of themselves, crying unto Him for pure grace only, feeling at the same time that they deserve every thing that is the contrary. In this state was Augustine often; and in the same state was Bernard, when, at the point of death, he said, "I have lost my time, because I have lived wrong." I do not see, here, that there was any power spoken of which could apply itself unto Grace, but that all power was condemned as being only averse; although those same saints, at the time when they disputed concerning "Free-will," spoke otherwise. And the same I see has happened unto all, that, when they are engaged in words and disputations, they are one thing; but another, when they came to experience and practice. In the former, they speak differently from what they felt before; in the latter, they feel differently from what they spoke before. But men, good as well as bad, are to be judged of, more from what they feel, than from what they say.

But we will indulge you still further. We will not require miracles, the Spirit, and sanctity. We return to the doctrine itself. We only require this of you:—that you would at least explain to us, what work, what word, what thought, that power of "Free-will" can move, attempt, or perform, in order to apply itself unto grace. For it is not enough to say, there is! there is! there is a certain power of "Free-will! " For what is more easily said than this? Nor does such a way of proceeding become men the most learned, and the most holy, who have been approved by so many ages, but must be called baby-like (as we say in a German proverb.) It must be defined, what that power is, what it can do, in what it is passive, and what takes place. To give you an example (for I shall press you most homely) this is what is required:—Whether that power must pray, or fast, or labour, or chastise the body, or give alms; or what other work of this kind it must do, or attempt. For if it be a power it must do some kind of work. But here you are more dumb than Seriphian frogs and fishes. And how should you give the definition, when, according to your own testimony, you are at an uncertainty about the power itself, at difference among each other, and inconsistent with yourselves? And what must become of the definition, when the thing to be defined has no consistency in itself?

But be it so, that since the time of Plato, you are at length agreed among yourselves concerning the power itself; and that its work may be defined to be praying, or fasting, or something of the same kind, which perhaps, still lies undiscovered in the ideas of Plato. Who shall certify us that such is truth, that it pleases God, and that we are doing right, in safety? Especially when you yourselves assert that there is a human cause which has not the testimony of the Spirit, because of its having been handled by philosophers, and having existed in the world before Christ came, and before the Spirit was sent down from heaven. It is most certain, then, that this doctrine was not sent down from heaven with the Spirit, but sprung from the earth long before: and therefore, there is need of weighty testimony, whereby it may be confirmed to be true and sure.

We will grant, therefore, that we are private individuals and few, and you public characters and many; we ignorant, and you the most learned: we stupid, and you the most acute; we creatures of yesterday, and you older than Deucalion; we never received, and you approved by so many ages; in a word, we sinners, carnal, and dolts, and you awe-striking to the very devils, for your sanctity, spirit, and miracles.— Yet allow us the right at least of Turks and Jews, to ask of you that reason for your doctrine, which your favourite Peter has commanded you to give. We ask it of you in the most modest way: that is, we do not require it to be proved by sanctity, by the Spirit, and by miracles, (which however, we could do in our own right, seeing that you yourselves require that of others): nay, we even indulge you so far, as not to require you to produce any example of a work, a word, or a thought, in confirmation of your doctrine but only to explain to us the doctrine itself, and merely to tell us plainly, what you would have to be understood by it, and what the form of it is. If you will not, or cannot do this, then let us at least attempt to set forth an example of it ourselves. For you are as bad as the Pope himself, and his followers, who say, "You are to do as we *say,* but not to do, as we *do.*" In the same manner you say, that that power requires a work to be done: and so, we shall be set on to work, while you remain at your ease. But will you not grant us this, that the more you are in numbers, the longer you are in standing, the greater you are, the farther you are on all accounts superior to us, the more disgraceful it is to you, that we, who in every respect are as nothing in your eyes, should desire to learn and practise your doctrine, and that you should not be able to prove it, either by any miracle, or by the killing of a louse, or by any the least motion of the Spirit, or by any the least work of sanctity, nor even to bring forth any example of it, either in work or word? And further, (a thing unheard of before) that you should not be able to tell us plainly of what form the doctrine is, and how it is to be understood? –O excellent teachers of "Free-will! " What are *you*, now, but *"Sound only! "* Who now, Erasmus, are they who "boast of the Spirit but shew it not forth? " Who "say only, and then wish men to believe them? " Are not your friends they, who are thus extolled to the skies, and who can say nothing, and yet boast of, and exact such great things?

We entreat, therefore, you and yours, my friend Erasmus, that you will allow us to stand aloof and tremble with fear, alarmed at the peril of our conscience; or, at least, to wave our assenting to a doctrine, which, as you yourself see, even though you should succeed to the utmost, and all your arguments should be proved and established, is nothing but an empty term, and a sounding of these syllables–'There is a power of "Free-will! " '–There is a power of "Free-will! "–Moreover, it still remains an uncertainty among your own friends themselves, whether it be *a term* even, or *not*: for they differ from each other, and are inconsistent with themselves. It is most iniquitous, therefore, nay, the greatest of miseries, that our consciences, which Christ has redeemed by His blood, should be tormented by the ghost of one term, and that, a term which has no certainty in it. And yet, if we should not suffer ourselves to be thus tormented, we should be held as guilty of unheard-of pride, for disregarding so many fathers of so many ages, who have asserted "Free-will." Whereas, the truth is, as you see from what has been said, they never defined any thing whatever concerning "Free-will": but the doctrine of "Free-will" is erected under the covering, and upon the basis of their name: of which, nevertheless, they can shew no form, and for which, they can fix no term: and thus they delude the world with a term, that is a lie!

Sect. XXXI.—And here, Erasmus, I call to your remembrance your own advice. You just now advised–'that questions of this kind be omitted; and that, Christ crucified be rather taught, and those things which suffice unto Christian piety'–but this, we are now seeking after and doing. What are we contending for, but that the simplicity and purity of the Christian doctrine should prevail, and that those things should be left and disregarded, which have been invented, and introduced with it, by men? But you who give this advice, do not act according to it yourself: nay you act contrary to it: you write Diatribes: you exalt the decrees of the Popes: you honour the authority of men: and you try all means to draw us aside into these strange things and contrary to the Holy Scriptures: but you consider not the things that are necessary, how that, by so doing we should corrupt the simplicity and sincerity of the Scriptures, and confound them with the added inventions of men. From which, we plainly discover, that you did not give us that advice, from your heart; and that you write nothing seriously, but take it for granted that you can, by the empty bulls of your words, turn the world as you please. Whereas you turn them no where: for you say nothing whatever but mere contradictions, in all things, and every where. So that he would be most correct, who should call you, the very Proteus himself, or Vertumnus: or should say with Christ, 'Physician, heal thyself.'—'The teacher, whose own faults his ignorance prove, has need to hide his head! '—

Until, therefore, you shall have proved your affirmative, we stand fast in our negative. And in the judgment, even of all that company of saints of whom you boast, or rather, of the whole world, we dare to say, and we glory in saying, that it is our duty not to admit that which is nothing, and which cannot, to a certainty, be proved what it is. And you must all be possessed of incredible presumption or of madness, to demand that to be admitted by us, for no other reason, than because you, as being many, great, and of long standing, choose to assert that, which you yourselves acknowledge to be nothing. As though it were a conduct becoming Christian teachers, to mock the miserable people, in things pertaining to godliness, with that which is nothing, as if it were a matter that essentially concerned their salvation. Where is that former acumen of the Grecian talent, which heretofore, at least covered lies under some elegant semblage of truth— it now lies in open and naked words! Where is that former dexteriously laboured Latinity—it now thus deceives, and is deceived, by one most empty *term!*

But thus it happens to the senseless, or the malicious readers, of books: all those things which were the infirmities of the fathers or of the saints, they make to be of the highest authority: the fault, therefore, is not in the authors, but in the readers. It is as though one relying on the holiness and the authority of St. Peter, should contend that all that St. Peter ever said was true: and should even attempt to persuade us that it was truth, when, (Matt. xvi. 22,) from the infirmity of the flesh, he advised Christ not to suffer. Or that: where he commanded Christ to depart from him out of the ship. (Luke v. 8.) And many other of those things, for which he was rebuked of Christ.

Men of this sort are like unto them, who, for the sake of ridicule, idly say, that all things that are in the Gospel are not true. And they catch hold of that, (John viii. 48): where the Jews say unto Christ, "Do we not say well that thou art a Samaritan, and hast a devil? " Or that: "He is guilty of death." Or that: "We found this fellow perverting our nation, and forbidding to give tribute to Caesar." These, do the same thing as those assertors of "Free-will," but for a different end, and not wilfully, but from blindness and ignorance; for they, so catch at that which the fathers, falling by the infirmity of the flesh, have said in favour of "Free-will," that they even oppose it to that which the same fathers have elsewhere, in the power of the Spirit, said against "Free-will": nay, they so urge and force it, that the better is made to give way to the worse. Hence it comes to pass, that they give authority to the worse expressions, because they fall in with their fleshly mind; and take it from the better, because they make against their fleshly mind.

But why do we not rather select the better? For there are many such in the fathers.—To produce an example. What can be more carnally, nay, what more impiously, sacrilegiously, and blasphemously spoken, than that which Jerome is wont to say—'Virginity peoples heaven, and marriage, the earth.' As though the earth, and not heaven, was intended for the patriarchs, the apostles, and Christian husbands. Or, as though heaven was designed for gentile vestal virgins, who are without Christ. And yet, these things and others of the same kind, the Sophists collect out of the fathers that they may procure unto them authority, carrying all things more by numbers than by judgment. As that disgusting carpenter of Constance did, who lately made that jewel of his, the Stable of Augeas, a present to the public, that there might be a something to cause nausea and vomit in the pious and the learned.

Sect. XXXII.—And now, while I am making these observations, I will reply to that remark of yours, where you say—'that it is not to be believed, that God would overlook an error in His Church for so many ages, and not reveal to any one of His saints that, which we contend for as being the grand essential of the Christian doctrine'—

In the first place, we do not say that this error was overlooked of God in His Church, or in any one of His Saints. For the Church is ruled by the Spirit of God, and the Saints are led by the Spirit of God. (Rom. viii. 14.) And Christ is with His Church even unto the end of the world. (Matt. xxviii. 20.) And the Church is the pillar and ground of the truth. (1 Tim. iii. 15.) These things, I say, we know; for the Creed which we all hold runs thus, "I believe in the Holy Catholic Church;" so that, it is impossible that she can err even in the least article. And even if we should grant, that some of the Elect are held in error through the whole of their life; yet they must, of necessity, return into the way of truth before their death; for Christ says, (John x. 28.) "No one shall pluck them out of My hand." But this is the labour, this the point—whether it can be proved to a certainty, that those, whom you call the church, were the Church; or, rather, whether, having been in error throughout their whole life, they were at last brought back before death. For this will not easily be proved, if God suffered all those most learned men whom you adduce, to remain in error through so long a series of ages—Therefore, God suffered His Church to be in error.

But, look at the people of Israel: where, during so many kings and so long a time, not one king is mentioned who never was in error. And under Elijah the Prophet, all the people and every thing that was public among them, had so gone away into idolatry, that he thought that he himself was the only one left: whereas, while the kings, the princes, the prophets, and whatever could be called the people or the Church of God was going to destruction, God was reserving to Himself "seven thousand." (Rom. xi. 4.) But who could see these or know them to be the people of God? And who, even now, dares to deny that God, under all these great men, (for you make mention of none but men in some high office, or of some great name,) was reserving to Himself a Church among the commonalty, and suffering all those to perish after the example of the kingdom of Israel? For it is peculiar to God, to restrain the elect of Israel, and to slay their fat ones: but, to preserve the refuse and remnant of Israel, (Ps. lxxviii. 31; Isaiah i. 9., x. 20-22., xi. 11-16.)

What happened under Christ Himself, when all the Apostles were offended at Him, when He was denied and condemned by all the people, and there were only a Joseph, a Nicodemus, and a thief upon the cross preserved? Were *they* then said to be the people of God? There was, indeed, a people of God remaining, but it was not called the people of God; and that which was so called, was not the people of God. And who knows who are the people of God, when throughout the whole world, from its origin, the state of the church was always such, that those were called the people and saints of God who were not so; while others among them, who were as a refuse, and were not called the people and saints of God, were the People and Saints of God? as is manifest in the histories of Cain and Abel, of Ishmael and Isaac, of Esau and Jacob.

Look again at the age of the Arians, when scarcely five catholic bishops were preserved throughout the whole world, and they, driven from their places, while the Arians reigned, every where bearing the public name and office of the church. Nevertheless, under these heretics, Christ preserved His Church: but so, that it was the least thought or considered to be the Church.

Again, shew me, under the kingdom of the Pope, one bishop discharging his office. Shew me one council in which their transactions were, concerning the things pertaining to godliness, and not rather, concerning gowns, dignities, revenues, and other baubles, which they could not say, without being mad, pertained to the Holy Spirit! Nevertheless they are called the church, when all, at least who live as they do, must be reprobates and any thing but the church. And yet, even under them Christ preserved His Church, though it was not called the Church. How many Saints must you imagine those of the inquisition have, for some ages, burnt and killed, as John Huss and others, in whose time, no doubt there lived many holy men of the same spirit!

Why do you not rather wonder at this, Erasmus, that there ever were, from the beginning of the world, more distinguished talents, greater erudition, more ardent pursuit among the world in general than among Christians or the people of God? As Christ Himself declares, "The children of this world are wiser than the children of light." (Luke xvi. 8.) What Christian can be compared (to say nothing of the Greeks) with Cicero alone for talents, for erudition, or for indefatigability? What shall we say, then, was the preventive cause that no one of them was able to attain unto grace, who certainly exerted "Free-will" with its utmost powers? Who dares say, that there was no one among them who contended for truth with all his efforts? And yet we must affirm that no one of them all attained unto it. Will you here too say, it is not to be believed, that God would utterly leave so many great men, throughout such a series of ages, and permit them to labour in vain? Certainly, if "Free-will" were any thing, or could do any thing, it must have appeared and wrought something in those men, at least in some one instance. But it availed nothing, nay it always wrought in the contrary direction. Hence by this argument only, it may be sufficiently proved, that "Free-will" is nothing at all, since no proof of it can be produced even from the beginning of the world to the end!

Sect. XXXIII.—But to return—What wonder, if God should leave all the elders of the church to go their own ways, who thus permitted all the nations to go *their* own ways, as Paul saith, Acts xiv. 16, xvii. 30? —But, my friend Erasmus, THE CHURCH OF GOD INDEED, IS NOT SO COMMON A THING AS THIS TERM, CHURCH OF GOD: NOR ARE THE SAINTS OF GOD INDEED, EVERY WHERE TO BE FOUND LIKE THE TERM, SAINTS OF GOD. THEY ARE PEARLS AND PRECIOUS JEWELS, WHICH THE SPIRIT DOES NOT CAST BEFORE SWINE; BUT WHICH, (AS THE SCRIPTURE EXPRESSES IT,) HE KEEPS HIDDEN, THAT THE WICKED SEE NOT THE GLORY OF GOD! Otherwise, if they were openly known of all, how could it come to pass that they should be thus vexed and afflicted in the world? As Paul saith, (1 Cor. ii. 8,) "Had they known Him, they would not have crucified the Lord of glory."

I do not say these things, because I deny that those whom you mention are the saints and church of God; but because it cannot be proved, if any one should deny it, that they really are saints, but must be left quite in uncertainty; and because, therefore, the position deduced from their holiness, is not sufficiently credible for the confirmation of my doctrine. I call them saints, and look upon them as such: I call them the church, and look upon them as such—according to the law of Charity, but not according to the law of Faith. That is, charity, which always thinks the best of every one, and suspects not, but believeth and presumes all things for good concerning its neighbour, calls every one who is baptized, a saint. Nor is there any peril if she err, for charity is liable to err; seeing that she is exposed to all the uses and abuses of all; an universal handmaid, to the good and to the evil, to the believing and to the unbelieving, to the true and to the false.—But faith, calls no one a saint but him who is declared to be so by the judgment of God, for faith is not liable to be deceived. Therefore, although we ought all to be looked upon as saints by each other by the law of charity, yet no one ought to be decreed a saint by the law of faith, so as to make it an article of faith that such or such an one is a Saint. For in this way, that adversary of God, the Pope, canonized his minions whom he knows not to be saints, setting himself in the place of God. (2 Thess. ii. 4.)

All that I say concerning those saints of yours, or rather, ours, is this:—that since they have spoken differently from each other, those should rather be selected who have spoken the best: that is, who have spoken in defense of Grace, and against "Free-will": and those left, who, through the infirmity of the flesh, have borne witness of the flesh rather than of the Spirit. And also, that those who are inconsistent with themselves, should be selected and caught at, in those parts of their writings where they speak from the Spirit, and left, where they savour of the flesh. This is what becomes a Christian reader, and a 'clean beast dividing the hoof and chewing the cud.' (Lev. xi. 3., Deut. xiv. 6.) Whereas now, laying aside judgment, we swallow down all things together, or, what is worse, by a perversion of judgment, we cast away the best and receive the worst, out of the same authors; and moreover, affix to those worst parts, the title and authority of their sanctity; which sanctity, they obtained, not on account of "Free-will" or the flesh, but on account of the best things, even of the Spirit only.

Sect. XXXIV.—But you say—"what therefore shall we do? The Church is hidden, the Saints are unknown! What, and whom shall we believe? Or, as you most sharply dispute, who will certify us? How shall we search out the Spirit? If we look to erudition, all are rabbins! If we look to life, all are sinners! If we look to the Scripture, they each claim it as belonging to them! But however, our discussion is not so much concerning the Scripture (which is not itself sufficiently clear,) but concerning the sense of the Scripture. And though there are men of every order at hand, yet, as neither numbers, nor erudition, nor dignity, is of any service to the subject, much less can paucity, ignorance, and mean rank avail any thing."—

Well then! I suppose the matter must be left in doubt, and the point of dispute remain before the judge: so that, we should seem to act with policy if we should go over to the sentiments of the Sceptics. Unless, indeed, we were to act as you wisely do, for you pretend that you are so much in doubt, that you professedly desire to seek and learn the truth; while, at the same time, you cleave to those who assert "Free-will," until the truth be made glaringly manifest.

But no! I here in reply to you observe, that you neither say all, nor nothing. For we shall not search out the Spirit by the arguments of erudition, of life, of talent, of multitude, of dignity, of ignorance, of inexperience, of paucity, or of meanness of rank. And yet, I do not approve of those, whose whole resource is in a boasting of the Spirit. For I had the last year, and have still, a sharp warfare with those fanatics who subject the Scriptures to the interpretation of their own boasted spirit. On the same account also, I have hitherto determinately set myself against the Pope, in whose kingdom, nothing is more common, or more generally received than this saying:—'that the Scriptures are obscure and ambiguous; and that the Spirit, as the Interpreter, should be sought from the apostolical see of Rome! ' than which, nothing could be said that was more destructive; for by means of this saying, a set of impious men have exalted themselves above the Scriptures themselves; and by the same, have done whatever pleased them; till at length, the Scriptures are absolutely trodden under foot, and we compelled to believe and teach nothing but the dreams of men that are mad. In a word, that saying is no human invention, but a poison poured forth into the world by a wonderful malice of the devil himself, the prince of all demons.

We hold the case thus:—that the spirits are to be tried and proved by a twofold judgment. The one, internal; by which, through the Holy Spirit, or a peculiar gift of God, any one may illustrate, and to a certainty, judge of, and determine on, the doctrines and sentiments of all men, for himself and his own personal salvation: concerning which it is said, (1 Cor. ii. 15,) "The spiritual man judgeth all things, but he himself is judged of no man." This belongs to faith, and is necessary for every, even private, Christian. This, we have above called, 'the internal clearness of the Holy Scripture.' And it was this perhaps to which *they* alluded, who, in answer to you said, that all things must be determined by the judgment of the Spirit. But this judgment cannot profit another, nor are we speaking of this judgment in our present discussion; for no one, I think, doubts its reality.

The other, then, is the external judgment; by which, we judge, to the greatest certainty, of the spirits and doctrines of all men; not for ourselves only, but for others also, and for their salvation. This judgment is peculiar to the public ministry of the Word and the external office, and especially belongs to teachers and preachers of the Word. Of this we make use, when we strengthen the weak in faith, and when we refute adversaries. This is what we before called, 'the external clearness of the Holy Scripture.' Hence we affirm that all spirits are to be proved in the face of the church, by the judgment of Scripture. For this ought, above all things, to be received, and most firmly settled among Christians:—that the Holy Scriptures are a spiritual light by far more clear than the sun itself, especially in those things which pertain unto salvation or necessity.

Sect. XXXV.—But, since we have been persuaded to the contrary of this, by that pestilent saying of the Sophists, 'the Scriptures are obscure and ambiguous;' we are compelled, first of all, to prove that first grand principle of ours, by which all other things are to be proved: which 'among the Sophists, is considered absurd and impossible to be done.'

First then, Moses saith, (Deut. xvii. 8,) that, 'if there arise a matter too hard in judgment, men are to go to the place which God shall choose for His name, and there to consult the priests, who are to judge of it according to the law of the Lord.'

He saith, "according to the law of the Lord"—but how will they judge thus, if the law of the Lord be not externally most clear, so as to satisfy them concerning it? Otherwise, it would have been sufficient, if he had said, according to their own spirit. Nay, it is so in every government of the people, the causes of all are adjusted according to laws. But how could they be adjusted, if the laws were not most certain, and absolutely, very lights to the people? But if the laws were ambiguous and uncertain, there would not only be no causes settled, but no certain consistency of manners. Since, therefore, laws are enacted that manners may be regulated according to a certain form, and questions in causes settled, it is necessary that that, which is to be the rule and standard for men in their dealings with each other, as the law is, should of all things be the most certain and most clear. And if that light and certainty in laws, in profane administrations where temporal things only are concerned, are necessary, and have been, by the goodness of God, freely granted to the whole world; how shall He not have given to Christians, that is to His own Elect, laws and rules of much greater light and certainty, according to which they might adjust and settle both themselves and all their causes? And that more especially, since He wills that all temporal things should, by *His,* be despised. And "if God so clothe the grass of the field, which to-day is, and to-morrow is cast into the oven," how much more shall He clothe us? (Matt. vi, 30)—But, let us proceed, and drown that pestilent saying of the Sophists, in Scriptures.

Psalm xix. 8, saith, "The commandment of the Lord is clear (or pure), enlightening the eyes." And surely, that which enlightens the eyes, cannot be obscure or ambiguous!

Again, Psalm cxix. 130, "The door of thy words giveth light; it giveth understanding to the simple." Here, it is ascribed unto the words of God, that they are a door, and something open, which is quite plain to all and enlightens even the simple.

Isaiah viii. 20, sends all questions "to the law and to the testimony;" and threatens that if we do not this, the light of the east shall be denied us.

In Malachi, ii. 7, commands, 'that they should seek the law from the mouth of the priest, as being the messenger of the Lord of Hosts.' But a most excellent messenger indeed of the Lord of Hosts he must be, who should bring forth those things, which were both so ambiguous to himself and so obscure to the people, that neither he should know what he himself said, nor they what they heard!

And what, throughout the Old Testament, in the 119th Psalm especially, is more frequently said in praise of the Scripture, than that, it is itself a most certain and most clear light? For Ps. cxix. 105, celebrates its clearness thus: "Thy word is a lamp unto my feet and a light unto my paths." He does not say only—thy Spirit is a lamp unto my feet; though he ascribes unto Him also His office, saying, "Thy good Spirit shall lead me into the land of uprightness." (Ps. cxliii. 10.) Thus the Scripture is called a "way" and a "path:" that is from its most perfect certainty.

Sect. XXXVI.—Now let us come to the New Testament. Paul saith, (Rom. i. 2,) that the Gospel was promised "by the Prophets in the Holy Scriptures." And, (Rom. iii. 21,) that the righteousness of faith was testified "by the law and the Prophets." But what testimony is that, if it be obscure? Paul, however, throughout all his epistles makes the Gospel, the word of light, the Gospel of clearness; and he professedly and most copiously sets it forth as being so, 2 Cor. iii. and iv.; where he treats most gloriously concerning the clearness both of Moses and of Christ.

Peter also saith, (2 Pet. i. 19,) "And we certainly have more surely the word of prophecy; unto which, ye do well that ye take heed, as unto a light shining in a dark place." Here Peter makes the Word of God a clear lamp, and all other things darkness: whereas, we make obscurity and darkness of the Word.

Christ also often calls Himself, the "light of the world;" (John viii. 12. ix. 5,) and John the Baptist, a "burning and a shining light." (John v. 35.) Certainly, not on account of the holiness of his life, but on account of the word which he ministered. In the same manner Paul calls the Philippians shining "lights of the world," (Phil. ii. 15), because (says he,) ye "hold forth the word of life." (16.) For life without the word is uncertain and obscure.

And what is the design of the apostles in proving their preaching by the Scriptures? Is it that they may obscure their own darkness by still greater darkness? What was the intention of Christ, in teaching the Jews to "search the Scriptures" (John v. 39,) as testifying of Him? Was it that He might render them doubtful concerning faith in Him? What was *their* intention, who having heard Paul, searched the Scriptures night and day, "to see if these things were so? " (Acts xvii. 11.) Do not all these things prove that the Apostles, as well as Christ Himself, appealed to the Scriptures as the most clear testimonies of the truth of their discouses? With what face then do we make them 'obscure? '

Are these words of the Scripture, I pray you, obscure or ambiguous: "God created the heavens and the earth" (Gen. i. 1.) "The Word was made flesh." (John i. 14,) and all those other words which the whole world receives as articles of faith? Whence then, did they receive them? Was it not from the Scriptures? And what do those who at this day preach? Do they not expound and declare the Scriptures? But if the Scripture which they declare, be obscure, who shall certify us that their declaration is to be depended on? Shall it be certified by another new declaration? But who shall make that declaration? —And so we may go on *ad infinitum.*

In a word, if the Scripture be obscure or ambiguous, what need was there for its being sent down from heaven? Are we not obscure and ambiguous enough in ourselves, without an increase of it by obscurity, ambiguity, and darkness being sent down unto us from heaven? And if this be the case, what will become of that of the apostle, "All Scripture is given by inspiration of God, and is profitable for doctrine, for reproof, for correction? " (2 Tim. iii. 16.) Nay, Paul, thou art altogether useless, and all those things which thou ascribest unto the Scripture, are to be sought for out of the fathers approved by a long course of ages, and from the Roman see! Wherefore, thy sentiment must be revoked, where thou writest to Titus, (chap. i. 9,) 'that a bishop ought to be powerful in doctrine, to exhort and to convince the gainsayers, and to stop the mouths of vain talkers, and deceivers of minds.' For how shall he be powerful, when thou leavest him the Scriptures in obscurity—that is, as arms of tow and feeble straws, instead of a sword? And Christ must also, of necessity, revoke His word where He falsely promises us, saying, "I will give you a mouth and wisdom which all your adversaries shall not be able to resist," (Luke xxi. 15.) For how shall they not resist when we fight against them with obscurities and uncertainties? And why do you also, Erasmus, prescribe to us a form of Christianity, if the Scriptures be obscure to you!

But I fear I must already be burdensome, even to the insensible, by dwelling so long and spending so much strength upon a point so fully clear; but it was necessary, that that impudent and blasphemous saying, 'the Scriptures are obscure,' should thus be drowned. And you, too, my friend Erasmus, know very well what you are saying, when you deny that the Scripture is clear, for you at the same time drop into my ear this assertion: 'it of necessity follows therefore, that all your saints whom you adduce, are much less clear.' And truly it would be so. For who shall certify us concerning their light, if you make the Scriptures obscure? Therefore they who deny the all-clearness and all-plainness of the

Scriptures, leave us nothing else but darkness.

Sect. XXXVII.—But here perhaps, you will say—all that you have advanced is nothing to me. I do not say that the Scriptures are every where obscure (for who would be so mad?) but that they are obscure in this, and the like parts.—I answer: I do not advance these things against you only, but against all who are of the same sentiments with you. Moreover, I declare against you concerning the whole of the Scripture, that I will have no one part of it called obscure: and, to support me, stands that which I have brought forth out of Peter, that the word of God is to us a "lamp shining in a dark place." (2 Peter i. 19.) But if any part of this lamp do not shine, it is rather a part of the dark place than of the lamp itself. For Christ has not so illuminated us, as to wish that any part of His word should remain obscure, even while He commands us to attend to it: for if it be not shiningly plain, His commanding us to attend to it is in vain.

Wherefore, if the doctrine concerning "Free-will" be obscure and ambiguous, it does not belong unto Christians and the Scriptures, and is, therefore to be left alone entirely, and classed among those "old wives' fables" (1 Tim. iv. 7,) which Paul condemns in contentious Christians. But if it do belong unto Christians and the Scriptures, it ought to be clear, open, and manifest, and in every respect like unto all the other most evident articles of faith. For all the articles of faith which belong unto Christians ought to be such, as may not only be most evident to themselves but so defended by manifest and clear Scriptures against the adversaries, as to stop the mouths of them all, that they shall not be able in any thing to gainsay. And this Christ has promised us, saying, "I will give you a mouth and wisdom which all your adversaries shall not be able to resist." But if our mouth be weak in this part, that the adversaries are able to resist, his saying, that no adversary shall be able to resist our mouth, is false. In the doctrine of "Free-will," therefore, we shall either have no adversaries, (which will be the case if it belong unto us;) or, if it belong unto us, we shall have adversaries indeed, but such as will not be able to resist.

But concerning the inability of our adversaries to resist, (as that particular falls in here,) I would, by the way, observe that it is thus:—It does not mean, that they are forced to yield with the heart, or to confess, or be silent. For who can compel men against their will to yield, confess their error, and be silent? 'What (saith Augustine), is more loquacious than vanity? ' But what is meant by their mouths being stopped, their not having a word to gainsay, and their saying many things, and yet, in the judgment of common sense, saying nothing, will be best illustrated by examples.—

When Christ, put the Sadduces to silence by proving the resurrection from the dead, out of that Scripture of Moses. (Matt. xxii. 23-32,) "I am the God of Abraham, &c., God is not the God of the dead but of the living;" (Exod. iii. 6,) this they were not able to resist, nor had they a word to gainsay. But did they, therefore, cease from their opinion?

And how often did He, by the most evident Scriptures and arguments, so confute the Pharisees, that the very people saw them to be confuted openly, and they themselves felt it. Nevertheless, they still perseveringly continued His adversaries.

Stephen, (Acts vi. 10,) so spoke, that, according to the testimony of Luke, "they could not resist the spirit and the wisdom with which he spake." But what did they? Did they yield? No! from their shame of being overcome and their inability to resist, they became furious, and shutting their eyes and ears they suborned false witnesses against him. (Acts vi. 11-13.)

Behold how the same apostle, standing in the council, confutes his adversaries, while he enumerates to that people the mercies of God unto them from their beginning, and proves to them, that God never commanded a temple to be built unto Him: (for it was upon that point they then held him as guilty, and that was the subject in dispute.) At length however, he grants, that there was a temple built under Solomon. But then he takes up the point in this way: "but the Most High dwelleth not in temples made with hands." And to prove this, he brings forward Isaiah the prophet, lxvi. 1, "What is the house that ye build unto Me? " And, tell me, what could they here say against a Scripture so manifest? Yet still, not at all moved by it, they stood fixed in their own opinion. Wherefore, he then launches forth on them saying, "Ye uncircumcised in heart and ears, ye do always resist the Holy Ghost, &c." (Acts vii. 51.) He saith, "ye do resist," although they were not able to resist.

But let us come to our own times. John Huss preached thus against the Pope from Matt. xvi. 18–'The gates of hell shall not prevail against my church.' Is there there any obscurity or ambiguity? But the gates of hell do prevail against the Pope and his, for they are notorious throughout the world of their open impiety and iniquities. Is there any obscurity here either? ERGO: THE POPE AND HIS, ARE NOT THE CHURCH CONCERNING WHICH CHRIST SPEAKS.'–What could they gainsay here? How could they resist the mouth that Christ had given him? Yet, they did resist, and persist until they had burnt him: so far were they from yielding to Him, in heart. And this is the kind of resistance to which Christ alludes when He saith, "Your adversaries shall not be able to resist." (Luke xxi. 15.) He says they are "adversaries;" therefore they will resist, for otherwise, they would not remain adversaries, but would become friends. And yet He says, they "shall not be able to resist." What is this else but saying–though they resist, they shall not be able to resist?

If therefore, I also shall be enabled so to refute the doctrine of "Free-will," that the adversaries shall not be able to resist, although they persist in their opinion, and go on to resist contrary to their conscience, I shall have done enough. For I know well, by experience, how unwilling every one is to be overcome; and (as Quintillian says,) 'that there is no one, who would not rather appear to know, than to be taught. Although, now a-days all men, in all places, have this proverb on their tongue, but more from use, or rather abuse, than from heart-reality–'I am willing to learn, and I am ready to follow what is better, when I am taught it by admonition: I am man, and liable to err.' Because, under this mask, this fair semblance of humility, they can with plausible confidence say; 'I am not fully satisfied of it.' 'I do not comprehend it.' 'He does violence to the Scriptures.' 'He asserts so obstinately.' And they nestle under this confidence, taking it for granted, that no one would ever suspect, that souls of so much humility could, ever pertinaciously resist and determinately impugn the known truth. Hence their not yielding in heart, is not to be imputed to their malice, but to the obscurity and duplicity of their arguments.

In the same manner did the philosophers of the Greeks, act; who, that the one might not appear to give up to the other, though evidently confuted, began, as Aristotle records, to deny first principles. In the same way we would mildly persuade ourselves and others, that there are in the world many good men, who would willingly embrace the truth, if there were but one who could plainly shew which it is; and that, it is not to be supposed, that so many learned men, in such a course of ages, were all in error, and did not know that truth.–As though we knew not, that the world is the kingdom of Satan, where, in addition to the natural blindness that is engendered in our flesh, and those most wicked spirits also which have dominion over us, we grow hardened in that very blindness, and are bound in a darkness, no longer human, but devilish.

Sect. XXXVIII.–But you ask–"if then the Scripture be quite clear, why have men of renowned talent, through so many ages, been blind upon this point? "–

I answer: they have been thus blind, to the praise and glory of "Free-will;" in order that, that highly boasted-of 'power,' by which a man is able to apply himself unto those things that pertain unto eternal salvation, might be eminently displayed; that very exalted power, which neither sees those things which it sees, nor hears those things which it hears, and much less, understands and seeks after them. For to this power, applies that which Christ and the evangelists so often bring forward out of Isaiah vi. 9, "Hearing ye shall hear and shall not understand, and seeing ye shall see and shall not perceive." What is this else but saying, that "Free-will," or the human heart, is so bound by the power of Satan, that, unless it be quickened up in a wonderful way by the Spirit of God, it cannot of itself see or hear those things which strike against the eyes and ears so manifestly, as to be as it were palpable by the hand? So great is the misery and blindness of the human race! Thus also the Evangelists themselves, when they wondered how it could be that the Jews were not won over by the works and words of Christ, which were evidently incontrovertible and undeniable, satisfied themselves from that place of the Scripture, where it is shewn, that man, left to himself, seeing seeth not, and hearing heareth not. And what can be more monstrous! "The light (saith Christ) shineth in darkness, and the darkness comprehendeth it not." (John i. 5.) Who could believe this? Who hath heard the like—that the light should shine in darkness, and yet, the darkness still remain darkness, and not be enlightened!

Wherefore, it is no wonder in divine things, that through so many ages, men renowned for talent remained blind. It might have been a wonder in human things, but in divine things, it would rather have been a wonder if there had been one here and there that did not remain blind: that they all remained utterly blind alike, is no wonder at all. For what is the whole human race together, without the Spirit, but the kingdom of the devil (as I have said) and a confused chaos of darkness? And therefore it is, that Paul, (Ephes. vi. 12,) calls the devils, "the rulers of this darkness." And, (1 Cor. ii. 8,) he saith, that none of the princes of this world knew the wisdom of God. What then must *he* think of the rest, who asserts that the princes of this world are the slaves of darkness? For by princes, he means those greatest and highest ones, whom you call 'men renowned for talent.' And why were all the Arians blind? Were there not among them men renowned for talent? Why was Christ foolishness to the nations? Are there not among the nations men renowned for talent? "God (saith Paul) knoweth the thoughts of the wise that they are vain," (1 Cor. iii. 20.) He chose not to say "of men," as the text to which he refers has it, but would point to the first and greatest among men, that from them we might form a judgment of the rest.—But upon these points more at large, perhaps, hereafter.

Suffice it thus to have premised, in Exordium, that the Scriptures are most clear, and that by them, our doctrines can be so defended that the adversaries cannot resist: but those doctrines that cannot be thus defended, are nothing to us, for they belong not unto Christians. But if there be any who do not see this clearness, and are blind, or offend under this sun, they, if they be wicked, manifest how great that dominion and power of Satan is over the sons of men, when they can neither hear nor comprehend the all-clear words of God, but are as one cheated by a juggler, who is made to think that the sun is a cold cinder, or to believe that a stone is gold. But if they fear God, they are to be numbered among those elect, who, to a certain degree, are led into error that the power of God may be manifest in us, without which, we can neither see nor do any thing whatever. For the not comprehending the words of God, does not arise, as you pretend, from weakness of mind; nay, nothing is better adapted to the receiving of the words of God, than a weakness of mind; for it was on account of these weak ones, and to these weak ones, that Christ came, and it is to them he sends his Word. But it is the wickedness of Satan enthroned and reigning in our weakness, and resisting the Word of God:—for if Satan did not do this, a whole world of men might be converted by one Word of God once heard, nor could there be need of more.

Sect. XXXIX.—But why do I go on enlarging? Why do I not conclude this discussion with this Exordium, and give my sentence against you in your own words, according to that saying of Christ, "By thy words thou shalt be justified, and by thy words thou shalt be condemned? " (Matt. xii. 37.) For you say that the Scripture is not quite clear upon this point. And then, suspending all declaration of your own sentiment, you discuss each *side* of the subject, what may be said for, and what against, and nothing else whatever do you do, in the whole of this book of yours; which, for that very reason, you wished to call DIATRIBE (The Collation) rather than APOPHASIS (The Denial), or something of that kind; because, you wrote with a design to *collect all things,* and *to assert nothing.*

But if the Scripture be not quite clear upon this point, why do those of whom you boast, not only remain blind to their side of the subject, but rashly and as fools, define and assert "Free-will," as though proved by a certain and all-sure testimony of Scripture,—that numberless series of the most learned men, I mean, whom the consent of so many ages has approved, even unto this day, and many of whom, in addition too an admirable acquaintance with the Sacred Writings, a piety of life commends? —Some have given, by their blood, a testimony of that doctrine of Christ, which they had defended by Scriptures. If you say what you say, from your heart, it is surely a settled point with you, that "Free-will" has assertors, who are endowed with a wonderful understanding in the Sacred Writings, and who even gave testimony of that doctrine by their blood. If this be true, they certainly had clear Scripture on their side, else, where would be their admirable understanding in the Sacred Writings? Moreover, what lightness and temerity of spirit must it be, to shed ones blood for a matter uncertain and obscure? This is not to be the martyrs of Christ, but the martyrs of devils!

Now then, do you just set the matter before you, and weigh it in your mind, and say, to which of the two you consider the greater credit should be given; to the prejudices of so many learned men, so many orthodox divines, so many saints, so many martyrs, so many theologians old and recent, so many colleges, so many councils, so many bishops and high-priest Popes, who were of opinion that the Scriptures are quite clear, and who (according to you) confirmed the same by their writings and by their blood; or to your own private judgment, who deny that the Scriptures are quite clear, and who, perhaps, never spent one single tear or sigh for the doctrine of Christ, in the whole of your life? If you believe they were right in their opinion, why do you not follow them in it? If you do not believe they were right, why do you boast of them with such a trumpeting mouth, and such a torrent of language, as though you would overwhelm us head and ears with a certain storm or flood of eloquence? Which flood, however, will the more heavily rush back upon your own head, whilst my Ark is borne along in safety on the top of the waters! Moreover, you attribute to so many and great men, the utmost folly and temerity. For when you speak of them as being men of the greatest understanding in the Scripture, and as having asserted it by their pen, by their life, and by their death; and yet at the same time contend yourself, that the same Scripture is obscure and ambiguous, this is nothing less than making those men most ignorant in understanding, and most stupid in assertion. Thus I, their poor private despiser, do not pay them such an ill compliment, as you do, their public flatterer.

Sect. XL.—Here, therefore, I hold you fast in a last-pinch syllogism (as they say). For either the one or the other of your assertions must be false. Either that, where you say, 'those men were admirable for their understanding in the Sacred Writings, for their life, and for their martyrdom;' or that, where you say, that 'the Scriptures are not quite clear.' But since you are drawn more this latter way, that is, to believe that the Scriptures are not quite clear, (for this is what you harp upon throughout the whole of your book), it remains evident, that it was either from your own natural inclination towards them, or for the sake of flattering them, but by no means from seriousness, that you called those men, 'men of the greatest understanding in the Scripture, and martyrs of Christ;' merely in order that you might blind the eyes of the inexperienced commonalty, and make work for Luther by loading his cause with empty words, odium, and contempt. But, however, I aver that *neither* of your assertions are true, and that *both* are false. For, first of all, I aver, that the Scriptures are quite clear: and next, that those men, as far as they asserted "Free-will," were most ignorant of the Sacred Writings: and moreover, that they neither asserted it by their life, nor by their death, but by their pen only; and that, while their heart was travelling another road.

Wherefore this small part of the Disputation I conclude thus.—By the Scripture, as being obscure, nothing ever has hitherto, nor ever can be defined concerning "Free-will;" according to your own testimony. Moreover, nothing has ever been manifested in confirmation of "Free-will," in the lives of all the men from the beginning of the world; as we have proved above. To teach, then, *a something* which is neither described by one word within the Scriptures, nor evidenced by one fact without the Scriptures, is that, which does not belong to the doctrines of Christians, but to the very fables of Lucian. Except, however, that Lucian, as he *amuses only* with ludicrous stories from wit and policy, *deceives* and *injures* no one. But these friends of ours, in a matter of importance which concerns eternal salvation, madly trifle to the perdition of souls innumerable.

Thus I might here have concluded the whole of this discussion, even with the testimony of my adversaries making *for* me, and *against* themselves. For no proof can be more decisive, than the very confession and testimony of the guilty person against himself. But however, as Paul commands us to stop the mouths of vain talkers, let us now enter upon the Discussion itself, and handle the subject in the order in which the Diatribe proceeds: that we may, FIRST, confute the arguments adduced in support of "Free-will": SECONDLY, defend our arguments that are confuted: and, LASTLY, contend for the Grace of God against "Free-will."

DISCUSSION.

FIRST PART.

Sect. XLI.—And, first of all, let us begin regularly with your *definition*: according to which, you define "Free-will" thus,

– "Moreover I consider Free-will in this light: that it is a power in the human will, by which, a man may apply himself to those things which lead unto eternal salvation, or turn away from the same."–

With a great deal of policy indeed, you have here stated a mere naked definition, without declaring any *part* of it, (as all others do); because, perhaps, you feared more shipwrecks than one. I therefore am compelled to state the several parts myself. The thing defined itself, if it be closely examined, has a much wider extent than the definition of it: and such a definition, the Sophists would call faulty: that is, when the definition does not fully embrace the thing defined. For I have shown before, that "Free-will" cannot be applied to any one but to God only. You may, perhaps, rightly assign to man some kind of will, but to assign unto him "Free-will" in divine things, is going too far. For the term "Free-will," in the judgment of the ears of all, means, that which can, and does do God-ward, whatever it pleases, restrainable by no law and no command. But you cannot call him *free*, who is a servant acting under the power of the Lord. How much less, then, can we rightly call men or angels *free*, who so live under the all-overruling command of God, (to say nothing of sin and death,) that they cannot consist one moment by their own power.

Here then, at the outset, the definition of *the term*, and the definition of *the thing* termed, militate against each other: because the term signifies one thing, and the thing termed is, by experience, found to be another. It would indeed be more properly termed "Vertible-will," or "Mutable-will." For in this way Augustine, and after him the Sophists, diminished the glory and force of the term, *free;* adding thereby this detriment, that they assign *vertibility* to "Free-will." And it becomes us thus to speak, lest, by inflated and lofty terms of empty sound, we should deceive the hearts of men. And, as Augustine also thinks, we ought to speak according to a certain rule, in sober and proper words; for in teaching, simplicity and propriety of argumentation is required, and not highflown figures of rhetorical persuasion.

Sect. XLII.—But that we might not seem to delight in a mere war of words, we cede to that abuse, though great and dangerous, that "Free-will" means "Vertible-will." We will cede also that to Erasmus, where he makes "Free-will" 'a power of the human will:' (as though angel had not as "Free-will" too, merely because he designed in this book to treat only on the "Free-will" of men!) We make this remark, otherwise, even in this part, the definition would be too narrow to embrace the thing defined.

We come then to those parts of the definition, which are the hinge upon which the matter turns. Of these things some are manifest enough; the rest shun the light, as if conscious to themselves that they had every thing to fear: because, nothing ought to be expressed more clearly, and more decisively, than a definition; for to define obscurely, is the same thing as defining nothing at all.

The clear parts of the definition then are these:—'power of human will:' and 'by which a man can:' also, 'unto eternal salvation.' But these are Andabatae:—'to apply:' and, 'to those things which lead:' also, 'to turn away.' What shall we divine that this 'to apply' means? And this 'to turn away,' also? And also what these words mean, 'which pertain unto eternal salvation? ' Into what dark corner have these withdrawn their meaning? I seem as if I were engaged in dispute with a very Scotinian, or with Heraclitus himself, so as to be in the way of being worn out by a twofold labour. First, that I shall have to find out my adversary by groping and feeling about for him in pits and darkness, (which is an enterprize both venturous and perilous,) and if I do not find him, to fight to no purpose with ghosts, and beat the air in the dark. And, secondly, if I should bring him out into the light, that then, I shall have to fight with him upon equal ground, when I am already worn out with hunting after him.

I suppose, then, what you mean by the 'power of the human will' is this:—a power, or faculty, or disposition, or aptitude, to will or not to will, to choose or refuse, to approve or disapprove, and what other actions soever belong to the will. Now then, what it is for this same power 'to apply itself,' or 'to turn away,' I do not see: unless it be the very willing or not willing, choosing or refusing, approving or disapproving; that is, the very action itself of the will. But may we suppose, that this power is a kind of medium, between the will itself and the action itself; such as, that by which the will itself allures forth the action itself of willing or not willing, or by which the action itself of willing or not willing is allured forth? Any thing else beside this, it is impossible for one to imagine or think of. And if I am deceived, let the fault be my author's who has given the definition, not mine who examine it. For it is justly said among lawyers, 'his words who speaks obscurely, when he can speak more plainly, are to be interpreted against himself.' And here I wish to know nothing of our moderns and their subtleties, for we must come plainly to close quarters in what we say, for the sake of understanding and teaching.

And as to those words, 'which lead unto eternal salvation,' I suppose by them are meant the words and works of God, which are offered to the human will, that it might either apply itself to them, or turn away from them. But I call both the Law and the Gospel the words of God. By the Law, works are required; and by the Gospel, faith. For there are no other things which lead either unto the grace of God, or unto eternal salvation, but the word and the work of God: because grace or the spirit is the life itself, to which we are led by the word and the work of God.

Sect. XLIII.—But this life or salvation is an eternal matter, incomprehensible to the human capacity: as Paul shews, out of Isaiah, (1 Cor. ii. 9.) "Eye hath not seen nor ear heard, neither hath it entered into the heart of man to conceive, the things which God hath prepared for them that love him." For when we speak of eternal life, we speak of that which is numbered among the chiefest articles of our faith. And what "Free-will" avails in this article Paul testifies, (1 Cor. ii. 10.) Also: "God (saith he) hath revealed them unto us by His Spirit." As though he had said, the heart of no man will ever understand or think of any of those things, unless the Spirit shall reveal them; so far is it from possibility, that he should ever apply himself unto them or seek after them.

Look at experience. What have the most exalted minds among the nations thought of a future life, and of the resurrection? Has it not been, that the more exalted they were in mind, the more ridiculous the resurrection and eternal life have appeared to them? Unless you mean to say, that those philosophers and Greeks at Athens, who, (Acts xvii. 18,) called Paul, as he taught these things, a "babbler" and a "setter forth of strange gods," were not of exalted minds. Portius Festus, (Acts xxvi. 24,) calls out that Paul is "mad," on account of his preaching eternal life. What does Pliny bark forth, Book vii? What does Lucian also, that mighty genius? Were not they men wondered at? Moreover to this day there are many, who, the more renowned they are for talent and erudition, the more they laugh at this article; and that openly, considering it a mere fable. And certainly, no man upon earth, unless imbued with the Holy Spirit, ever secretly knows, or believes in, or wishes for, eternal salvation, how much soever he may boast of it by his voice and by his pen. And may you and I, friend Erasmus, be free from this boasting leaven. So rare is a believing soul in this article! —Have I got the sense of this definition?

Sect. XLIV.—Upon the authority of Erasmus, then, *"Free-will,"* is a power of the *human will, which can, of itself, will and not will to embrace the word and work of God, by which it is to be led to those things which are beyond its capacity and comprehension.* If then, it can will and not will, it can also love and hate. And if it can love and hate, it can, to a certain degree, do the Law and believe the Gospel. For it is impossible, if you can will and not will, that you should not be able by that will to begin some kind of work, even though, from the hindering of another, you should not be able to perfect it. And therefore, as among the work of God which lead to salvation, death, the cross, and all the evils of the world are numbered, human will can will its own death and perdition. Nay, it can will all things while it can will the embracing of the word and work of God. For what is there that can be any where beneath, above, within, and without the word and work of God, but God Himself? And what is there here left to grace and the Holy Spirit? This is plainly to ascribe *divinity* to "Free-will." For to will to embrace the Law and the Gospel, not to will sin, and to will death, belongs to the power of God alone: as Paul testifies in more places than one.

Wherefore, no one, since the Pelagians, has written more rightly concerning "Free-will" than Erasmus. For I have said above, that "Free-will" is a divine term, and signifies a divine power. But no one hitherto, except the Pelagians, has ever assigned to it that power. Hence, Erasmus by far outstrips the Pelagians themselves: for they assign that divinity to the whole of "Free-will," but Erasmus to the half of it only. They divide "Free-will" into two parts: *the power of discerning,* and *the power of choosing;* assigning the one to reason, and the other to will; and the Sophists do the same. But Erasmus, setting aside the power of discerning, exalts the power of choosing alone, and thus makes a lame, half-membered "Free-will," God himself! What must we suppose then he would have done, had he set about describing the whole of "Free-will."

But, not contented with this, he outstrips even the philosophers. For it has never yet been settled among them, whether or not any thing can give motion to itself; and upon this point, the Platonics and Peripatetics are divided in the whole body of philosophy. But according to Erasmus, "Free-will" not only of its own power gives motion to itself, but 'applies itself' to those things which are eternal; that is, which are incomprehensible to itself! A new and unheard-of definer of "Free-will," truly, who leaves the philosophers, the Pelagians, the Sophists, and all the rest of them, far behind him! Nor is this all. He does not even spare himself, but dissents from, and militates against himself, more than against all the rest together. For he had said before, that 'the human will is utterly ineffective without grace:' (unless perhaps this was said only in joke!) but here, where he gives a serious definition, he says, that 'the human will has that power by which it can effectively apply itself to those things which pertain unto eternal salvation;' that is, which are incomparably beyond that power. So that, in this part, Erasmus outstrips even himself!

Sect. XLV.—Do you see, friend Erasmus, that by this definition, you (though unwittingly I presume,) betray yourself, and make it manifest that you either know nothing of these things whatever, or that, without any consideration, and in a mere air of contempt, you write upon the subject, not knowing what you say nor whereof you affirm? And as I said before, you say less about, and attribute more to "Free-will," than all others put together; for you do not describe the whole of "Free-will," and yet you assign unto it all things. The opinion of the Sophists, or at least of the father of them, Peter Lombard, is far more tolerable: he says, ' "Free-will" is the faculty of discerning, and then choosing also good, if with grace, but evil if grace be wanting.' He plainly agrees in sentiment with Augustine, that ' "Free-will," of its own power, cannot do any thing but fall, nor avail unto any thing but to sin.' Wherefore Augustine also, Book ii., against Julian, calls "Free-will" 'under bondage,' rather than 'free.'—But you make the power of "Free-will" equal in both respect: that it can, by its own power, without grace, both apply itself unto good, and turn itself from evil. For you do not imagine how much you assign unto it, by this pronoun *itself,* and *by itself,* when you say 'can apply itself:' for you utterly exclude the Holy Spirit with all His power, as a thing superfluous and unnecessary. Your definition, therefore, is condemnable even by the Sophists; who, were they not so blinded by hatred and fury against me, would be enraged at your book rather than at mine. But now, as your intent is to oppose Luther, all that you say is holy and catholic, even though you speak against both yourself and them,—so great is the patience of holy men!

Not that I say this, as approving the sentiments of the Sophists concerning "Free-will," but because I consider them more tolerable, for they approach nearer to the truth. For though they do not say, as I do, that "Free-will" is nothing at all, yet since they say that it can of itself do nothing without grace, they militate against Erasmus, nay, they seem to militate against themselves, and to be tossed to and fro in a mere quarrel of words, being more earnest for contention than for the truth, which is just as Sophists should be. But now, let us suppose that a Sophist of no mean rank were brought before me, with whom I could speak upon these things apart, in familiar conversation, and should ask him for his liberal and candid judgment in this way:—'If any one should tell you, that that was *free,* which of its own power could only go one way, that is, the bad way, and which could go the other way indeed, that is, the right way, but not by its own power, nay, only by the help of another—could you refrain from laughing in his face, my friend? '—For in this way, I will make it appear, that a stone, or a log of wood has "Free-will," because it can go upwards and downwards; although, by its own power, it can go only downwards, but can go upwards only by the help of another. And, as I said before, by meaning at the same time the thing itself, and also something else which may be joined with it or added to it, I will say, consistently with the use of all words and languages—all men are no man, and all things are nothing!

Thus, by a multiplicity of argumentation, they at last make "Free-will," free *by accident;* as being that, which may at some time be set free by another. But our point in dispute is concerning the thing itself, concerning the reality of "Free-will." If this be what is to be solved, there now remains nothing, let them say what they will, but the empty name of "Free-will."

The Sophists are deficient also in this—they assign to "Free-will," the power of discerning good from evil. Moreover, they set light by regeneration, and the renewing of the Spirit, and give that other *external aid,* as it were, to "Free-will:" but of this hereafter.—Let this be sufficient concerning the definition. Now let us look into the arguments that are to exalt this empty thing of a TERM.

Sect. XLVI.—First of all, we have that of Ecclesiasticus xv. 15-18.—"God from the beginning made man, and left him in the hand of his own counsel. He gave him also His commandments, and His precepts: saying, If thou wilt keep My commandments, and wilt keep continually the faith that pleaseth Me, they shall preserve thee. He hath set before thee fire and water; and upon which thou wilt, stretch forth thine hand. Before man is life and death, good and evil; and whichsoever pleaseth him, shall be given unto him."—

Although I might justly refuse this book, yet, nevertheless, I receive it; lest I should, with loss of time, involve myself in a dispute concerning the books that are received into the canon of the Hebrews: which canon you do not a little reproach and deride, when you compare the Proverbs of Solomon, and the Love-song, (as, with a double-meaning sneer, you call it,) with the two books Esdras and Judith, the History of Susannah, of the Dragon, and the Book of Esther, though they have this last in their canon, and according to my judgment, it is much more worthy of being there, than any one of those that are considered not to be in the canon.

But I would briefly answer you here in your own words, 'The Scripture, in this place, is obscure and ambiguous;' therefore, it proves nothing to a certainty. But however, since I stand in the negative, I call upon you to produce that place which declares, in plain words, what "Free-will" is, and what it can do. And this perhaps you will do by about the time of the Greek Calends.—In order to avoid this necessity, you spend many fine sayings upon nothing; and moving along on the tip-toe of prudence, cite numberless opinions concerning "Free-will," and make of Pelagius almost an Evangelist. Moreover, you vamp up a four-fold grace, so as to assign a sort of faith and charity even to the philosophers. And also that new fable, a three-fold law; of nature, of works, and of faith, so as to assert with all boldness, that the precepts of the philosophers agree with the precepts of the Gospel. Again, you apply that of Psalm iv. 6, "The light of Thy countenance is settled upon us," which speaks of the knowledge of the very countenance of the Lord, that is, of faith, to blinded reason. All which things together, if taken into consideration by any Christian, must compel him to suspect, that you are mocking and deriding the doctrines and religion of Christians. For to attribute these things as so much ignorance to him, who has illustrated all our doctrines with so much diligence, and stored them up in memory, appears to me very difficult indeed. But however, I will here abstain from open exposure, contented to wait until a more favourable opportunity shall offer itself. Although I entreat you, friend Erasmus, not to tempt me in this way like one of those who say—who sees us? For it is by no means safe in so great a matter, to be continually mocking every one with Vertumnities of words. But to the subject.

Sect. XLVII.—Out of the ONE opinion concerning "Free-will" you make THREE. You say—'that THE FIRST OPINION, of those who deny that man can will good without special grace, who deny that it can begin, who deny that it can make progress, perfect, &c., seems to you *severe*, though it may be VERY PROBABLE.' And this you prove, as leaving to man the desire and the effort, but not leaving what is to be ascribed to his own power. 'That THE SECOND OPINION of those who contend, that "Free-will" avails unto nothing but to sin, and that grace alone works good in us, &c., is *more severe still.'* And THIRDLY 'that the opinion of those who say that "Free-will" is an empty term, for that God works in us both good and evil, is *most severe*." And that, it is against these last that you profess to write.'—

Do you know what you are saying, friend Erasmus? You are here making three different opinions as if belonging to three different sects: because you do not know that it is the same subject handled by us same professors of the same sect, only by different persons, in a different way and in other words. But let me just put you in remembrance, and set before you the yawning inconsiderateness, or stupidity of your judgment.

How does that definition of "Free-will," let me ask you, which you gave us above, square with this first opinion which you confess to be, 'very probable?' For you said that ' "Free-will" is a power of the human will, by which a man can apply himself unto good;' whereas here, you say and approve the saying that, 'man, without grace, cannot will good!' The definition, therefore, affirms what its example denies. And hence there are found in your "Free-will" both a YEA and a NAY: so that, in one and the same doctrine and article, you approve and condemn us, and approve and condemn yourself. For do you think, that to 'apply itself to those things which pertain unto eternal salvation,' which power your definition assigns to "Free-will," is not to do good, when, if there were so much good in "Free-will," that it could apply itself unto good, it would have no need of grace? Therefore, the "Free-will" which you define is one, and the "Free-will" you defend is another. Hence then, Erasmus, outstripping all others, has two "Free-wills;" and they, militating against each other!

Sect. XLVIII.—But, setting aside that "Free-will" which the definition defines, let us consider that which the opinion proposes as contrary to it. You grant, that man, without special grace, cannot will good: (for we are not now discussing what the grace of God can do, but what man can do without grace:) you grant, then, that "Free-will" cannot will good. This is nothing else but granting that it cannot 'apply itself to those things which pertain unto eternal salvation,' according to the tune of your definition. Nay, you say a little before, 'that the human will after sin, is so depraved, that having lost its liberty, it is compelled to serve sin, and cannot recall itself into a better state.' And if I am not mistaken, you make the Pelagians to be of this opinion. Now then I believe, my Proteus has here no way of escape: he is caught and held fast in plain words:—'that the will, having lost its liberty, is tied and bound a slave to sin.' O noble Free-will! which, having lost its liberty, is declared by Erasmus himself, to be the slave of sin! When Luther asserted this, 'nothing was every heard of so absurd;' 'nothing was more useless, than that this paradox should be proclaimed abroad! ' So much so, that even a Diatribe must be written against him!

But perhaps no one will believe me, that these things are said by Erasmus. If the Diatribe be read in this part, it will be admired: but I do not so much admire it. For he who does not treat this as a serious subject, and is not interested in the cause, but is in mind alienated from it, and grows weary of it, cold in it, and disgusted with it, how shall not such an one everywhere speak absurdities, follies, and contrarieties, while, as one drunk or slumbering over the cause, he belches out in the midst of his snoring, It is so! it is not so! just as the different words sound against his ears? And therefore it is, that rhetoricians require a feeling of the subject in the person discussing it. Much more then does theology require such a feeling, that it may make the person vigilant, sharp, intent, prudent, and determined.

If therefore "Free-will" without grace, when it has lost its liberty, is compelled to serve sin and cannot will good, I should be glad to know, what that desire is, what that endeavour is, which that first 'probable opinion' leaves it. It cannot be a good desire or a good endeavour, because it cannot will good, as the opinion affirms, and as you grant. Therefore, it is an evil desire and an evil endeavour that is left, which, when the liberty is lost, is compelled to serve sin.—But above all, what, I pray, is the meaning of this saying: 'this opinion leaves the desire and the endeavour, but does not leave what is to be ascribed to its own power.' Who can possibly conceive in his mind what this means? If the desire and the endeavour be left to the power of "Free-will," how are they not ascribed to the same? If they be not ascribed to it, how can they be left to it? Are then that desire and that endeavour before grace, left to grace itself that comes after, and not to "Free-will" so as to be at the same time left, and not left, to the same "Free-will? " If these things be not paradoxes, or rather enormities, then pray what are enormities?

Sect. XLIX.—But perhaps the Diatribe is dreaming this, that between these two 'can will good' and 'cannot will good' there may be a medium; seeing that, *to will* is absolute, both in respect of good, and evil. So that thus, by a certain logical subtlety, we may steer clear of the rocks, and say, in the will of man there is a certain *willing*, which cannot indeed will good without grace, but which, nevertheless, being without grace, does not immediately will nothing but evil, but is a sort of *mere abstracted willing*, vertible, upwards unto good by grace, and downwards unto evil by sin. But then, what will become of that which you have said, that, 'when it has lost its liberty it is compelled to serve sin? ' What will become of that desire and endeavour which are left? Where will be that power of 'applying itself to those things which pertain unto eternal salvation? ' For that power of applying itself unto salvation, cannot be a mere *willing*, unless the salvation itself be said to be a nothing. Nor, again, can that desire and endeavour be a mere *willing*; for *desire* must strive and attempt something, (as good perhaps,) and cannot go forth into nothing, nor be absolutely inactive.

In a word, which way soever the Diatribe turns itself, it cannot keep clear of inconsistencies and contradictory assertions; nor avoid making that very "Free-will" which it defends, as much a bond-captive as it is a bond-captive itself. For, in attempting to liberate "Free-will," it is so entangled, that it is bound, together with "Free-will," in bonds indissoluble.

Moreover, it is a mere logical figment that in man there is a medium, *a mere willing*, nor can they who assert this prove it; it arose from an *ignorance* of *things* and an *observance* of *terms*. As though the thing were always in reality, as it is set forth in terms; and there are with the Sophists many such misconceptions. Whereas the matter rather stands as Christ saith, "He that is not with Me is against Me." (Matt. xii. 30.) He does not say, He that is not with Me is yet not *against* Me, but *in the medium*. For if God be in us, Satan is from us, and it is present with us to will nothing but good. But if God be not in us, Satan is in us, and it is present with us to will evil only. Neither God nor Satan admit of a *mere abstracted willing* in us; but, as you yourself rightly said, when our liberty is lost we are compelled to serve sin: that is, we *will* sin and evil, we *speak* sin and evil, we *do* sin and evil.

Behold then! invincible and all-powerful truth has driven the witless Diatribe to that dilemma, and so turned its wisdom into foolishness, that whereas, its design was to speak against me, it is compelled to speak *for* me *against* itself; just in the same way as "Free-will" does any thing good; for when it attempts so to do, the more it acts against evil the more it acts against good. So that the Diatribe is, in *saying*, exactly what "Free-will" is in *doing*. Though the whole Diatribe itself, is nothing else but a notable effort of "Free-will," condemning by defending, and defending by condemning: that is, being a twofold fool, while it would appear to be wise.

This, then, is the state of the first opinion compared with itself:—*it denies that a man can will any thing good; but yet that a desire remains; which desire, however, is not his own!*

Sect. L.—Now let us compare this opinion with the remaining two.

The next of these, is that opinion 'more severe still,' which holds, that "Free-will" avails unto nothing but to sin. And this indeed is Augustine's opinion, expressed, as well in many other places, as more especially, in his book "Concerning the Spirit and the Letter;" in (if I mistake not) the fourth or fifth chapter, where he uses those very words.

The third, is that 'most severe' opinion; that "Free-will" is a mere empty term, and that every thing which we do, is done from necessity under the bondage of sin.—It is with these two that the Diatribe conflicts.

I here observe, that perhaps it may be, that I am not able to discuss this point intelligibly, from not being sufficiently acquainted with the Latin or with the German. But I call God to witness, that I wish nothing else to be said or to be understood by the words of the last two opinions than what is said in the first opinion: nor does Augustine wish any thing else to be understood, nor do I understand any thing else from his words, than that which the first opinion asserts: so that, the *three opinions* brought forward by the Diatribe are with me nothing else than my *one sentiment*. For when it is granted and established, that "Free-will," having once lost its liberty, is compulsively bound to the service of sin, and cannot will any thing good: I, from these words, can understand nothing else than that "Free-will" is a mere empty term, whose reality is lost. And a lost liberty, according to my grammar, is no liberty at all. And to give the name of liberty to that which has no liberty, is to give it an empty term. If I am wrong here, let him set me right who can. If these observations be obscure or ambiguous, let him who can, illustrate and make them plain. I for my part, cannot call that health which is lost, health; and if I were to ascribe it to one who was sick, I should think I was giving him nothing else than an empty name.

But away with these enormities of words. For who would bear such an abuse of the manner of speaking, as that we should say a man has "Free-will," and yet at the same time assert, that when that liberty is once lost, he is compulsively bound to the service of sin, and cannot will any thing good? These things are contrary to common sense, and utterly destroy the common manner of speaking. The Diatribe is rather to be condemned, which in a drowsy way, foists forth its own words without any regard to the words of others. It does not, I say, consider what it is, nor how much it is to assert, that man, when his liberty is lost, is compelled to serve sin and cannot will any thing good. For if it were at all vigilant or observant, it would plainly see, that the sentiment contained in the three opinions is one and the same, which it makes to be diverse and contrary. For if a man, when he has lost his liberty, is compelled to serve sin, and cannot will good, what conclusion concerning him can be more justly drawn, than that he can do nothing but sin, and will evil? And such a conclusion, the Sophists themselves would draw, even by *their* syllogisms. Wherefore, the Diatribe, unhappily, contends against the last two opinions, and approves the first; whereas, that is precisely the same as the other two; and thus again, as usual, it condemns itself and approves my sentiments, in one and the same article.

Sect. LI.—Let us now come to that passage in Ecclesiasticus, and also with it compare that first 'probable opinion.' The opinion saith, 'Free-will cannot will good.' The passage in Ecclesiasticus is adduced to prove, that "Free-will" is something, and can do something. Therefore, the opinion which is to be proved by Ecclesiasticus' asserts one thing; and Ecclesiasticus, which is adduced to prove it, asserts another. This is just as if any one, setting about to prove that Christ was the Messiah, should adduce a passage which proves that Pilate was governor of Syria, or any thing else equally discordant. It is in the same way that "Free-will" is here proved. But, not to mention my having above made it manifest, that nothing clear or certain can be said or proved concerning "Free-will," as to what it is, or what it can do, it is worth while to examine the whole passage thoroughly.

First he saith, "God made man in the beginning." Here he speaks of the creation of man; nor does he say any thing, as yet, concerning either "Free-will" or the commandments.

Then he goes on, "and left him in the hand of his own counsel." And what is here? Is "Free-will" built upon this? But there is not here any mention of commandments, for the doing of which "Free-will" is required; nor do we read any thing of this kind in the creation of man. If any thing be understood by "the hand of his own counsel," that should rather be understood which is in Genesis i. and ii.: that man was made lord of all things that he might freely exercise dominion over them: and as Moses saith, "Let us make man, and let him have dominion over the fishes of the sea:" nor can any thing else be proved from those words: for it is in these things only that man may act of his own will, as being subject unto him. And moreover, he calls this *man's counsel,* in contradiction as it were to the *counsel of God.* But after this, when He has said, that man was made and left thus in the hand of his own counsel— he adds,

"He added moreover His commandments and His precepts." Unto what did He add them? Certainly unto that counsel and will of man, and over and above unto that constituting of His dominion over other things. By which commandments He took from man the dominion over one part of His creatures, (that is, over the tree of knowledge of good and evil,) and willed rather that he should *not* be free.—Having added the commandments, He then comes to the will of man towards God and towards the things of God.

"If thou wilt keep the commandments they shall preserve thee," &c. From this part, therefore, "If thou wilt," begins the question concerning "Free-will." So that, from Ecclesiasticus we learn, that man is constituted as divided into two kingdoms.—The one, is that in which he is led according to his own will and counsel, without the precepts and the commandments of God: that is, in those things which are beneath him. Here he has dominion and is lord, as "left in the hand of his own counsel." Not that God so leaves him to himself, as that He does not co-operate with him; but He commits unto him the free use of things according to his own will, without prohibiting him by any laws or injunctions. As we may say, by way of similitude, the Gospel has left us in the hands of our own counsel, that we may use, and have dominion over all things as we will. But Moses and the Pope left us not in that counsel, but restrained us by laws, and subjected us rather to *their* own will.—But in the other kingdom, he is not left in the hand of his own counsel, but is directed and led according to the Will and Counsel of God. And as, in his own kingdom, he is led according to his own will, without the precepts of another; so, in the kingdom of God, he is led according to the precepts of another, without his own will.

And this is what Ecclesiasticus means, when he says, "He added moreover His commandments and His precepts: saying, If thou wilt," &c.

If, therefore, these things be satisfactorily clear, I have made it fully evident, that this passage of Ecclesiasticus does not make for "Free-will," but directly against it: seeing that, it subjects man to the precepts and will of God, and takes from him his "Free-will." But if they be not satisfactorily clear, I have at least made it manifest, that this passage cannot make for "Free-will;" seeing that, it may be understood in a sense different from that which they put upon it, that is, in my sense already stated, which is not absurd, but most holy and in harmony with the whole Scripture. Whereas, their sense militates against the whole Scripture, and is fetched from this one passage only, contrary to the tenor of the whole Scripture. I stand therefore, secure in the good sense, the negative of "Free-will," until they shall have confirmed their strained and forced affirmative.

When, therefore, Ecclesiasticus says, "If thou wilt keep the commandments, and keep the faith that pleaseth Me, they shall perserve thee," I do not see that "Free-will" can be proved from those words. For, "if thou wilt," is a verb of the subjunctive mood, which asserts nothing: as the logicians say, 'a conditional asserts nothing indicatively:' such as, if the devil be God, he is deservedly worshipped: if an ass fly, an ass has wings, so also, if there be "Free-will," grace is nothing at all. Therefore, if Ecclesiasticus had wished to assert "Free-will," he ought to have spoken thus:—man *is able* to keep the commandments of God, or, man, *has the power* to keep the commandments.

Sect. LII.—But here the Diatribe will sharply retort—"Ecclesiasticus by saying, "if thou wilt keep," signifies that there is a will in man, to keep, and not to keep: otherwise, what is the use of saying unto him who has no will, "if thou wilt?" Would it not be ridiculous if any were to say to a blind man, if thou wilt see, thou mayest find a treasure? Or, to a deaf man, if thou wilt hear, I will relate to thee an excellent story? This would be to laugh at their misery"—

I answer: These are the arguments of human reason, which is wont to shoot forth many such sprigs of wisdom. Wherefore, I must dispute now, not with Ecclesiasticus, but with human reason concerning a conclusion; for she, by her conclusions and syllogisms, interprets and twists the Scriptures of God just which way she pleases. But I will enter upon this willingly, and with confidence, knowing, that she can prate nothing but follies and absurdities; and that more especially, when she attempts to make a shew of her wisdom in these divine matters.

First then, if I should demand of her how it can be proved, that the freedom of the will in man is signified and inferred, wherever these expressions are used, 'if thou wilt,' 'if thou shalt do,' 'if thou shalt hear;' she would say, because the nature of words, and the common use of speech among men, seem to require it. Therefore, she judges of divine things and words according to the customs and things of men; than which, what can be more perverse; seeing that, the former things are heavenly, the latter earthly. Like a fool, therefore, she exposes herself, making it manifest that she has not a thought concerning God but what is human.

But, what if I prove, that the nature of words and the use of speech even among men, are not always of that tendency, as to make a laughing stock of those to whom it is said, 'if thou wilt,' 'if thou shalt do it,' 'if thou shalt hear?'—How often do parents thus play with their children, when they bid them come to them, or do this or that, for this purpose only, that it may plainly appear to them how unable they are to do it, and that they may call for the aid of the parent's hand? How often does a faithful physician bid his obstinate patient do or omit those things which are either injurious to him or impossible, to the intent that, he may bring him, by an experience, to the knowledge of his disease or his weakness? And what is more general and common, than to use words of insult or provocation, when we would show either enemies or friends, what they can do and what they cannot do?

I merely go over these things, to shew Reason her own conclusions, and how absurdly she tacks them to the Scriptures: moreover, how blind she must be not to see, that they do not always stand good even in human words and things. But the case is, if she see it to be done once, she rushes on headlong, taking it for granted, that it is done generally in all the things of God and men, thus making, according to the way of her wisdom, of a particularity an universality.

If then God, as a Father, deal with us as with sons, that He might shew us who are in ignorance our impotency, or as a faithful physician, that He might make our disease known unto us, or that He might insult His enemies who proudly resist His counsel; and for this end, say to us by proposed laws (as being those means by which He accomplishes His design the most effectually) 'do,' 'hear,' 'keep,' or, 'if thou wilt,' 'if thou wilt do,' 'if thou wilt hear;' can this be drawn herefrom as a just conclusion—therefore, either we have free power to act, or God laughs at us? Why is this not rather drawn as a conclusion—therefore, God tries us, that by His law He might bring us to a knowledge of our impotency, if we be His friends; or, He thereby righteously and deservedly insults and derides us, if we be His proud enemies. For this, as Paul teaches, is the intent of the divine legislation. (Rom. iii. 20, v. 20; Gal. iii. 19, 24.) Because human nature is blind, so that it knows not its own powers, or rather its own diseases. Moreover, being proud, it self-conceitedly imagines, that it knows and can do all things. To remedy which pride and ignorance, God can use no means more effectual than His proposed law: of which we shall say more in its place: let it suffice to have thus touched upon it here, to refute this conclusion of carnal and absurd wisdom:—'if thou wilt'—therefore thou art able to will freely.

The Diatribe dreams, that man is whole and sound, as, to human appearance, he is in his own affairs; and therefore, from these words, 'if thou wilt,' 'if thou wilt do,' 'if thou wilt hear,' it pertly argues, that man, if his will be not free, is laughed at. Whereas, the Scripture describes man as corrupt and a captive; and added to that, as proudly contemning and ignorant of his corruption and captivity: and therefore, by those words, it goads him and rouses him up, that he might know, by a real experience, how unable he is to do any one of those things.

Sect. LIII.—But I will attack the Diatribe itself. If thou really think, O Madam Reason! that these conclusions stand good, 'If thou wilt—therefore thou hast a free power,' why dost thou not follow the same thyself? For thou sayest, according to that 'probable opinion,' that "Free-will" cannot will any thing good. By what conclusion then can such a sentiment flow from this passage also, 'if thou wilt keep,' when thou sayest that the conclusion flowing from this, is, that man can will and not will freely? What! can bitter and sweet flow from the same fountain? Dost thou not here much more deride man thyself, when thou sayest, that he can keep that, which he can neither will nor choose? Therefore, neither dost thou, from thy heart, believe that this is a just conclusion, 'if thou wilt—therefore thou hast a free power,' although thou contendest for it with so much zeal, or, if thou dost believe it, then thou dost not, from thy heart, say, that that opinion is 'probable,' which holds that man cannot will good. Thus, reason is so caught in the conclusions and words of her own wisdom, that she knows not what she says, nor concerning what she speaks: nay, knows nothing but that which it is most right she should know—that "Free-will" is defended with such arguments as mutually devour, and put an end to each other; just as the Midianites destroyed each other by mutual slaughter, when they fought against Gideon and the people of God. Judges vii.

Nay, I will expostulate more fully with this wisdom of the Diatribe. Ecclesiasticus does not say, 'if thou shalt have the desire and the endeavour of keeping,' (for this is not to be ascribed to that power of yours, as you have concluded) but he says, "if thou wilt keep the commandments they shall preserve thee." Now then, if we, after the manner of your wisdom, wish to draw conclusions, we should infer thus:—therefore, man is able to keep the commandments. And thus, we shall not here make a certain small degree of desire, or a certain little effort of endeavour to be left in man, but we shall ascribe unto him the whole, full, and abundant power of keeping the commandments. Otherwise, Ecclesiasticus will be made to laugh at the misery of man, as commanding *him* to 'keep,' who, he knows, is not able to 'keep.' Nor would it have been sufficient if he had supposed the desire and the endeavour to be in the man, for he would not then have escaped the suspicion of deriding him, unless he had signified his having the full power of keeping.

But however, let us suppose that that desire and endeavour of "Free-will" are a real something. What shall we say to those, (the Pelagians, I mean) who, from this passage, have denied grace *in toto,* and ascribed all to "Free-will?" If the conclusion of the Diatribe stand good, the Pelagians have evidently established their point. For the words of Ecclesiasticus speak of *keeping,* not of *desiring* or *endeavouring.* If, therefore, you deny the Pelagians their conclusion concerning *keeping,* they, in reply, will much more rightly deny you your conclusion concerning *endeavouring.* And if you take from them the whole of "Free-will," they will take from you your remnant particle of it: for you cannot assert a remnant particle of that, which you deny *in toto.* In what degree soever, therefore, you speak against the Pelagians, who from this passage ascribe the whole to "Free-will," in the same degree, and with much more determination, shall we speak against that certain small remnant desire of your "Free-will." And in this, the Pelagians themselves will agree with us, that, if their opinion cannot be proved from this passage, much less will any other of the same kind be proved from it: seeing, that if the subject be to be conducted by conclusions, Ecclesiasticus above all makes the most forcibly for the Pelagians: for he speak in plain words concerning *keeping* only, "If thou wilt *keep* the commandments:" nay, he speaks also concerning *faith,* "If thou wilt *keep the faith:*" so that, by the same conclusion, keeping the faith ought also to be in our power, which, however, is the peculiar and precious gift of God.

In a word, since so many opinions are brought forward in support of "Free-will," and there is no one that does not catch at this passage of Ecclesiasticus on defense of itself; and since they are diverse from, and contrary to each other, it is impossible but that they must make Ecclesiasticus contradictory to, and diverse from themselves in the self same words; and therefore, they can from him prove nothing. Although, if that conclusion of yours be admitted, it will make for the Pelagians against all the others; and consequently, it makes against the Diatribe; which, in this passage, is stabbed by its own sword!

Sect. LIV.—But, as I said at first, so I say here: this passage of Ecclesiasticus is in favour of no one of those who assert "Free-will," but makes against them all. For that conclusion is not to be admitted, 'If thou wilt—therefore thou art able;' but those words, and all like unto them, are to be understood thus:—that by them man is admonished of his impotency; which, without such admonitions, being proud and ignorant, he would neither know nor feel.

For he here speaks, not concerning the first man only, but concerning any man: though it is of little consequence whether you understand it concerning the first man, or any others. For although the first man was not impotent, from the assistance of grace, yet, by this commandment, God plainly shews him how impotent he would be without grace. For if that man, who had the Spirit, could not by his new will, will good newly proposed, that is, obedience, because the Spirit did not add it unto him, what can we do without the Spirit toward the good that is lost! In this man, therefore, it is shewn, by a terrible example for the breaking down of our pride, what our "Free-will" can do when it is left to itself, and not continually moved and increased by the Spirit of God. *He* could do nothing to increase the Spirit who had its first-fruits, but fell from the first-fruits of the Spirit. What then can *we* who are fallen, do towards the first-fruits of the Spirit which are taken away! Especially, since Satan now reigns in us with full power, who cast *him* down, not then reigning in him, but by temptation alone! Nothing can be more forcibly brought against "Free-will," than this passage of Ecclesiasticus, considered together with the fall of Adam. But we have no room for these observations here, an opportunity may perhaps offer itself elsewhere. Meanwhile, it is sufficient to have shewn, that

Ecclesiasticus, in this place, says nothing whatever in favour of "Free-will" (which nevertheless they consider as their principal authority), and that these expressions and the like, 'if thou wilt,' 'if thou hear,' 'if thou do,' shew, not what men *can do*, but what they *ought to do!*

Sect. LV.—Another passage is adduced by our Diatribe out of Gen. iv. 7: where the Lord saith unto Cain, "Under thee shall be the desire of sin, and thou shalt rule over it."—"Here it is shewn (saith the Diatribe) that the motions of the mind to evil can be overcome, and that they do not carry with them the necessity of sinning."—

These words, 'the motions of the mind to evil can be overcome,' though spoken with ambiguity, yet, from the scope of the sentiment, the consequence, and the circumstances, must mean this:—that "Free-will," has the power of overcoming its motions to evil; and that, those motions do not bring upon it the necessity of sinning. Here, again, what is there excepted which is not ascribed unto "Free-will? " What need is there of the Spirit, what need of Christ, what need of God, if "Free-will" can overcome the motions of the mind to evil! And where, again, is that 'probable opinion' which affirms, that "Free-will" cannot so much as will good? For here, the victory over evil is ascribed unto that, which neither wills nor wishes for good. The inconsiderateness of our Diatribe is really—too—too bad!

Take the truth of the matter in a few words. As I have before observed, by such passages as these, it is shewn to man what he *ought to do*, not what he *can do*. It is said, therefore, unto Cain, that he ought to rule over his sin, and to hold its desires in subjection under him. But this he neither did nor could do, because he was already pressed down under the contrary dominion of Satan.—It is well known, that the Hebrews frequently use the *future indicative* for the *imperative*: as in Exod. xx. 1-17, "Thou shalt have none other gods but Me," "Thou shalt not kill," "Thou shalt not commit adultery," and in numberless other instances of the same kind. Otherwise, if these sentences were taken indicatively, as they really stand, they would be *promises* of God; and as He cannot lie, it would come to pass that no man could sin; and then, as *commands*, they would be unnecessary; and if this were the case, then our interpreter would have translated this passage more correctly thus:—"let its desire be under thee, and rule thou over it," (Gen. iv. 7.) Even as it then ought also to be said concerning the woman, "Be thou under thy husband, and let him rule over thee," (Gen. iii. 16.) But that it was not spoken indicatively unto Cain is manifest from this:—it would then have been a *promise*. Whereas, it was not a promise; because, from the conduct of Cain, the event proved the contrary.

Sect. LVI.—The third passage is from Moses, (Deut. xxx. 19.) "I have set before thy face life and death, choose what is good, &c."—"What words (says the Diatribe) can be more plain? It leaves to man the liberty of choosing."—

I answer: What is more plain, than, that you are blind? How, I pray, does it leave the liberty of choosing? Is it by the expression 'choose'? —Therefore, as Moses saith 'choose,' does it immediately come to pass that they do choose? Then, there is no need of the Spirit. And as you so often repeat and inculcate the same things, I shall be justified in repeating the same things also.—If there be a liberty of choosing, why has the 'probable opinion' said that "Free-will" cannot will good? Can it choose *not willing* or *against its will?* But let us listen to the similitude,—

—"It would be ridiculous to say to a man standing in a place where two ways met, Thou seest two roads, go by which thou wilt, when one only was open."—

This, as I have before observed, is from the arguments of human reason, which thinks, that a man is mocked by a command impossible: whereas I say, that the man, by this means, is admonished and roused to see his own impotency. True it is, that we are in a place where two ways meet, and that one of them only is open, yea rather neither of them is open. But by the law it is shewn how impossible the one is, that is, to good, unless God freely give His Spirit; and how wide and easy the other is, if God leave us to ourselves. Therefore, it would not be said ridiculously, but with a necessary seriousness, to the man thus standing in a place where two ways meet, 'go by which thou wilt,' if he, being in reality impotent, wished to seem to himself strong, or contended that neither way was hedged up.

Wherefore, the words of the law are spoken, not that they might assert the power of the will, but that they might illuminate the blindness of reason, that it might see that its own light is nothing, and that the power of the will is nothing. "By the law (saith Paul) is the knowledge of sin," (Rom. iii. 20.): he does not say—is the abolition of, or the escape from sin. The whole nature and design of the law is to give knowledge only, and that of nothing else save of sin, but not to discover or communicate any power whatever. For knowledge is not power, nor does it communicate power, but it teaches and shows how great the impotency must there be, where there is no power. And what else can the knowledge of sin be, but the knowledge of our evil and infirmity? For he does not say—by the law comes the knowledge of strength or of good. The whole that the law does, according to the testimony of Paul, is to make known sin.

And this is the place, where I take occasion to enforce this my general reply:—that man, by the words of the law, is admonished and taught what *he ought to do*, not what *he can do*: that is, that he is brought to know his sin, but not to believe that he has any strength in himself. Wherefore, friend Erasmus, as often as you throw in my teeth the words of the law, so often I throw in yours that of Paul, "By the law is the knowledge of sin,"—not of the power of the will. Heap together, therefore, out of the large Concordances all the imperative words into one chaos, provided that, they be not words of the promise but of the requirement of the law only, and I will immediately declare, that by them is always shewn what men *ought to do*, not what they *can do*, or *do do*. And even common grammarians and every little school-boy in the street knows, that by verbs of the imperative mood, nothing else is signified than that which ought to be done, and that, what is done or can be done, is expressed by verbs of the indicative mood.

Thus, therefore, it comes to pass, that you theologians, are so senseless and so many degrees below even school-boys, that when you have caught hold of one imperative verb you infer an indicative sense, as though what was commanded were immediately and even necessarily done, or possible to be done. But how many *slips* are there *between the cup and the lip!* So that, what you command to be done, and is therefore quite possible to be done, is yet never done at all. Such a difference is there, between verbs imperative and verbs indicative, even in the most common and easy things. Whereas you, in these things which are as far above those, as the heavens are above the earth, so quickly make indicatives out of imperatives, that the moment you hear the voice of him commanding, saying, "do," "keep," "choose," you will have, that it is immediately kept, done, chosen, or fulfilled, or, that our powers are able so to do.

Sect. LVII.—In the fourth place, you adduce from Deuteronomy xxx. many passages of the same kind which speak of choosing, of turning away from, of keeping; as, 'If thou shalt keep,' 'if thou shalt turn away from,' 'if thou shalt choose.'—"All these expressions (you say) are made use of preposteriously if there be not a "Free-will" in man unto good"—

I answer: And you, friend Diatribe, preposterously enough also conclude from these expressions the freedom of the will. You set out to prove the *endeavour* and *desire* of "Free-will" only, and you have adduced no passage which proves such an endeavour. But now, you adduce those passages, which, if your conclusion hold good, will ascribe *all* to "Free-will."

Let me here then again make a distinction, between the words of the Scripture adduced, and the conclusion of the Diatribe tacked to them. The words adduced are imperative, and they say nothing but what *ought to be* done. For, Moses does not say, 'thou hast the power and strength to choose.' The words 'choose,' 'keep,' 'do,' convey the precept 'to keep,' but they do not describe the ability of man. But the conclusion tacked to them by that wisdom-aping Diatribe, infers thus:—therefore, man can do those things, otherwise the precepts are given in vain. To whom this reply must be made:—Madam Diatribe, you make a bad inference, and do not prove your conclusion, but the conclusion and the proof merely *seem* to be right to your blind and inadvertent self. But know, that these precepts are not given preposterously nor in vain; but that proud and blind man might, by them, learn the disease of his own impotency, if he should attempt to do what is commanded. And hence your similitude amounts to nothing where you say.

—"Otherwise it would be precisely the same, as if any one should say to a man who was so bound that he could only stretch forth his left arm,—Behold! thou hast on thy right hand excellent wine, thou hast on thy left poison; on which thou wilt stretch forth thy hand"—

These your similitudes I presume are particular favourites of yours. But you do not all the while see, that if the similitudes stand good, they prove much more than you ever purposed to prove, nay, that they prove what you deny and would have to be disproved:—that "Free-will" can do *all things.* For by the whole scope of your argument, forgetting what you said, 'that "Free-will" can do nothing without grace,' you actually prove that "Free-will" can do all things without grace. For your conclusions and similitudes go to prove this:—that either "Free-will" can of itself do those things which are said and commanded, or they are commanded in vain, ridiculously, and preposterously. But these are nothing more than the old songs of the Pelagians sung over again, which even the Sophists have exploded, and which you have yourself condemned. And by all this your forgetfulness and disorder of memory, you do nothing but evince how little you know of the subject, and how little you are affected by it. And what can be worse in a rhetorician, than to be continually bringing forward things wide of the nature of the subject, and not only so, but to be always declaiming against his subject and against himself?

Sect. LVIII.—Wherefore I observe, finally, the passages of Scripture adduced by you are imperative, and neither prove any thing, nor determine any thing concerning the ability of man, but enjoin only what things are to be done, and what are not to be done. And as to your conclusions or appendages, and similitudes, if they prove any thing they prove this:—that "Free-will" can do all things without grace. Whereas this you did not undertake to prove, nay, it is by you denied. Wherefore, these your proofs are nothing else but the most direct confutations.

For, (that I may, if I can, rouse the Diatribe from its lethargy) suppose I argue thus—If Moses say, 'Choose life and keep the commandment', unless man be able to choose life and keep the commandment, Moses gives that precept to man ridiculously. —Have I by this argument proved my side of the subject, that "Free-will" can do nothing good, and that it has no external endeavour separate from its own power? Nay, on the contrary, I have proved, by an assertion sufficiently forcible, that either man can choose life and keep the commandment as it is commanded, or Moses is a ridiculous law-giver? But who would dare to assert that Moses was a ridiculous law-giver? It follows therefore, that man can do the things that are commanded.

This is the way in which the Diatribe argues throughout, contrary to its own purposed design; wherein, it promised that it would not argue thus, but would prove a certain endeavour of "Free-will;" of which however, so far from proving it, it scarcely makes mention in the whole string of its arguments; nay, it proves the contrary rather; so that it may itself be more properly said to affirm and argue all things ridiculously.

And as to its making it, according to its own adduced similitude, to be ridiculous, that a man 'having his right arm bound, should be ordered to stretch forth his right hand when he could only stretch forth his left.'—Would it, I pray, be ridiculous, if a man, having both his arms bound, and proudly contending or ignorantly presuming that he could do any thing right or left, should be commanded to stretch forth his hand right and left, not that his captivity might be derided, but that he might be convinced of his false presumption of liberty and power, and might be brought to know his ignorance of his captivity and misery?

The Diatribe is perpetually setting before us such a man, who either *can do* what is commanded, or at least *knows* that he *cannot do* it. Whereas, no such man is to be found. If there were such an one, then indeed, either impossibilities would be ridiculously commanded, or the Spirit of Christ would be in vain.

The Scripture, however, sets forth such a man, who is not only bound, miserable, captive, sick, and dead, but who, by the operation of his lord, Satan, to his other miseries, adds that of blindness: so that he believes he is free, happy, at liberty, powerful, whole, and alive. For Satan well knows that if men knew their own misery he could retain no one of them in his kingdom: because, it could not be, but that God would immediately pity and succour their known misery and calamity: seeing that, He is with so much praise set forth, throughout the whole Scripture as, being near unto the contrite in heart, that Isaiah lxi. 1-3, testifies, that Christ was sent "to preach the Gospel to the poor, and to heal the broken hearted."

Wherefore, the work of Satan is, so to hold men, that they come not to know their misery, but that they presume that they can do all things which are enjoined. But the work of Moses the legislator is the contrary, even that by the law he might discover to man his misery, in order that he might prepare him, thus bruised and confounded with the knowledge of himself, for grace, and might send him to Christ to be saved. Wherefore, the office of the law is not ridiculous, but above all things serious and necessary.

Those therefore who thus far understand these things, understand clearly at the same time, that the Diatribe, by the whole string of its arguments effects nothing whatever; that it collects nothing from the Scriptures but imperative passages, when it understands, neither what they mean nor wherefore they are spoken; and that, moreover, by the appendages of its conclusions and carnal similitudes it mixes up such a mighty mass of flesh, that it asserts and proves more than it ever intended, and argues against itself. So that there were no need to pursue particulars any further, for the whole is solved by one solution, seeing that the whole depends on one argument. But however, that it may be drowned in the same profusion in which it attempted to drown me, I will proceed to touch upon a few particulars more.

Sect. LIX.—There is that of Isaiah i. 19., "If ye be willing and obedient, ye shall eat the fat of the land:"—'Where, (according to the judgment of the Diatribe,) if there be no liberty of the will, it would have been more consistent, had it been said, If I will, if I will not.'

The answer to this may be plainly found in what has been said before. Moreover, what consistency would there then have been, had it been said, 'If I will, ye shall eat the fat of the land?' Does the Diatribe from its so highly exalted wisdom imagine, that the fat of the land can be eaten contrary to the will of God? Or, that it is a rare and new thing, that we do not receive of the fat of the land but by the will of God.

So also, that of Isaiah xxx. 21. "If ye will inquire, inquire ye: return, come."—"To what purpose is it (saith the Diatribe) to exhort those who are not in any degree in their own power? It is just like saying to one bound in chains, Move thyself to this place."—

Nay, I reply, to what purpose is it to cite passages which of themselves prove nothing, and which, by the appendage of your conclusion, that is, by the perversion of their sense, ascribe all unto "Free-will," when a certain endeavour only was to be ascribed unto it, and to be proved?

—"The same may be said (you observe) concerning that of Isaiah xlv. 20. "Assemble yourselves and come." "Turn ye unto me and ye shall be saved." And that also of Isaiah lii. 1-2. "Awake! awake! " "shake thyself from the dust," "loose the bands of thy neck." And that of Jeremiah xv. 19. "If thou wilt turn, then will I turn thee; and if thou shalt separate the precious from the vile, thou shalt be as My mouth." And Malachi more evidently still, indicates the endeavour of "Free-will" and the grace that is prepared for him who endeavours, "Turn ye unto Me, saith the Lord of hosts, and I will turn unto you, saith the Lord." (Mal. iii. 7.)

Sect. LX.—In these passages, our friend Diatribe makes no distinction whatever, between the voice of the Law and the voice of the Gospel: because, forsooth, it is so blind and so ignorant, that it knows not what is the Law and what is the Gospel. For out of all the passages from Isaiah, it produces no one word of the law, save this, 'If thou wilt;' all the rest is Gospel, by which, as the word of offered grace, the bruised and afflicted are called unto consolation. Whereas, the Diatribe makes them the words of the law. But, I pray thee, tell me, what can that man do in theological matters, and the Sacred Writings, who has not even gone so far as to know what is Law and what is Gospel, or, who, if he does know, condemns the observance of the distinction between them? Such an one must confound all things, heaven with hell, and life with death; and will never labour to know any thing of Christ. Concerning which, I shall put my friend Diatribe a little in remembrance, in what follows.

Look then, first, at that of Jeremiah and Malachi "If thou wilt turn, then will I turn thee:" and, "turn ye unto me, and I will turn unto you." Does it then follow from "turn ye"—therefore, ye are able to turn? Does it follow also from "Love the Lord thy God with all thy heart"—therefore, thou art able to love with all thine heart? If these arguments stand good, what do they conclude, but that "Free-will" needs not the grace of God, but can do all things of its own power? And then, how much more right would it be that the words should be received as they stand—'If thou shalt turn, then will I also turn thee?' That is;—if thou shalt cease from sinning, I also will cease from punishing; and if thou shalt be converted and live well, I also will do well unto thee in turning away thy captivity and thy evils. But even in this way, it does not follow, that man can turn by his own power, nor do the words imply this; but they simply say, "If thou wilt turn;" by which, a man is admonished of what he ought to do. And when he has thus known and seen what he *ought to do* but *cannot do*, he would ask *how he is to do it*, were it not for that Leviathan of the Diatribe (that is, that appendage and conclusion it has here tacked on) which comes in and between and says,—'therefore, if man cannot turn of his own power, "turn ye" is spoken in vain.' But, of what nature all such conclusion is, and what it amounts to, has been already fully shewn.

It must, however, be a certain stupor or lethargy which can hold, that the power of "Free-will" is confirmed by these words "turn ye," "if thou wilt turn," and the like, and does not see, that for the same reason, it must be confirmed by this Scripture also, "Thou shalt love the Lord thy God with all thine heart," seeing that, the meaning of Him who commands and requires is the same in both instances. For the loving of God, is not less required than our conversion, and the keeping of all the commandments; because, the loving of God is our real conversion. And yet, no one attempts to prove "Free-will" from that command 'to love,' although from those words "if thou wilt," "if thou wilt hear," "turn ye", and the like, all attempt to prove it. If therefore from that word, "love the Lord thy God with all thy heart," it does not follow that "Free-will" is any thing or can do any thing, it is certain that it neither follows from these words, "if thou wilt," "if thou wilt hear," "turn ye," and the like, which either require less, or require with less force of importance, than these words "Love God! " "Love the Lord! "

Whatever, therefore, is said against drawing a conclusion in support of "Free-will" from this word "love God," the same must be said against drawing a conclusion in support of "Free-will" from every other word of command or requirement. For, if by the command 'to love,' the nature of the law only be shewn, and what we *ought to do*, but not the power of the will or what we *can do*, but rather, what we *cannot do*, the same is shewn by all the other Scriptures of requirement. For it is well known, that even the schoolmen, except the Scotinians and moderns, assert, that man cannot love God with all his heart. Therefore, neither can he perform any one of the other precepts, for all the rest, according to the testimony of Christ, hang on this one. Hence, by the testimony even of the doctors of the schools, this remains as a settled conclusion:—that the words of the law do not prove the *power of "Free-will,"* but shew what we *ought to do*, and what we *cannot do*.

Sect. LXI.—But our friend Diatribe, proceeding to still greater lengths of inconsiderateness, not only infers from that passage of Malachi iii. 7., "turn ye unto me," an indicative sense, but also, goes on with zeal to prove therefrom, the endeavour of "Free-will," and the grace prepared for the person endeavouring.

Here, at last, it makes mention of the endeavour and by a new kind of grammar, 'to *turn*,' signifies, with it, the same thing as 'to *endeavour*:' so that the sense is, "turn ye unto me," that is, endeavour ye to turn; "and I will turn unto you," that is, I will endeavour to turn unto you: so that, at last, it attributes an endeavour even unto God, and perhaps, would have grace to be prepared for Him upon His endeavouring: for if turning signify endeavouring in one place, why not in every place?

Again, it says, that from Jeremiah xv. 19., "If thou shalt separate the precious from the vile," not the endeavour only, but the liberty of choosing is proved; which, before, it declared was 'lost,' and changed into a 'necessity of serving sin.' You see, therefore, that in handling the Scriptures the Diatribe has a "Free-will" with a witness: so that, with it, words of the same kind are compelled to prove *endeavour* in one place, and *liberty* in another, just as the turn suits.

But, to away with vanities, the word TURN is used in the Scriptures in a twofold sense, the one *legal*, the other *evangelical*. In the legal sense, it is the voice of the exactor and commander, which requires, not an endeavour, but a change in the whole life. In this sense Jeremiah frequently uses it, saying, "Turn ye now every one of you from his evil way:" and, "Turn ye unto the Lord:" in which, he involves the requirement of all the commandments; as is sufficiently evident. In the evangelical sense, it is the voice of the divine consolation and promise, by which nothing is demanded of us, but in which the grace of God is offered unto us. Of this kind is that of Psalm cxxvi. 1, "When the Lord shall turn again the captivity of Zion;" and that of Psalm cxvi. 7, "Turn again into thy rest, O my soul." Hence, Malachi, in a very brief compendium, has set forth the preaching both of the law and of grace. It is the whole sum of the law, where he saith, "Turn ye unto me;" and it is grace, where he saith, "I will turn unto you." Wherefore, as much as "Free-will" is proved from this word, "Love the Lord," or from any other word of particular law, just so much is it proved from this word of summary law, "TURN YE." It becomes a wise reader of the Scriptures, therefore, to observe what are words of the law and what are words of grace, that he might not be involved in confusion like the unclean Sophists, and like this sleepily-yawning Diatribe.

Sect. LXII.—Now observe, in what way the Diatribe handles that single passage in Ezekiel xviii. 23, "As I live, saith the Lord, I desire not the death of a sinner, but rather that he should turn from his wickedness and live." In the first place—"if (it says) the expressions "shall turn away," "hath done," "hath committed," be so often repeated in this chapter, where are they who deny that man can do any thing?"—

Only remark, I pray, the excellent conclusion! It set out to prove the endeavour and the desire of "Free-will," and now it proves the whole work, that all things are fulfilled by "Free-will!" Where now, I pray, are those who need grace and the Holy Spirit? For it pertly argues thus: saying, 'Ezekiel says, "If the wicked man shall turn away, and shall do righteousness and judgment, he shall live." Therefore, the wicked man does that immediately and can do it.' Whereas Ezekiel is signifying, *what ought to be done*, but the Diatribe understands it as *being done*, and *having been done*. Thus teaching us, by a new kind of grammar, that *ought to be* is the same as *having been*, *being exacted* the same as *being performed*, *and being required* the same as *being rendered*.

And then, that voice of the all-sweet Gospel, "I desire not the death of a sinner," &c.,

it perverts thus:—"Would the righteous Lord deplore that death of His people which He Himself wrought in them? If, therefore, He wills not our death, it certainly is to be laid to the charge of our own will, if we perish. For, what can you lay to the charge of Him, who can do nothing either of good or evil? "

It was upon this same string that Pelagius harped long ago, when he attributed to "Free-will" not a desire nor an endeavour only, but the power of doing and fulfilling all things. For as I have said before, these conclusions prove that power, if they prove any thing; so that, they make with equal, nay with more force against the Diatribe which denies that power of "Free-will," and which attempts to establish the endeavour only, than they do, against us who deny "Free-will" altogether.—But, to say nothing of the ignorance of the Diatribe, let us speak to the subject.

It is the Gospel voice, and the sweetest consolation to miserable sinners, where Ezekiel saith, "I desire not the death of a sinner, but rather, that he should be converted and live," and it is in all respects like unto that of Psalm xxx. 5.; "For His wrath is but for a moment, in His willingness is life." And that of Psalm xxxvi. 7., "How sweet is thy loving-kindness, O God." Also, "For I am merciful," And that of Christ, (Matt. xi. 28.) "Come unto me, all ye that labour and are heavy laden, and I will give you rest." And also that of Exodus xx. 6, "I will shew mercy unto thousands of them that love me."

And what is more than half of the Holy Scripture, but mere promises of grace, by which, mercy, life, peace, and salvation, are extended from God unto men? And what else is the whole word of promise but this:—"I desire not the death of a sinner? " Is not His saying, "I am merciful," the same as saying, I am not angry, I am unwilling to punish, I desire not your death, My will is to pardon, My will is to spare? And if there were not these divine promises standing, by which consciences, afflicted with a sense of sin and terrified at the fear of death and judgment, might be raised up, what place would there be for pardon or for hope! What sinner would not sink in despair! But as "Free-will" is not proved from any of the other words of mercy, of promise, and of comfort, so neither is it from this:—"I desire not the death of a sinner," &c.

But our friend Diatribe, again making no distinction between the words of the law, and the words of the promise, makes this passage of Ezekiel the voice of the law, and expounds it thus:—"I desire not the death of a sinner:" that is, I desire not that he should sin unto death, or should become a sinner guilty of death; but rather, that he should be converted from sin, if he have committed any, and thus live. For if it do not expound the passage thus, it will make nothing to its purpose. But this is utterly to destroy and take away that most sweet place of Ezekiel, "I desire not the death." If we in our blindness will read and understand the Scriptures thus, what wonder if they be 'obscure and ambiguous.' Whereas God does not say, "I desire not the sin of man, but, I desire not the death of a sinner," which manifestly shews that He is speaking of the punishment of sin, of which the sinner has a sense on account of his sin, that is, of the fear of death; and that He is raising up and comforting the sinner lying under this affliction and desperation, that He might not "break the bruised reed nor quench the smoking flax," but raise him to the hope of pardon and salvation, in order that he might be further converted, that is, by the conversion unto salvation from the fear of death, and that he might live, that is, might be in peace and rejoice in a good conscience.

And this is also to be observed, that as the voice of the law is not pronounced but upon those who neither feel nor know their sins, as Paul saith, "By the law is the knowledge of sin;" (Rom. iii. 20,) so, the word of grace does not come but unto those, who, feeling their sins, are distressed and exercised with desperation. Therefore, in all the words of the law, you will find sin to be implied while it shews what we ought to do; as on the contrary, in all the words of the promise, you will find the evil to be implied under which the sinners, or those who are raised up, labour: as here, "I desire not the death of a sinner," clearly points out the death and the sinner, both the evil itself which is felt, and the sinner himself who feels it. But by this, 'Love God with all thine heart,' is shewn what *good* we *ought to do*, not what *evil* we *feel*, in order that we might know, how far we are *from doing good.*

Sect. LXIII.—Nothing, therefore, could be more absurdly adduced in support of "Free-will" than this passage of Ezekiel, nay, it makes with all possible force directly against "Free-will." For it is here shewn, in what state "Free-will" is, and what it can do under the knowledge of sin, and in turning itself from it:—that is, that it can only go on to worse, and add to its sins desperation and impenitency, unless God soon come in to help, and to call back, and raise up by the word of promise. For the concern of God in promising grace to recall and raise up the sinner, is itself an argument sufficiently great and conclusive, that "Free-will," of itself, cannot but go on to worse, and (as the Scripture saith) 'fall down to hell:' unless, indeed, you imagine that God is such a trifler, that He pours forth so great an abundance of the words of promise, not from any necessity of them unto our salvation, but from a mere delight in loquacity! Wherefore, you see, that not only all the words of law stand against "Free-will," but also, that all the words of the promise utterly confute it; that is, that the whole Scripture makes directly against it.

Hence, you see, this word, "I desire not the death of a sinner," does nothing else but preach and offer divine mercy to the world, which none receive with joy and gratitude but those who are distressed and exercised with the fears of death, for they are they in whom the law has now done its office, that is, in bringing them to the knowledge of sin. But they who have not yet experienced the office of the law, who do not yet know their sin nor feel the fears of death, despise the mercy promised in that word.

Sect. LXIV.—But, *why it is,* that some are touched by the law and some are not touched, why some receive the offered grace and some despise it, that is another question which is not here treated on by Ezekiel; because, he is speaking of THE PREACHED AND OFFERED MERCY OF GOD, not of that SECRET AND TO BE FEARED WILL OF GOD, who, according to His own counsel, ordains whom, and such as, He will to be receivers and partakers of the preached and offered mercy: which WILL, is not to be curiously inquired into, but to be adored with reverence as the most profound SECRET of the divine Majesty, which He reserves unto Himself and keeps hidden from us, and that, much more religiously than the mention of ten thousand Corycian caverns.

But since the Diatribe thus pertly argues—"Would the righteous Lord deplore that death of His people, which He Himself works in them? This would seem quite absurd"—

I answer, as I said before,—we are to argue in one way, concerning the WILL OF GOD preached, revealed, and offered unto us, and worshipped by us; and in another, concerning GOD HIMSELF not preached, not revealed, not offered unto us, and worshipped by us. In whatever, therefore, God hides Himself and will be unknown by us, that is nothing unto us: and here, that sentiment stands good—'What is above us, does not concern us.'

And that no one might think that this distinction is my own, I follow Paul, who, writing to the Thessalonians concerning Antichrist, saith, (2 Thess. ii. 4.) "that he should exalt himself above all that is God, as preached and worshipped:" evidently intimating, that any one might be exalted above God as He is preached and worshipped, that is, above the word and worship of God, by which He is known unto us and has intercourse with us. But, above God not worshipped and preached, that is, as He is in our own nature and majesty, nothing can be exalted, but all things are under His powerful hand.

God, therefore, is to be left to remain in His own Nature and Majesty; for in this respect, we have nothing to do with Him, nor does He wish us to have, in this respect, anything to do with Him: but we have to do with Him, as far as He is clothed in, and delivered to us by, His Word; for in that He presents Himself unto us, and that is His beauty and His glory, in which the Psalmist celebrates Him as being clothed. Wherefore, we say, that the righteous God does not 'deplore that death of His people which He Himself works in them;' but He deplores that death which He finds in His people, and which He desires to remove from them. For GOD PREACHED desires this:—that, our sin and death being taken away, we might be saved, "He sent His word and healed them." (Psalm cvii. 20.) But GOD HIDDEN IN MAJESTY neither deplores, nor takes away death, but works life and death and all things: nor has He, in this Character, defined Himself in His Word, but has reserved unto Himself, a free power over all things.

But the Diatribe is deceived by its own ignorance, in not making a distinction between GOD PREACHED and GOD HIDDEN: that is, between the word of God and God Himself. God does many things which He does not make known unto us in His word: He also wills many things which He does not in His word make known unto us that He wills. Thus, He does not 'will the death of a sinner,' that is, *in His word*; but He *wills* it by that *will inscrutable*. But in the present case, we are to consider His word only, and to leave that will inscrutable; seeing that, it is by His word, and not by that will inscrutable, that we are to be guided; for who can direct himself according to a will inscrutable and incomprehensible? It is enough to know only, that there is in God a certain will inscrutable: but *what, why,* and *how far* that will wills, it is not lawful to inquire, to wish to know, to be concerned about, or to reach unto—it is only to be feared and adored!

Therefore it is rightly said, 'if God does not desire our death, it is to be laid to the charge of our own will, if we perish:' this, I say, is right, if you speak of GOD PREACHED. For He desires that all men should be saved, seeing that, He comes unto all by the word of salvation, and it is the fault of the will which does not receive Him: as He saith. (Matt. xxiii. 37.) "How often would I have gathered thy children together, and thou wouldest not! " But WHY that Majesty does not take away or change this fault of the will IN ALL, seeing that, it is not in the power of man to do it; or why He lays that to the charge of the will, which the man cannot avoid, it becomes us not to inquire, and though you should inquire much, yet you will never find out: as Paul saith, (Rom. ix. 20,) "Who art thou that repliest against God! "—Suffice it to have spoken thus upon this passage of Ezekiel. Now let us proceed to the remaining particulars.

Sect. LXV.—The Diatribe next argues—"If what is commanded be not in the power of every one, all the numberless exhortations in the Scriptures, and also all the promises, threatenings, expostulations, reproofs, asseverations, benedictions and maledictions, together with all the forms of precepts, must of necessity stand coldly useless."—

The Diatribe is perpetually forgetting the subject point, and going on with that which is contrary to its professed design: and it does not see, that all these things make with greater force against itself than against us. For from all these passages, it proves the liberty and ability to fulfil all things, as the very words of the conclusion which it draws necessarily declare: whereas, its design was, to prove '*that "Free-will" is that, which cannot will any thing good without grace, and is a certain endeavour that is not to be ascribed to its own powers.*' But I do not see that such an endeavour is proved by any of these passages, but that as I have repeatedly said already, that only is required which ought to be done: unless it be needful to repeat it again, as often as the Diatribe harps upon the same string, putting off its readers with a useless profusion of words.

About the last passage which it brings forward out of the Old Testament, is that of Deut. xxx. 11-14. "This commandment which I command thee this day, is not above thee, neither is it far off. Neither is it in heaven, that thou shouldest say, Who of us shall ascend up into heaven and bring it down unto us, that we may hear it and do it. But the word is very nigh unto thee, in thy mouth and in thy heart, that thou mayest do it." The Diatribe contends—'that it is declared by this passage, that what is commanded is not only placed in us, but is down-hill work, that is, easy to be done, or at least, not difficult.'—

I thank the Diatribe for such wonderful erudition! For if Moses so plainly declare, that there is in us, not only an ability, but also a power to keep all the commandments with ease, why have I been toiling all this time! Why did I not at once produce this passage and assert "Free-will" before the whole world! What need now of Christ! What need of the Spirit! We have now found a passage which stops the mouths of all, and, which not only plainly asserts the liberty of the will, but teaches that the observance of all the commandments is easy! —What need was there for Christ to purchase for us, even with His own blood, the Spirit, as though necessary, in order that He might make the keeping of the commandments easy unto us, when we were already thus qualified by nature! Nay, here, the Diatribe itself recants its own assertions, where it affirmed, that ' "Free-will" cannot will any thing good without grace,' and now affirms, that "Free-will" is of such power, that it can, not only will good, but keep the greatest, nay, all the commandments, with ease.

Only observe, I pray, what a mind does, where the heart is not in the cause, and how impossible it is that it should not expose itself! And can there still be any need to confute the Diatribe? Who can more effectually confute it, than it confutes itself! This truly, is that beast that devours itself! How true is the proverb, that 'A liar should have a good memory! '

I have already spoken upon this passage of Deuteronomy, I shall now treat upon it briefly; if indeed, there be any need so far to set aside Paul, who, Rom. x. 5-11, so powerfully handles this passage.—You can see nothing here to be said, nor one single syllable to speak, either of the ease or difficulty, of the power or impotency of "Free-will" or of man, either to keep or not to keep the commandments. Except that those, who entangle the Scriptures in their own conclusions and cogitations, make them obscure and ambiguous to themselves, that they might thus make of them what they please. But, if you cannot turn your eyes this way, turn your ears, or feel out what I am about to say with your hands.—Moses saith, "it is not above thee," "neither is it far from thee," "neither is it in heaven," "neither is it beyond the sea." Now, what is the meaning of this, "above thee? " What, of this "far from thee? " What, of this "in heaven? " What, of this "beyond the sea? " Will they then make the most commonly used terms, and even grammar so obscure unto us, that we shall not be able to speak any thing to a certainty, merely that they might establish their assertion, that the Scriptures are obscure?

According to my grammar, these terms signify neither the quality nor the quantity of human powers, but the distance of places only. For "above thee" does not signify a certain power of the will, but a certain place which is above us. So also "far from thee," "in heaven," "beyond the sea," do not signify any thing of ability in man, but a certain place at a distance above us, or on our right hand, or on our left hand, or behind us, or over against us. Some one may perhaps laugh at me for disputing in so plain a way, thus setting, as it were, a ready-marked-out lesson before such great men, as though they were little boys learning their alphabet, and I were teaching them how to put syllables together—but what can I do, when I see darkness to be sought for in a light so clear, and those studiously desiring to be blind, who boastingly enumerate before us such a series of ages, so much talent, so many saints, so many martyrs, so many doctors, and who with so much authority boast of this passage, and yet will not deign to look at the syllables, or to command their cogitations so far, as to give the passage of which they boast one consideration? Let the Diatribe now go home and consider, and say, how it can be, that one poor private individual should see that, which escaped the notice of so many public characters, and of the greatest men of so many ages. This passage surely, even in the judgment of a school-boy, proves that they must have been blind not very unfrequently!

What therefore does Moses mean by these most plain and clear words, but, that he has worthily performed his office as a faithful law-giver; and that therefore, if all men have not before their eyes and do not know all the precepts which are enjoined, the fault does not rest with him; that they have no place left them for excuse, so as to say, they did not know, or had not the precepts, or were obliged to seek them elsewhere; that if they do not keep them, the fault rests not with the law, or with the law-giver, but with themselves, seeing that the law is before them, and the law-giver has taught them; and that they have no place left for excusation of ignorance, only for accusation of negligence and disobedience? It is not, saith he, necessary to fetch the laws down from heaven, nor from lands beyond the sea, nor from afar, nor can you frame as an excuse, that you never had them nor heard them, for you have them nigh unto you; they are they which God hath commanded, which you have heard from my mouth, and which you have had in your hearts and in your mouths continually; you have heard them treated on by the Levites in the midst of you, of which this my word and book are witnesses; this, therefore only remains—that you do them.—What, I pray you, is here attributed unto "Free-will? " What is there, but the demanding that it would do the laws which it has, and the taking away from it the excuse of ignorance and the want of the laws?

These passages are the sum of what the Diatribe brings forward out of the Old Testament in support of "Free-will," which being answered, there remains nothing that is not answered at the same time, whether it have brought forward, or wished to bring forward more; seeing that, it could bring forward nothing but imperative, or conditional, or optative passages, by which is signified, not what we *can do*, or *do do*, (as I have so often replied, to the so often repeating Diatribe) but what we *ought to do*, and what *is required of us*, in order that we might come to the knowledge of our impotency, and that there might be wrought in us the knowledge of our sin. Or, if they do prove any thing, by means of the appended conclusions and similitudes invented by human reason, they prove this:—that "Free-will" is not a certain small degree of endeavour or desire only, but a full and free ability and power to do all things, without the grace of God, and without the Holy Spirit.

Thus, nothing less is proved by the whole sum of that copious, and again and again reiterated and inculcated argumentation, than that which was aimed at to be proved, that is, the PROBABLE OPINION; by which, "Free-will" is defined to be of that impotency, 'that it cannot will any thing good without grace, but is compelled into the service of sin; though it has an endeavour, which, nevertheless, is not to be ascribed to its own powers.'—A monster truly! which, at the same time, can do nothing by its own power, and yet, has an endeavour within its own power: and thus, stands upon the basis of a most manifest contradiction!

Sect. LXVI.—We now come to the NEW TESTAMENT, where again, are marshalled up in defence of that miserable bondage of "Free-will," an host of imperative sentences, together with all the auxiliaries of carnal reason, such as, conclusions, similitudes, &c., called in from all quarters. And if you ever saw represented in a picture, or imagined in a dream, a king of flies attended by his forces armed with lances and shields of straw or hay, drawn up in battle array against a real and complete army of veteran warriors—it is just thus, that the human dreams of the Diatribe are drawn up in battle array against the hosts of the words of God!

First of all, marches forth in front, that of Matt. xxiii. 37-39, as it were the Achilles of these flies, "O Jerusalem, Jerusalem, how often would I have gathered thy children together, and thou wouldest not."—"If all things be done from necessity (says the Diatribe) might not Jerusalem here have justly said in reply to the Lord, Why dost thou weary thyself with useless tears? If thou didst not will that we should kill the prophets, why didst thou send them? Why dost thou lay that to our charge, which, from *will* in thee, was done of *necessity* by us? "—thus the Diatribe.—

I answer: Granting in the mean time that this conclusion and proof of the Diatribe is good and true, what, I ask, is proved thereby? —that 'probable opinion,' which affirms that "Free-will" cannot will good? Nay, the will is proved to be free, whole, and able to do all things which the prophets have spoken; and such a will the Diatribe never intended to prove. But let the Diatribe here reply to itself. If "Free-will" cannot will good, why is it laid to its charge, that it did not hear the prophets, whom, as they taught good, it could not hear by its own powers? Why does Christ in useless tears weep over those as though they could have willed that, which He certainly knew they could not will? Here, I say, let the Diatribe free Christ from the imputation of madness, according to its 'probable opinion,' and then my opinion is immediately set free from that Achilles of the flies.

Therefore, that passage of Matthew either forcibly proves "Free-will" altogether, or makes with equal force against the Diatribe itself, and strikes it prostrate with its own weapon!

But I here observe as I have observed before, that we are not to dispute concerning that SECRET WILL of the divine Majesty; and that, that human temerity, which, with incessant perverseness, is ever leaving those things that are necessary, and attacking and trying this point, is to be called off and driven back, that it employ not itself in prying into those secrets of Majesty which it is impossible to attain unto, seeing that, they dwell in that light which is inaccessible; as Paul witnesseth. (1 Tim. vi. 16.) But let the man acquaint himself with the God Incarnate, or, as Paul saith, with Jesus crucified, in whom are all the treasures of wisdom and knowledge—but hidden! for in Him, there is an abundance both of that which he ought to know, and of that which he ought not to know.

The God Incarnate, then, here speaks thus—"I WOULD and THOU WOULDST NOT! " The God Incarnate, I say, was sent for this purpose—that He might desire, speak, do, suffer, and offer unto all, all things that are necessary unto salvation, although He should offend many, who, being either left or hardened by that secret will of Majesty, should not receive Him thus desiring, speaking, doing, and offering: as John i. 5, saith, "The light shineth in darkness, and the darkness comprehended it not." And again, "He came unto His own, and His own received Him not." (11.) It belongs also to this same God Incarnate, to weep, to lament, and to sigh over the perdition of the wicked, even while that will of Majesty, from purpose, leaves and reprobates some, that they might perish. Nor does it become us to inquire *why* He does so, but to revere that God who can do, and wills to do, such things.

Nor do I suppose that any one will cavillingly deny, that that will which here saith, "How often would I! " was displayed to the Jews, even before God became Incarnate; seeing that, they are accused of having slain the prophets, before Christ, and having thus resisted His will. For it is well known among Christians, that all things were done by the prophets in the name of Christ to come, who was promised that He should become Incarnate: so that, whatever has been offered unto men by the ministers of the word from the foundation of the world, may be rightly called, the Will of Christ.

Sect. LXVII.—But here Reason, who is always very knowing and loquacious, will say,—This is an excellently invented scape-gap; that, as often as we are pressed close by the force of arguments, we might run back to that to-be-revered will of Majesty, and thus silence the disputant as soon as he becomes troublesome; just as astrologers, do, who, by their invented epicycles, elude all questions concerning the motion of the whole heaven.—

I answer: It is no invention of mine, but a command supported by the Holy Scriptures. Paul, (Rom. ix. 19,) speaks thus: "Why therefore doth God find fault; for who hath resisted His will? Nay, but O man, who art thou that contendeth with God? " "Hath not the potter power? " And so on. And before him, Isaiah lviii. 2, "Yet they seek Me daily, and desire to know My ways, as a nation that did righteousness: they ask of Me the ordinances of justice, and desire to approach unto God."

From these words it is, I think, sufficiently manifest, that it is not lawful for men to search into that will of Majesty. And this subject is of that nature, that perverse men are here the most led to pry into that to-be-revered will, and therefore, there is here the greatest reason why they should be exhorted to silence and reverence. In other subjects, where those things are handled for which we can give a reason, and for which we are commanded to give a reason, we do not this. And if any one still persist in searching into the reason of that will, and do not choose to hearken to our admonition, we let him go on, and, like the giants, fight against God; while we look on to see what triumph he will gain, persuaded in ourselves, that he will do nothing, either to injure our cause or to advance his own. For it will still remain unalterable, that he must either prove that "Free-will" can do all things, or that the Scriptures which he adduces must make against himself. And, which soever of the two shall take place, he vanquished, lies prostrate, while we as conquerors "stand upright! "

Sect. LXVIII.—Another passage is that of (Matt. xix. 17,) "If thou wilt enter into life, keep the commandments."—"With what face, (says the Diatribe,) can "if thou wilt" be said to him who has not a Free-will? "—

To which I reply:—Is, therefore, the will, according to this word of Christ, free? But you wish to prove, that "Free-will" cannot will any thing good; and that, without grace, it of necessity serves sin. With what face, then, do you now make will wholly free?

The same reply will be made to that also—"If thou wilt be perfect," "If any one will come after me," "He that will save his life," "If ye love me," "If ye shall continue." In a word, as I said before, (to ease the Diatribe's labour in adducing such a load of words) let all the *conditional ifs* and all the *imperative verbs* be collected together.—"All these precepts (says the Diatribe) stand coldly useless, if nothing be attributed to the human will. How ill does that conjunctive *if* accord with mere necessity? "—

I answer: If they stand coldly useless, it is your fault that they stand coldly useless, who, at one time, assert that nothing is to be attributed to "Free-will," while you make "Free-will" unable to will good, and who, on the contrary, here make the same "Free-will" able to will all good; nay, you thus make them to stand as nothing at all: unless, with you, the same words stand coldly useless and warmly useful at the same time, while they at once assert all things and deny all things.

I wonder how any author can delight in repeating the same things so continually, and to be as continually forgetting his subject design: unless perhaps, distrusting his cause, he wishes to overcome his adversary by the bulk of his book, or to weary him out with the tedium and toil of reading it. By what conclusion, I ask, does it follow, that *will* and *power* must immediately take place as often as it is said, 'If thou wilt,' 'If any one will,' 'If thou shalt? ' Do we not most frequently imply in such expressions impotency rather, and impossibility? For instance.—If thou wilt equal Virgil in singing, my friend Mevius, thou must sing in another strain.—If thou wilt surpass Cicero, friend Scotus, instead of thy subtle jargon, thou must have the most exalted eloquence. If thou wilt stand in competition with David, thou must of necessity produce Psalms like his. Here are plainly signified things impossible to our own powers, although by divine power, all these things may be done. So it is in the Scriptures, that by such expressions it might be shewn what we cannot do ourselves, but what can be done in us by the power of God.

Moreover, if such expressions should be used in those things which are utterly impossible to be done, as being those which God would never do, then, indeed, they might rightly be called either coldly useless, or ridiculous, because they would be spoken in vain. Whereas now, they are so used, that by them, not only the impotency of "Free-will" is shewn, by which no one of those things can be done, but it is also signified, that a time will come when all those things shall be done, but by a power not our own, that is, by the divine power; provided that, we fully admit, that in such expressions, there is a certain signification of things possible and to be done: as if any one should interpret them thus:—"If thou wilt keep the commandments, (that is, if thou shalt at any time have the will to keep the commandments, though thou wilt have it, not of thyself, but of God, who giveth it to whom He will,) they also shall preserve thee."

But, to take a wider scope.—These expressions, especially those which are conditional, seem to be so placed also, on account of the Predestination of God, and to involve that as being unknown to us. As if they should speak thus:—"If thou desire," "If thou wilt:" that is, if thou be such with God, that he shall deign to give thee this will to keep the commandments, thou shalt be saved. According to which manner of speaking, it is given us to understand both truths.—That we can do nothing ourselves; and that, if we do any thing, God works that in us. This is what I would say to those, who will not be content to have it said, that by these words our impotency only is shewn, and who will contend, that there is also proved a certain power and ability to do those things which are commanded.

And in this way, it will also appear to be truth, that we are not able to do any of the things which are commanded, and yet, that we are able to do them all: that is, speaking of the former, with reference to our own powers, and of the latter, with reference to the grace of God.

Sect. LXIX.—The third particular that moves the Diatribe is this:—"How there can be (it observes) any place for mere necessity there, where mention is so frequently made of good works and of bad works, and where there is mention made of reward, I cannot understand; for neither nature nor necessity can have merit."—

Nor can I understand any thing but this:—that that 'probable opinion,' asserts 'mere necessity' where it affirms that "Free-will" cannot will any thing good, and yet, nevertheless, here attributes to it even 'merit.' Hence, "Free-will" gains ground so fast, as the book and argumentation of the Diatribe increases, that now, it not only has an endeavour and desire of its own, 'though not by its own powers,' nay, not only wills good and does good, but also merits eternal life according to that saying of Christ, (Matt. v. 12,) "Rejoice and be exceeding glad, for great is your reward in heaven." "Your reward," that is, the reward of "Free-will." For the Diatribe so understands this passage, that Christ and the Spirit of God are nothing. For what need is there of them, if we have good works and merit by "Free-will! " I say these things, that we may see, that it is no rare thing for men of exalted talent, to be blind in a matter which is plainly manifest even to one of a thick and uninformed understanding; and that we may also see, how weak, arguments drawn from human authority are in divine things, where the authority of God alone avails.

But we have here to speak upon two things. First, upon the precepts of the New Testament. And next, upon merit. We shall touch upon each briefly, having already spoken upon them more fully elsewhere.

The New Testament, properly, consists of promises and exhortations, even as the Old, properly, consists of laws and threatenings. For in the New Testament, the Gospel is preached; which is nothing else than the word, by which, are offered unto us the Spirit, grace, and the remission of sins obtained for us by Christ crucified; and all entirely free, through the mere mercy of God the Father, thus favouring us unworthy creatures, who deserve damnation rather than any thing else.

And then follow exhortations, in order to animate those who are already justified, and who have obtained mercy, to be diligent in the fruits of the Spirit and of righteousness received, to exercise themselves in charity and good works, and to bear courageously the cross and all the other tribulations of this world. This is the whole sum of the New Testament. But how little Erasmus understands of this matter is manifest from this:—it knows not how to make any distinction between the Old Testament and the New, for it can see nothing any where but precepts, by which, men are formed to good manners only. But what the new-birth is, the new-creature, regeneration, and the whole work of the Spirit, of all this it sees nothing whatever. So that, I am struck with wonder and astonishment, that the man, who has spent so much time and study upon these things, should know so little about them.

This passage therefore, "Rejoice, and be exceeding glad, for great is your reward in heaven," agrees as well with "Free-will" as light does with darkness. For Christ is there exhorting, not "Free-will," but His apostles, (who were not only raised above "Free-will" in grace, and justified, but were stationed in the ministry of the Word, that is, in the highest degree of grace,) to endure the tribulations of the world. But we are now disputing about "Free-will," and that particularly, as it is without Grace; which, by laws and threats, or the Old Testament, is instructed in the knowledge of itself only, that it might flee to the promises presented to it in the New Testament.

Sect. LXX.—As to merit, or a proposed reward, what is it else but a certain promise? But that promise does not prove that we can do any thing; it proves nothing more than this:—if any one shall do this thing or that, he shall then have a reward. Whereas, our subject inquiry is, not what reward is to be given, or how it is to be given, but, whether or not we can do those things, for the doing of which the reward is to be given. This is the point to be settled and proved. Would not these be ridiculous conclusions? —The prize is set before all that run in the race: therefore, all can so run as to obtain.—If Caesar shall conquer the Turks, he shall gain the kingdom of Syria: therefore, Caesar can conquer, and does conquer the Turks.—If "Free-will" shall gain dominion over sin, it shall be holy before the Lord: therefore "Free-will" is holy before the Lord.

But away with things so stupid and openly absurd: (except that, "Free-will" deserves to be proved what it is by arguments so excellent) let us rather speak to this point:—'that necessity, has neither merit nor reward.' If we speak of the *necessity of compulsion*, it is true: if we speak of the *necessity of immutability*, it is false. For who would bestow a reward upon, or ascribe merit to, an unwilling workman? But with respect to those who do good or evil willingly, even though they cannot alter that necessity by their own power, the reward or punishment follows naturally and necessarily: as it is written "thou shalt render unto every man according to his works." (Pro. xxiv. 29.) It naturally follows—if thou remain under water, thou wilt be suffocated; if thou swim out, thou wilt be saved.

To be brief: As it respects merit or reward, you must speak, either *of the worthiness* or *of the consequence*. If you speak of the *worthiness*, there is no merit, no reward. For if "Free-will" cannot of itself will good, but wills good by grace alone, (for we are speaking of "Free-will" apart from grace and inquiring into the power which properly belongs to each) who does not see, that that good will, merit, and reward, belong to grace alone. Here then, again, the Diatribe dissents from itself, while it argues from merit the freedom of the will; and with me, against whom it fights, it stands in the same condemnation as ever; that is, its asserting that there is merit, reward, and liberty, makes the same as ever directly against itself; seeing that, it asserted above, that it could will nothing good, and undertook to prove that assertion.

If you speak of the *consequence*, there is nothing either good or evil which has not its reward. And here arise an error, that, in speaking of merits and rewards, we agitate opinions and questions concerning *worthiness*, which has not existence, when we ought to be disputing concerning *consequences*. For there remains, as a necessary consequence the judgment of God and a hell for the wicked, even though they themselves neither conceive nor think of such a reward for their sins, nay, they utterly detest it; and, as Peter saith, execrate it. (2 Pet. ii. 10-14.)

In the same manner, there remains a kingdom for the just, even though they themselves neither seek it nor think of it; seeing that, it was prepared for them by their Father, not only before they themselves existed, but before the foundation of the world. Nay, if they should work good in order to obtain the Kingdom, they never would obtain it, but would be numbered rather with the wicked, who, with an evil and mercenary eye, seek the things of self even in God. Whereas, the sons of God, do good with a free-will, seeking no reward, but the glory and will of God only; ready to do good, even if (which is impossible) there were neither a Kingdom nor a hell.

These things are, I believe, sufficiently confirmed even from that saying of Christ only, which I have just cited, Matt. xxv. 34, "Come, ye blessed of my Father, receive the kingdom which was prepared for you from the foundation of the world."—How can they merit that, which is theirs, and prepared for them before they had existence? So that we might much more rightly say, the kingdom of God merits us its possessors; and thus, place the merit where these place the reward, and the reward where these place the merit. For the kingdom is not merited, but before prepared: and the sons of the kingdom are before prepared for the kingdom, but do not merit the kingdom for themselves: that is, the kingdom merits the sons, not the sons the kingdom. So also hell more properly merits and prepares its sons, seeing that, Christ saith, "Depart, ye cursed, into eternal fire, prepared for the devil and his angels." (Matt. xxv. 41.)

Sect. LXXI.—But, says the Diatribe-"what then mean all those Scriptures which promise a kingdom and threaten hell? Why is the word reward so often repeated in the Scriptures; as, "Thou hast thy reward," "I am thy exceeding great reward? " Again, "Who rendereth unto every man according to his work;" and Paul, Rom. ii. 6, "Who by patient continuance in well doing, seek for eternal life," and many of the same kind? " (Rom. ii. 6-7.)—

It is answered: By all these passages, the *consequence of reward* is proved and nothing else, but by no means the *worthiness of merit*: seeing that, those who do good, do it not from a servile and mercenary principle in order to obtain eternal life, but they seek eternal life, that is, they are in that way, in which they shall come unto and find eternal life. So that seeking, is striving with desire, and pursuing with ardent diligence, that, which always leads unto eternal life. And the reason why it is declared in the Scriptures, that those things shall follow and take place after a good or bad life, is, that men might be instructed, admonished, awakened, and terrified. For as "by the law is the knowledge of sin" (Rom. iii. 20,) and an admonition of our impotency, and as from that, it cannot be inferred that we can do any thing ourselves; so, by these promises and threats, there is conveyed an admonition, by which we are taught, what will follow sin and that impotency made known by the law; but there is not, by them, any thing of worthiness ascribed unto our merit.

Wherefore, as the words of the law are for instruction and illumination, to teach us what we ought to do, and also what we are not able to do; so the words of reward, while they signify what will be hereafter, are for exhortation and threatening, by which the just are animated, comforted, and raised up to go forward, to persevere, and to conquer; that they might not be wearied or disheartened either in doing good or in enduring evil; as Paul exhorts his Corinthians, saying, "Be ye steadfast, knowing that your labour is not in vain in the Lord." (1 Cor. xv. 58.) So also God supports Abraham, saying "I am thy exceeding great reward." (Gen. xv. 1.) Just in the same manner as you would console any one, by signifying to him, that his works certainly pleased God, which kind of consolation the Scripture frequently uses; nor is it a small consolation for any one to know, that he so pleases God, that nothing but a good consequence can follow, even though it seem to him impossible.

Sect. LXXII.—To this point pertain all those words which are spoken concerning the *hope* and *expectation,* that those things which we hope for will certainly come to pass. For the pious do not hope because of these words themselves, nor do they expect such things because they hope for them. So also the wicked by the words of threatening, and of a future judgment, are only terrified and cast down that they might cease and abstain from sin, and not become proud, secure, and hardened in their sins.

But if Reason should here turn up her nose and say—Why does God will these things to be done by His words, when by such words nothing is effected, and when the will can turn itself neither one way nor the other? Why does He not do what He does without the Word, when He can do all things without the Word? For the will is of no more power, and does no more with the Word, if the Spirit to move within be wanting; nor is it of less power, nor does it do less without the Word, if the Spirit be present, seeing that, all depends upon the power and operation of the Holy Spirit.

I answer: Thus it pleaseth God—not to give the Spirit without the Word, but through the Word; that He might have us as workers together with Him, while we sound forth in the Word without, what He alone works by the breath of His Spirit within, wheresoever it pleaseth Him; which, nevertheless, He could do without the Word, but such is not His *will.* And who are we that we should inquire into the cause of the divine will? It is enough for us to know, that such is the will of God; and it becomes us, bridling the termerity of reason, to reverence, love, and adore that will. For Christ, (Matt. xi. 25-26,) gives no other reason why the Gospel is hidden from the wise, and revealed unto babes, than this:—So it pleased the Father! In the same manner also, He might nourish us without bread; and indeed He has given a power which nourishes us without bread, as Matt. iv. 4, saith, "Man doth not live by bread alone, but by the Word of God:" but yet, it hath pleased Him to nourish us by His Spirit within, by means of the bread, and instead of the bread used without.

It is certain, therefore, that merit cannot be proved from the reward, at least out of the Scriptures; and that, moreover, "Free-will" cannot be proved from merit, much less such a "Free-will" as the Diatribe set out to prove, that is, 'which of itself cannot will any thing good!' And even if you grant merit, and add to it, moreover, those usual similitudes and conclusions of reason, such as, 'it is commanded in vain,' 'the reward is promised in vain,' 'threatenings are denounced in vain, if there be no "Free-will:"' all these, I say, if they prove any thing, prove this:—that "Free-will" can of itself do all things. But if it cannot of itself do all things, then that conclusion of reason still remains—therefore, the precepts are given in vain, the promises are made in vain, and the threatenings are denounced in vain.

Thus, the Diatribe is perpetually arguing against itself, as often as it attempts to argue against me. For God alone by His Spirit works in us both merit and reward, but He makes known and declares each, by His external Word, to the whole world; to the intent that, His power and glory and our impotency and vileness might be proclaimed even among the wicked, the unbelieving, and the ignorant, although those alone who fear God receive these things into their heart, and keep them faithfully; the rest despise them.

Sect. LXXIII.—It would be too tedious to repeat here each imperative passage which the Diatribe enumerates out of the New Testament, always tacking to them her own conclusions, and vainly arguing, that those things which are so said are 'to no purpose,' are 'superfluous,' are 'coldly useless,' are 'ridiculous,' are 'nothing at all,' if the will be not free. And I have already repeatedly observed, even to disgust, that nothing whatever is effected by such arguments; and that if any thing be proved, the whole of "Free-will" is proved. And this is nothing less than overthrowing the Diatribe altogether; seeing that, it set out to prove such a "Free-will" as cannot of itself do good, but serves sin; and then goes on to prove such a "Free-will" as can do all things; thus, throughout, forgetting and not knowing itself.

It is mere cavillation where it makes these remarks—"By their fruits," saith the Lord, "ye shall know them." (Matt. vii. 16, 20.) He calls works fruits, and He calls them ours, but they are not ours if all things be done by necessity."—

I pray you, are not those things most rightly called ours, which we did not indeed make ourselves, but which we received from others? Why should not those works be called ours, which God has given unto us by His Spirit? Shall we then not call Christ ours, because we did not make Him, but only received Him? Again: if we made all those things which are called ours—therefore, we made our own eyes, we made our own hands, we made our own feet: unless you mean to say, that our eyes, our hands, and our feet are not called our own! Nay, "What have we that we did not receive," saith Paul. (1 Cor. iv. 7.) Shall we then say, that those things are either not ours, or else we made them ourselves? But suppose they are called our fruits because we made them, where then remain grace and the Spirit? —Nor does He say, "By their fruits, which are in a certain small part their own, ye shall know them." This cavillation rather is ridiculous, superfluous, to no purpose, coldly useless, nay, absurd and detestable, by which the holy words of God are defiled and profaned.

In the same way also is that saying of Christ upon the cross trifled with, "Father, forgive them, for they know not what they do." (Luke xxiii. 34.) Here, where some assertion might have been expected which should make for "Free-will," recourse is again had to conclusions—"How much more rightly (says the Diatribe) would He have excused them on this ground—because they have not a Free-will, nor can they if they willed it, do otherwise."—

No! nor is that "Free-will" which 'cannot will any thing good,' concerning which we are disputing, proved by this conclusion either; but that "Free-will" is proved by it which can do all things; concerning which no one disputes, to except the Pelagians.

Here, where Christ openly saith, "they know not what they do," does He not testify that they could not will good? For how can you will that which you do not know? You certainly cannot desire that of which you know nothing! What more forcible can be advanced against "Free-will", than that it is such a thing of nought, that it not only cannot will good, but cannot even know what evil it does, and what good is? Is there then any obscurity in this saying, "they know not what they do? " What is there remaining in the Scriptures which may not, upon the authority of the Diatribe, declare for "Free-will," since this word of Christ is made to declare for it, which is so clearly and so directly against it? In the same easy way any one might affirm that this word declares for "Free-will"—"And the earth was without form and void:" (Gen. i. 2.) or this, "And God rested on the seventh day:" (Gen. ii. 2,) or any word of the same kind. Then, indeed, the Scriptures would be obscure and ambiguous, nay, would be nothing at all. But to dare to make use of the Scriptures in this way, argues a mind that is in a signal manner, a contemner both of God and man, and that deserves no forbearance whatever.

Sect. LXXIV.—Again the Diatribe receives that word of John i. 12, "To them gave He power to become the sons of God," thus—"How can there be power given unto them, to become the sons of God, if there be no liberty in our will? "—

This word also, is a hammer that beats down "Free-will," as is nearly the whole of the evangelist John, and yet, even this is brought forward in support of "Free-will." Let us, I pray you, just look into this word. John is not speaking concerning any work of man, either great or small but concerning the very renewal and transformation of the old man who is a son of the devil, into the new man who is a son of God. This man is merely passive (as the term is used), nor does he do any thing, but is wholly made: and John is speaking of being made: he saith we are made the sons of God by a power given unto us from above, not by the power of "Free-will" inherent in ourselves.

Whereas, our friend Diatribe here concludes, that "Free-will" is of so much power, that it makes us the sons of God; if not, it is prepared to aver, that the word of John is ridiculous and stands coldly useless. But who ever so exalted "Free-will" as to assign unto it the power of making us the sons of God, especially such a "Free-will" as cannot even will good, which "Free-will" it is that the Diatribe has taken upon itself to establish? But let this conclusion be gone after the rest which have been so often repeated; by which, nothing else is proved, if any thing be proved at all, than that which the Diatribe denies—that "Free-will" can do all things.

The meaning of John is this.—That by the coming of Christ into the world by His Gospel, by which grace was offered, but not works required, a full opportunity was given to all men of becoming the sons of God, if they would believe. But as to this willing and this believing on His name, as "Free-will" never knew it nor thought of it before, so much less could it then do it of its own power. For how could reason then think that faith in Jesus as the Son of God and man was necessary, when even at this day it could neither receive nor believe it, though the whole Creation should cry out together—there is a certain person who is both God and man! Nay it is rather offended at such a saying, as Paul affirms. (1 Cor. i. 17-31.) so far is it from possibility that it should either will it, or believe it.

John, therefore, is preaching, not the power of "Free-will," but the riches of the kingdom of God offered to the world by the Gospel; and signifying at the same time, how few there are who receive it; that is, from the enmity of the "Free-will" against it; the power of which is nothing else than this:—Satan reigning over it and causing it to reject grace, and the Spirit which fulfils the law. So excellently do its 'endeavour' and 'desire' avail unto the fulfilling of the law.

But we shall hereafter shew more fully what a thunderbolt this passage of John is against "Free-will." Yet I am not a little astonished that passages which make so signally and so forcibly against "Free-will" are brought forward by the Diatribe in support of "Free-will;" whose stupidity is such, that it makes no distinction whatever between the promises, and the words of the law: for it most ridiculously sets up "Free-will" by the words of the law, and far more absurdly still confirms it by the words of the promise. But how this absurdity is, may be immediately solved, if it be but considered with what an unconcerned and contemptuous mind the Diatribe is here disputing: With whom, it matters not, whether grace stand or fall, whether "Free-will" lie prostrate or sit in state, if it can but, by words of vanity, serve the turn of tyrants, to the odium of the cause!

Sect. LXXV.—After this, it comes to Paul also, the most determined enemy to "Free-will," and even he is dragged in to confirm "Free-will;" "Or despisest thou the riches of His goodness, and patience, and long-suffering, not knowing that the goodness of God leadeth to repentance? "—(Rom. ii. 4.)—"How (says the Diatribe) can the despising of the commandment be imputed where there is not a Free-will? How can God invite to repentance, who is the author of impenitence? How can the damnation be just, where the judge compels unto evil doing? "—

I answer: Let the Diatribe see to these questions itself. What are they unto us! The Diatribe said according to that 'probable opinion.' 'that "Free-will" cannot will good, and is of necessity compelled to serve sin.' How, therefore, can the despising of the commandment be charged on the will, if it cannot will good, and has no liberty, but is necessarily compelled to the service of sin? How can God invite to repentance who is the author of the reason why it cannot repent, while it leaves, or does not give grace to, that, which cannot of itself will good? How can the damnation be just, where the judge, by taking away his aid, compels the wicked man to be left in his wickedness who cannot of his own power do otherwise?

All these conclusions therefore recoil back upon the head of the Diatribe. Or, if they prove any thing, as I said, they prove that "Free-will" can do all things: which, however, is denied by the Diatribe and by all. Thus these conclusions of reason torment the Diatribe, throughout all the passages of Scripture: seeing that, it must appear ridiculous and coldly useless, to enforce and exact with so much vehemence, when there is no one to be found who can perform: for the apostle's intent is, by means of these threats, to bring the impious and proud to a knowledge of themselves and of their impotency, that he might prepare them for grace when humbled by the knowledge of sin.

And what need is there to speak of, singly, all those parts which are brought forward out of Paul, seeing that, they are only a collection of imperative or conditional passages, or of those by which Paul exhorts Christians to the fruits of faith? Whereas the Diatribe, by its appended conclusions, forms to itself a power of "Free-will," such and so great, which can, without grace, do all things which Paul in his exhortations prescribes. Christians, however, are not led by "Free-will," but by the Spirit of God (Rom. viii. 14): and to be led, is not to lead, but to be impelled, as a saw or an axe is impelled by a carpenter.

And that no one might doubt whether or not Luther asserted things so absurd, the Diatribe recites his own words; which, indeed, I acknowledge. For I confess that that article of Wycliffe, 'all things take place from necessity, that is, from the immutable will of God, and our will is not compelled indeed, but it cannot of itself do good,' was falsely condemned by the Council of Constance, or that conspiracy or cabal rather. Nay the Diatribe itself defends the same together with me, while it asserts, 'that Free-will cannot by its own power will any thing good,' and that, it of necessity serves sin:' although in furnishing this defence, it all the while designs the direct contrary.

Suffice it to have spoken thus in reply to the FIRST PART of the Diatribe, in which it has endeavoured to establish "Free-will." Let us now consider the latter part in which our arguments are refuted, that is, those by which "Free-will" is utterly overthrown.—Here you will see, what the smoke of man can do, against the thunder and lightning of God!

SECOND PART.

Sect. LXXVI.–The Diatribe, having thus first cited numberless passages of Scripture, as it were a most formidable army in support of "Free-will," in order that it might inspire courage into the confessors and martyrs, the men saints and women saints on the side of "Free-will," and strike terror into all the fearful and trembling deniers of, and transgressors against "Free-will," imagines to itself a poor contemptible handful only standing up to oppose "Free-will:" and therefore it brings forward no more than two Scriptures, which seem to be more prominent than the rest, to stand up on their side: intent only upon slaughter, and that, to be executed without much trouble. The one of these passages is from Exod. ix. 13, "The Lord hardened the heart of Pharaoh:" the other is from Malachi i. 2-3, "Jacob have I loved, but Esau have I hated." Paul has explained at large both these passages in the Romans ix. 11-17. But, according to the judgment of the Diatribe, what a detestable and useless discussion has he made of it! So that, did not the Holy Spirit know a little something of rhetoric, there would be some danger, lest, being broken at the outset by such an artfully managed show of contempt, he should despair of his cause, and openly yield to "Free-will" before the sound of the trumpet for the battle. But, however, I, as a recruit taken into the rear of those two passages, will display the forces on our side. Although, where the state of the battle is such, that one can put to flight ten thousand, there is no need of forces. If therefore, one passage shall defeat "Free-will," its numberless forces will profit it nothing.

Sect. LXXVII.–In this part of the discussion, then, the Diatribe has found out a new way of eluding the most clear passages: that is, it will have that there is, in the most simple and clear passages, a *trope*. And as, before, when speaking in defence of "Free-will," it eluded all the imperative and conditional sentences of the law by means of conclusions tacked, and similitudes added to them; so now, where it designs to speak against us, it twists all the words of the divine promise and declaration just which way it pleases, by means of a trope which it has invented; thus, being every where an incomprehensible Proteus! Nay, it demands with a haughty brow, that this permission should be granted it, saying, that we ourselves, when pressed closely, are accustomed to get off by means of invented tropes: as in these instances:–"On which thou wilt, stretch forth thine hand:" (Ex. viii. 5,) that is, grace shall extend thine hand on which it will. "Make you a new heart:" (Ezek. xviii. 31,) that is, grace shall make you a new heart: and the like. It seems, therefore, an indignity offered, that Luther should be allowed to give forth an interpretation so forced and twisted, and that it should not be far more allowable to follow the interpretations of the most approved doctors.

You see then, that here, the contention is not for the text itself, no, nor for conclusions and similitudes, but for tropes and interpretations. When then shall we ever have any plain and pure text, without tropes and conclusions, either for or against "Free-will?" Has the Scriptures no such texts anywhere? And shall the cause of "Free-will" remain for ever in doubt, like a reed shaken with the wind, as being that which can be supported by no certain text, but which stands upon conclusions and tropes only, introduced by men mutually disagreeing with each other?

But let our sentiment rather be this:–that neither conclusion nor trope is to be admitted into the Scriptures, unless the evident state of the particulars, or the absurdity of any particular as militating against an article of faith, require it: but, that the simple, pure, and natural meaning of the words is to be adhered to, which is according to the rules of grammar, and to that common use of speech which God has given unto men. For if every one be allowed, according to his own lust, to invent conclusions and tropes in the Scriptures, what will the whole Scripture together be, but a reed shaken with the wind, or a kind of Vertumnus? Then, in truth, nothing could, to a certainty, be determined on or proved concerning any one article of faith, which you might not subject to cavillation by means of some trope. But every trope ought to be avoided as the most deadly poison, which is not absolutely required by the Scriptures itself.

See what happened to that trope-inventor, Origen, in expounding the Scriptures. What just occasion did he give the calumniator Porphery, to say, 'those who favour Origen, can be no great friends to Hieronymus.' What happened to the Arians by means of that trope, according to which, they made Christ *God nominally*? What happened in our own times to those new prophets concerning the words of Christ, "This is my body?" One invented a trope in the word "this," another in the word "is," another in the word "body." I have therefore observed this:—that all heresies and errors in the Scriptures, have not arisen from the simplicity of the words, as is the general report throughout the world, but from men not attending to the simplicity of the words, and hatching tropes and conclusions out of their own brain.

For example. "On which soever thou wilt, stretch forth thine hand." I, as far as I can remember, never put upon these words so violent an interpretation, as to say, 'grace shall extend thine hand on which soever it will:' "Make yourselves a new heart," 'that is, grace shall make you a new heart, and the like;' although the Diatribe traduces me thus in a public work, from being so carried away with, and illuded by its own tropes and conclusions, that it knows not what it says about any thing. But I said this:—that by the words, 'stretch forth thine hand,' simply taken as they are, without tropes or conclusions, nothing else is signified than what is required of us in the stretching forth of our hand, and what we ought to do; according to the nature of an imperative expression, with grammarians, and in the common use of speech.

But the Diatribe, not attending to this simplicity of the word, but with violence adducing conclusions and tropes, interprets the words thus:—"Stretch forth thine hand;" that is, thou art able by thine own power to stretch forth thine hand. "Make you a new heart," that is, ye are able to make a new heart. 'Believe in Christ,' that is, ye are able to believe in Christ. So that, with it, what is spoken imperatively, and what is spoken indicatively, is the same thing; or else, it is prepared to aver, that the Scripture is ridiculous and to no purpose. And these interpretations, which no grammarian will bear, must not be called, in Theologians, violent or invented, but the productions of the most approved doctors received by so many ages.

But it is easy for the Diatribe to admit and follow tropes in this part of the discussion, seeing that, it cares not at all whether what is said be certain or uncertain. Nay, it aims at making all things uncertain; for its design is, that the doctrines concerning "Free-will" should be left alone, rather than searched into. Therefore, it is enough for it, to be enabled in any way to avoid those passages by which it finds itself closely pressed.

But as for me, who am maintaining a serious cause, and who am inquiring what is, to the greatest certainty, the truth, for the establishing of consciences, I must act very differently. For me, I say, it is not enough that you say there may be a trope here: but I must inquire, whether there ought to be, or can be a trope there. For if you cannot prove that there must, of necessity, be a trope in that passage, you will effect nothing at all. There stands there this word of God—"I will harden the heart of Pharaoh." (Ex. iv. 21, Rom. ix. 17-18.) If you say that it can be understood or ought to be understood thus:—I will permit it to be hardened: I hear you say, indeed, that it may be so understood. And I hear this trope used by every one, 'I destroyed you, because I did not correct you immediately when you began to do wrong.' But here, there is no place for that interpretation. We are not here inquiring, whether that trope be in use; we are not enquiring whether any one can use it in that passage of Paul: but this is the point of inquiry—whether or not it be sure and safe to use this passage plainly as it stands, and whether Paul would have it so used. We are not inquiring into the use of an indifferent reader of this passage, but into the use of the author Paul himself.

What will you do with a conscience inquiring thus? —Behold God, as the Author, saith, "I will harden the heart of Pharaoh:" the meaning of the word "harden" is plain and well known. But a man, who reads this passage, tells me, that in this place, 'to harden,' signifies 'to give an occasion of becoming hardened,' because, the sinner is not immediately corrected. But by what authority does he this? With what design, by what necessity, is the natural signification of this passage thus twisted? And suppose the reader and interpreter should be in error, how shall it be proved that such a turn ought to be given to this passage? It is dangerous, nay, impious, thus to twist the Word of God, without necessity and without authority. Would you then comfort a poor soul thus labouring, in this way? —Origen thought so and so. Cease to search into such things, because they are curious and superfluous. But he would answer you, this admonition should have been given to Moses or Paul before they wrote, and so also to God Himself, for it is they who vex us with these curious and superfluous Scriptures.

Sect. LXXVIII.—This miserable scape-gap of tropes, therefore, profits the Diatribe nothing. But this Proteus of ours must here be held fast, and compelled to satisfy us fully concerning the trope in this passage; and that, by Scriptures the most clear, or by miracles the most evident. For as to its mere opinion, even though supported by the laboured industry of all ages, we give no credit to that whatever. But we urge on and press it home, that there can be here no trope whatever, but that the Word of God is to be understood according to the plain meaning of the words. For it is not given unto us (as the Diatribe persuades itself) to turn the words of God backwards and forwards according to our own lust: if that were the case, what is there in the whole Scripture, that might not be resolved into the philosophy of Anaxagoras—'that any thing might be made from any thing?' And thus I will say, "God created the heavens and the earth:" that is, He stationed them, but did not make them out of nothing. Or, "He created the heavens and the earth;" that is, the angels and the devils; or the just and the wicked. Who, I ask, if this were the case, might not become a theologian at the first opening of a book?

Let this, therefore, be a fixed and settled point:—that since the Diatribe cannot prove, that there is a trope in these our passages which it utterly destroys, it is compelled to cede to us, that the words are to be understood according to their plain meaning; even though it should prove, that the same trope is contained in all the other passages of Scripture, and used in common by every one. And by the gaining of this one point, all our arguments are at the same time defended, which the Diatribe designed to refute; and thus, its refutation is found to effect nothing, to do nothing, and to be nothing.

Whenever, therefore, this passage of Moses, "I will harden the heart of Pharaoh," is interpreted thus:—My long-suffering, by which I bear with the sinner, leads, indeed, others unto repentance, but it shall render Pharaoh more hardened in iniquity:—it is a pretty interpretation, but it is not proved that it ought to be so interpreted. But I am not content with what is said, I must have the proof.

And that also of Paul, "He hath mercy on whom He will have mercy, and whom He will He hardeneth," (Rom. ix. 18,) is plausibly interpreted thus:-that is, God hardens when He does not immediately punish the sinner; and He has mercy when He immediately invites to repentance by afflictions.—But how is this interpretation proved?

And also that of Isaiah lxiii. 17, "Why hast Thou made us to err from Thy ways and hardened our heart from Thy fear?" Be it so, that Jerome interprets it thus from Origen:—*He* is said to 'make to err' who does not immediately recall from error. But who shall certify us that Jerome and Origen interpret rightly? It is, therefore, a settled determination with me, not to argue upon the authority of any teacher whatever, but upon that of the Scripture alone. What Origens and Jeromes does the Diatribe, then, forgetting its own determination, set before us! especially when, among all the ecclesiastical writers, there are scarcely any who have handled the Holy Scriptures less to the purpose, and more absurdly, than Origen and Jerome.

In a word: this liberty of interpretation, by a new and unheard-of kind of grammar, goes to confound all things. So that, when God saith, "I will harden the heart of Pharaoh," you are to change the persons and understand it thus:—Pharaoh hardens himself by My long-suffering. God hardeneth our hearts;—that is, we harden ourselves by God's deferring the punishment. Thou, O Lord, has made us to err;—that is, we have made ourselves to err by Thy not punishing us. So also, God's having mercy, no longer signifies His giving grace, or showing mercy, or forgiving sin, or justifying, or delivering from evil, but, on the contrary, signifies bring on evil and punishing.

In fact, by these tropes matters will come to this:—you may say, that God had mercy upon the children of Israel when He sent them into Assyria and to Babylon; because, He there punished the sinners, and there invited them, by afflictions, to repentance: and that, on the other hand, when He delivered them and brought them back, He had not then mercy upon them, but hardened them; that is, by His long-suffering and mercy He gave them an occasion of becoming hardened. And also, God's sending the Saviour Christ into the world, will not be said to be the mercy, but the hardening of God; because, by this mercy, He gave men an occasion of hardening themselves. On the other hand, His destroying Jerusalem, and scattering the Jews even unto this day, is His having mercy on them; because, He punishes the sinners and invites them to repentance. Moreover, His carrying the saints away into heaven at the day of judgment, will not be in mercy, but in hardening; because, by His long-suffering, He will give them an occasion of abusing it. But His thrusting the wicked down to hell, will be His mercy; because, He punishes the sinners.—Who, I pray you, ever heard of such examples of the mercy and wrath of God as these?

And be it so, that good men are made better both by the long-suffering and by the severity of God; yet, when we are speaking of the good and the bad promiscuously, these tropes, by an utter perversion of the common manner of speaking, will make, out of the mercy of God His wrath, and His wrath out of His mercy; seeing that, they call it the wrath of God when He does good, and His mercy when He afflicts.

Moreover, if God be said then to harden, when He does good and endures with long-suffering, and then to have mercy when He afflicts and punishes, why is He more particularly said to harden Pharaoh than to harden the children of Israel, or than the whole world? Did He not do good to the children of Israel? Does He not do good to the whole world? Does He not bear with the wicked? Does He not rain upon the evil and upon the good? Why is He rather said to have mercy upon the children of Israel than upon Pharaoh? Did He not afflict the children of Israel in Egypt, and in the desert? —And be it so, that some abuse, and some rightly use, the goodness and the wrath of God; yet, according to your definition, to harden, is the same as, to indulge the wicked by long-suffering and goodness; and to have mercy, is, not to indulge, but to visit and punish. Therefore, with reference to God, He, by His continual goodness, does nothing but harden; and by His perpetual punishment, does nothing but shew mercy.

Sect. LXXIX.—But this is the most excellent statement of all—'that God is said to harden, when He indulges sinners by long-suffering; but to have mercy upon them, when He visits and afflicts, and thus, by severity, invites to repentance.'—

What, I ask, did God leave undone in afflicting, punishing, and calling Pharaoh to repentance? Are there not, in His dealings with him, ten plagues recorded? If, therefore, your definition stand good, that shewing mercy, is punishing and calling the sinner immediately, God certainly had mercy upon Pharaoh! Why then does not God say, I will have mercy upon Pharaoh? Whereas He saith, "I will harden the heart of Pharaoh." For, in the very act of having mercy upon him, that is, (as you say) afflicting and punishing him, He saith, "I will harden" him; that is, as you say, I will bear with him and do him good. What can be heard of more enormous! Where are now your tropes? Where are your Origens? Where are your Jeromes? Where are all your most approved doctors whom one poor creature, Luther, daringly contradicts? —But at this rate the flesh must unawares impel the man to talk, who trifles with the words of God, and believes not their solemn importance!

The text of Moses itself, therefore, incontrovertibly proves, that here, these tropes are mere inventions and things of nought, and that by those words, "I will harden the heart of Pharaoh," some thing else is signified far different from, and of greater importance than, doing good, or affliction and punishment; because, we cannot deny, that both were tried upon Pharaoh with the greatest care and concern. For what wrath and punishment could be more instant, than his being stricken by so many wonders and with so many plagues, that, as Moses himself testifies, the like had never been? Nay, even Pharaoh himself, repenting, was moved by them more than once; but he was not effectually moved, nor did he persevere. And what long-suffering or goodness of God could be greater, than His taking away the plagues so easily, hardening his sin so often, so often bringing back the good, and so often taking away the evil? Yet neither is of any avail, He still saith, "I will harden the heart of Pharaoh! " You see, therefore, that even if *your* hardening and mercy, that is your glosses and tropes, be granted to the greatest extent, as supported by use and by example, and as seen in the case of Pharaoh, there is yet a hardening that still remains; and that the hardening of which Moses speaks must, of necessity, be one, and that of which you dream, another.

Sect. LXXX.—But since I have to fight with fiction-framers and ghosts, let me turn to ghost-raising also. Let me suppose (which is an impossibility) that the trope of which the Diatribe dreams avails in this passage; in order that I may see, which way the Diatribe will elude the being compelled to declare, that all things take place according to the will of God alone, and from necessity in us; and how it will clear God from being Himself the author and cause of our becoming hardened. For if it be true that God is then said to "harden" when He bears with long-suffering, and does not immediately punish, these two positions still stand firm.

First, that man, nevertheless, *of necessity* serves sin. For when it is granted that "Free-will" cannot will any thing good, (which kind of Free-will the Diatribe undertook to prove) then, by the goodness of a long-suffering God, it becomes nothing better, but of necessity worse.—Wherefore, it still remains that all that we do, is done *from necessity.*

And next, that God appears to be just as cruel in this *bearing with us by His long-suffering,* as He does by being preached, as *willing to harden, by that will inscrutable.* For when He sees that "Free-will" cannot will good, but becomes worse by His enduring with long-suffering; by this very long-suffering He appears to be most cruel, and to delight in our miseries; seeing that, He could remedy them if He willed, and might not thus endure with long-suffering if He willed, nay, that He could not thus endure unless He willed; for who can compel Him against His will? That will, therefore, without which nothing is done, being admitted, and it being admitted also, that "Free-will" cannot will any thing good, all is advanced in vain that is advanced, either in excusation of God, or in accusation of "Free-will." For the language of "Free-will" is ever this:—I *cannot*, and God *will not*. What can I do! If He have mercy upon me by affliction, I shall be nothing benefited, but must of necessity become worse, unless He give me His Spirit. But this He gives me not, though He might give it me if He willed. It is certain, therefore, that He *wills, not to give.*

Sect. LXXXI.—Nor do the similitudes adduced make any thing to the purpose, where it is said by the Diatribe—"As under the same sun, mud is hardened and wax melted; as by the same shower, the cultivated earth brings forth fruit, and the uncultivated earth thorns; so, by the same long-suffering of God, some are hardened and some converted."—

For, we are not now dividing "Free-will" into two different natures, and making the one like mud, the other like wax; the one like cultivated earth, the other like uncultivated earth; but we are speaking concerning that one "Free-will" equally impotent in all men; which, as it cannot will good, is nothing but mud, nothing but uncultivated earth. Nor does Paul say that God, as the potter, makes one vessel unto honour, and another unto dishonour, out of different kinds of clay, but He saith, "Out of the same lump, &c." (Rom. ix. 21.) Therefore, as mud always becomes harder, and uncultivated earth always becomes more thorny; even so "Free-will," always becomes worse, both under the hardening sun of long-suffering, and under the softening shower of rain.

If, therefore, "Free-will" be of one and the same nature and impotency in all men, no reason can be given why it should attain unto grace in one, and not in another; if nothing else be preached to all, but the goodness of a long-suffering and the punishment of a mercy-shewing God. For it is a granted position, that "Free-will" in all, is alike defined to be, 'that which cannot will good.' And indeed, if it were not so, God could not elect any one, nor would there be any place left for Election; but for "Free-will" only, as choosing or refusing the long-suffering and anger of God. And if God be thus robbed of His power and wisdom to elect, what will there be remaining but that idol Fortune, under the name of which, all things take place at random! Nay, we shall at length come to this: that men may be saved and damned without God's knowing any thing at all about it; as not having determined by certain election who should be saved and who should be damned; but having set before all men in general His hardening goodness and long-suffering, and His mercy shewing correction and punishment, and left them to choose for themselves whether they would be saved or damned; while He, in the mean time, should be gone, as Homer says, to an Ethiopian feast!

It is just such a God as this that Aristotle paints out to us; that is, who sleeps Himself, and leaves every one to use or abuse His long-suffering and punishment just as He will. Nor can reason, of herself, form any other judgment than the Diatribe here does. For as she herself snores over, and looks with contempt upon, divine things; she thinks concerning God, that He sleeps and snores over them too; not exercising His wisdom, will, and presence, in choosing, separating, and inspiring, but leaving the troublesome and irksome business of accepting or refusing His long-suffering and His anger, entirely to men. This is what we come to, when we attempt, by human reason, to limit and make excuses for God, not revering the secrets of His Majesty, but curiously prying into them—being lost in the glory of them, instead of making one excuse for God, we pour forth a thousand blasphemies! And forgetting ourselves, we prate like madmen, both against God and against ourselves; when we are all the while supposing, that we are, with a great deal of wisdom, speaking both for God and for ourselves.

Here then you see, what that trope and gloss of the Diatribe, will make of God. And moreover, how excellently consistent the Diatribe is with itself; which before, by its one definition, made "Free-will" one and the same in all men: and now, in the course of its argumentation, forgetting its own definition, makes one "Free-will" to be cultivated and the other uncultivated, according to the difference of works, of manners, and of men: thus making two different "Free-wills"; the one, that which cannot do good, the other, that which can do good, and that by its own powers before grace: whereas, its former definition declared, that it could not, by those its own powers, will any thing good whatever. Hence, therefore, it comes to pass, that while we do not ascribe unto the will of God only, the will and power of hardening, shewing mercy, and doing all things; we ascribe unto "Free-will" itself the power of doing all things without grace; which, nevertheless, we declared to be unable to do any good whatever without grace.

The similitudes, therefore, of the sun and of the shower, make nothing at all to the purpose. The Christian would use those similitudes more rightly, if he were to make the sun and the shower to represent the Gospel, as Psalm xix. does, and as does also Hebrews vi. 7; and were to make the cultivated earth to represent the elect, and the uncultivated the reprobate; for the former are, by the word, edified and made better, while the latter are offended and made worse. Or, if this distinction be not made, then, as to "Free-will" itself, that, is in all men uncultivated earth and the kingdom of Satan.

Sect. LXXXII.—But let us now inquire into the reason why this trope was invented in this passage.—"It appears absurd (says the Diatribe) that God, who is not only just but also good, should be said to have hardened the heart of a man, in order that, by his iniquity, He might shew forth His own power. The same also occurred to Origen; who confesses, that the *occasion* of becoming hardened was given of God, but throws all the fault upon Pharaoh. He has, moreover, made a remark upon that which the Lord saith, "For this very purpose have I raised thee up." He does not say, (he observes) For this very purpose have I *made* thee: otherwise, Pharaoh could not have been wicked, if God had made him such an one as he was, for God beheld all His works, and they were "very good"—thus the Diatribe.

It appears then, that one of the principal causes why the words of Moses and of Paul are not received, is their absurdity. But against what article of faith does that absurdity militate? Or, who is offended at it? It is human Reason that is offended; who, being blind, deaf, impious, and sacrilegious in all the words and works of God, is, in the case of this passage, introduced as a judge of the words and works of God. According to the same argument of absurdity, you will deny all the Articles of Faith: because, it is of all things the most absurd, and as Paul saith, foolishness to the Gentiles, and a stumbling-block to the Jews, that God should be man, the son of a virgin, crucified, and sitting at the right hand of His Father: it is, I say, absurd to believe such things. Therefore, let us invent some tropes with the Arians, and say, that Christ is not truly God. Let us invent some tropes with the Manichees, and say, that He is not truly man, but a phantom introduced by means of a virgin; or a reflection conveyed by glass, which fell, and was crucified. And in this way, we shall handle the Scriptures to excellent purpose indeed!

After all, then, the tropes amount to nothing; nor is the absurdity avoided. For it still remains absurd, (according to the judgment of reason,) that that God, who is just and good, should exact of "Free-will" impossibilities: and that, when "Free-will" cannot will good and of necessity serves sin, that sin should yet be laid to its charge: and that, moreover, when He does not give the Spirit, He should, nevertheless, act so severely and unmercifully, as to harden, or permit to become hardened: these things, Reason will still say, are not becoming a God good and merciful. Thus, they too far exceed her capacity; nor can she so bring herself into subjection as to believe, and judge, that the God who does such things, *is* good; but setting aside faith, she wants to feel out, and see, and comprehend *how* He can be good, and not cruel. But she will comprehend that, when this shall be said of God:—He hardens no one, He damns no one; but He has mercy upon all, He saves all; and He has so utterly destroyed hell, that no future punishment need be dreaded. It is thus that Reason blusters and contends, in attempting to clear God, and to defend Him as just and good.

But faith and the Spirit judge otherwise; who *believe*, that God would be good, even though he should destroy all men. And to what profit is it, to weary ourselves with all these reasonings, in order that we might throw the fault of hardening upon "Free-will"! Let all the "Free-will" in the world, do all it can with all its powers, and yet, it never will give one proof, either that it can avoid being hardened where God gives not His Spirit, or merit mercy where it is left to its own powers. And what does it signify whether it *be hardened*, or *deserve being hardened*, if the hardening be of necessity, as long as it remains in that impotency, in which, according to the testimony of the Diatribe, it cannot will good? Since, therefore, the absurdity is not taken out of the way by these tropes; or, if it be taken out of the way, greater absurdities still are introduced in their stead, and all things are ascribed unto "Free-will"; away with such useless and seducing tropes, and let us cleave close to the pure and simple Word of God!

Sect. LXXXIII.—As to the other point—'that those things which God has made, are very good: and that God did not say, for this purpose have I *made* thee, but "For this purpose have I *raised* thee *up*." '—

I observe, first of all, that this, Gen. i., concerning the works of God being very good, was said before the fall of man. But it is recorded directly after, in Gen. iii. how man became evil,—when God departed from him and left him to himself. And from this one man thus corrupt, all the wicked were born, and Pharaoh also: as Paul saith, "We were all by nature the children of wrath even as others." (Eph. ii. 3). Therefore God *made*

Pharaoh wicked; that is, from a wicked and corrupt seed: as He saith in the Proverbs of Solomon, xvi. 4, "God hath made all things for Himself, yea, even the wicked for the day of evil:" that is, not by creating evil in them, but by forming them out of a corrupt seed, and ruling over them. This therefore is not a just conclusion—God made man wicked: therefore, he is not wicked. For how can he not be wicked from a wicked seed? As Ps. li. 5, saith, "Behold I was conceived in sin." And Job xiv. 4, "Who can make that clean which is conceived from unclean seed?" For although God did not make sin, yet, He ceases not to form and multiply that nature, which, from the Spirit being withdrawn, is defiled by sin. And as it is, when a carpenter makes statues of corrupt wood; so such as the nature is, such are the men made, when God creates and forms them out of that nature. Again: If you understand the words, "They were very good," as referring to the works of God after the fall, you will be pleased to observe, that this was said, not with reference to us, but with reference to God. For it is not said, Man saw all the things that God had made, and behold they were very good. Many things seem very good unto God, and are very good, which seem unto us very evil, and are considered to be very evil. Thus, afflictions, evils, errors, hell, nay, all the very best works of God, are, in the sight of the world, very evil, and even damnable. What is better than Christ and the Gospel? But what is more execrated by the world? And therefore, how those things are good in the sight of God, which are evil in our sight, is known only unto God and unto those who see with the eyes of God; that is, who have the Spirit. But there is no need of argumentation so close as this, the preceding answer is sufficient.

Sect. LXXXIV.—But here, perhaps, it will be asked, how can God be said to work evil in us, in the same way as He is said to harden us, to give us up to our own desires, to cause us to err, &c.?

We ought, indeed, to be content with the *Word* of God, and simply to believe what that saith; seeing that, the *works* of God are utterly unspeakable. But however, in compliance with Reason, that is, human foolery, I will just act the fool and the stupid fellow for once, and try, by a little babbling, if I can produce any effect upon her.

First, then, both Reason and the Diatribe grant, that God works all in all; and that, without Him, nothing is either done or effective, because He is Omnipotent; and because, therefore, all things come under His Omnipotence, as Paul saith to the Ephesians.

Now then, Satan and man being fallen and left of God, cannot will good; that is, those things which please God, or which God wills; but are ever turned the way of their own desires, so that they cannot but seek their own. This, therefore, their will and nature, so turned from God, cannot be a nothing: nor are Satan and the wicked man a nothing: nor are the nature and the will which they have a nothing, although it be a nature corrupt and averse. That remnant of nature, therefore, in Satan and the wicked man, of which we speak, as being the creature and work of God, is not less subject to the divine omnipotence and action, than all the rest of the creatures and works of God.

Since, therefore, God moves and does all in all, He necessarily moves and does all in Satan and the wicked man. But He so does all in them, as they themselves are, and as He finds them: that is, as they are themselves averse and evil, being carried along by that motion of the Divine Omnipotence, they cannot but do what is averse and evil. Just as it is with a man driving a horse lame on one foot, or lame on two feet; he drives him just so as the horse himself is; that is, the horse moves badly. But what can the man do? He is driving along this kind of horse together with sound horses; he, indeed, goes badly, and the rest well; but it cannot be otherwise, unless the horse be made sound.

Here then you see, that, when God works in, and by, evil men, the evils themselves are inwrought, but yet, God cannot do evil, although He thus works the evils by evil men; because, being good Himself He cannot do evil; but He uses evil instruments, which cannot escape the sway and motion of His Omnipotence. The fault, therefore, is in the instruments, which God allows not to remain actionless; seeing that, the evils are done as God Himself moves. Just in the same manner as a carpenter would cut badly with a saw-edged or broken-edged axe. Hence it is, that the wicked man cannot but always err and sin; because, being carried along by the motion of the Divine Omnipotence, he is not permitted to remain motionless, but must will, desire, and act according to his nature. All this is fixed certainty, if we believe that God is Omnipotent!

It is, moreover, as certain, that the wicked man is the creature of God; though being averse and left to himself without the Spirit of God, he cannot will or do good. For the Omnipotence of God makes it, that the wicked man cannot evade the motion and action of God, but, being of necessity subject to it, he yields; though his corruption and aversion to God, makes him that he cannot be carried along and moved unto good. God cannot suspend His Omnipotence on account of his aversion, nor can the wicked man change his aversion. Wherefore it is, that he must continue of necessity to sin and err, until he be amended by the Spirit of God. Meanwhile, in all these, Satan goes on to reign in peace, and keeps his palace undisturbed under this motion of the Divine Omnipotence.

Sect. LXXXV.—But now follows the *act itself* of *hardening*, which is thus:—The wicked man (as we have said) like his prince Satan, is turned totally the way of selfishness, and his own; he seeks not God, nor cares for the things of God; he seeks his own riches, his own glory, his own doings, his own wisdom, his own power, and, in a word, his own kingdom; and wills only to enjoy them in peace. And if any one oppose him or wish to diminish any of these things, with the same aversion to God under which he seeks these, with the same is he moved, enraged, and roused to indignation against his adversary. And he is as much unable to overcome this rage, as he is to overcome his desire of self-seeking; and he can no more avoid this seeking, than he can avoid his own existence; and this he cannot do, as being the creature of God, though a corrupt one.

The same is that fury of the world against the Gospel of God. For, by the Gospel, comes that "stronger than he," who overcomes the quiet possessor of the palace, and condemns those desires of glory, of riches, of wisdom, of self-righteousness, and of all things in which he trusts. This very irritation of the wicked, when God speaks and acts contrary to what they willed, is their hardening and their galling weight. For as they are in this state of aversion from the very corruption of nature, so they become more and more averse, and worse and worse, as this aversion is opposed or turned out of its way. And thus, when God threatened to take away from the wicked Pharaoh His power, he irritated and aggravated him, and hardened his heart the more, the more He came to him with His word by Moses, making known His intention to take away his kingdom and to deliver His own people from his power: because He did not give him His Spirit within, but permitted his wicked corruption, under the dominion of Satan, to grow angry, to swell with pride, to burn with rage, and to go on still in a certain secure contempt.

Sect. LXXXVI.—Let no one think, therefore, that God, where He is said to *harden*, or to *work evil in us* (for to harden is to do evil), so does the evil as though He created evil in us anew, in the same way as a malignant liquor-seller, being himself bad, would pour poison into, or mix it up in, a vessel that was not bad, where the vessel itself did nothing but receive, or passively accomplish the purpose of the malignity of the poison-mixer. For when people hear it said by us, that God works in us both good and evil, and that we from mere necessity passively submit to the working of God, they seem to imagine, that a man who is good, or not evil himself, is *passive* while God *works* evil *in* him: not rightly considering that God, is far from being inactive in all His creatures, and never suffers any one of them to keep holiday.

But whoever wishes to understand these things let him think thus:—that God works evil in us, that is, by us, not from the fault of God, but from the fault of evil in us:—that is, as we are evil by nature, God, who is truly good, carrying us along by His own action, according to the nature of His Omnipotence, cannot do otherwise than do evil by us, as instruments, though He Himself be good; though by His wisdom, He overrules that evil well, to His own glory and to our salvation.

Thus God, *finding* the will of Satan evil, not *creating* it so, but leaving it while Satan sinningly commits the evil, carries it along by His working, and moves it which way He will; though that will ceases not to be evil by this motion of God.

In this same way also David spoke concerning Shimei. "Let him curse, for God hath bidden him to curse David." (2 Samuel xvi. 10). How could God bid to curse, an action so evil and virulent! There was no where an external precept to that effect. David, therefore, looks to this:—the Omnipotent God *saith* and it is *done*: that is, He does all things by His external word. Wherefore here, the divine action and omnipotence, the good God Himself, carries along the will of Shimei, already evil together with all his members, and before incensed against David, and, while David is thus opportunely situated and deserving such blasphemy, commands the blasphemy, (that is, by his word which is his act, that is, the motion of his action), by this evil and blaspheming instrument.

Sect. LXXXVII.—It is thus God hardens Pharaoh—He presents to his impious and evil will His word and His work, which that will hates; that is, by its engendered and natural corruption. And thus, while God does not change by His Spirit that will within, but goes on presenting and enforcing; and while Pharaoh, considering his own resources, his riches and his power, trusts to them from the same naturally evil inclination; it comes to pass, that being inflated and uplifted by the imagination of his own greatness on the one hand, and swollen into a proud contempt of Moses coming in all humility with the unostentatious word of God on the other, he becomes hardened; and then, the more and more irritated and chafed, the more Moses advances and threatens: whereas, this his evil will would not, of itself, have been moved or hardened at all. But as the omnipotent Agent moved it by that His inevitable motion, it must of necessity will one way or the other.—And thus, as soon as he presented to it outwardly, that which naturally irritated and offended it, then it was, that Pharaoh could not avoid becoming hardened; even as he could not avoid the action of the Divine Omnipotence, and the aversion or enmity of his own will.

Wherefore, the hardening of Pharaoh's heart by God, is wrought thus,:—God presents outwardly to his enmity, that which he naturally hates; and then, He ceases not to move within, by His omnipotent motion, the evil will which He there finds. He, from the enmity of his will, cannot but hate that which is contrary to him, and trust to his own powers; and that, so obstinately, that he can neither hear nor feel, but is carried away, in the possession of Satan, like a madman or a fury.

If I have brought these things home with convincing persuasion, the victory in this point is mine. And having exploded the tropes and glosses of men, I understand the words of God simply; so that, there is no necessity for clearing God or accusing Him of iniquity. For when He saith, "I will harden the heart of Pharaoh," He speaks simply: as though He should say, I will so work, that the heart of Pharaoh shall be hardened: or, by My operation and working, the heart of Pharaoh shall be hardened. And how this was to be done, we have heard:—that is, by My general motion, I will so move his very evil will, that he shall go on in his course and lust of willing, nor will I cease to move it, nor can I do otherwise. I will, nevertheless, present to him My word and work; against which, that evil impetus will run; for he, being evil, cannot but will evil while I move him by the power of My Omnipotence.

Thus God with the greatest certainty knew, and with the greatest certainty declared, that Pharaoh would be hardened; because, He with the greatest certainty knew, that the will of Pharaoh could neither resist the motion of His Omnipotence, nor put away its own enmity, nor receive its adversary Moses; and that, as that evil will still remained, he must, of necessity, become worse, more hardened, and more proud, while, by his course and impetus, trusting to his own powers, he ran against that which he would not receive, and which he despised.

Here therefore, you see, it is confirmed even by this very Scripture, that "Free-will" can do nothing but evil, while God, who is not deceived from ignorance nor lies from iniquity, so surely promises the hardening of Pharaoh; because, He was certain, that an evil will could will nothing but evil, and that, as the good which it hated was presented to it, it could not but wax worse and worse.

Sec. LXXXVIII.—It now then remains, that perhaps some one may ask—Why then does not God cease from that motion of His Omnipotence, by which the will of the wicked is moved to go on in evil, and to become worse? I answer: this is to wish that God, for the sake of the wicked, would cease to be God; for this you really desire, when you desire His power and action to cease; that is, that He should cease to be good, lest the wicked should become worse.

Again, it may be asked—Why does He not then change, in His motion, those evil wills which He moves? —This belongs to those secrets of Majesty, where "His judgments are past finding out." Nor is it ours to search into, but to adore these mysteries. If "flesh and blood" here take offence and murmur, let it murmur, but it will be just where it was before. God is not, on that account, changed! And if numbers of the wicked be offended and "go away," yet, the elect shall remain!

The same answer will be given to those who ask—Why did He permit Adam to fall? And why did He make all of us to be infected with the same sin, when He might have kept him, and might have created us from some other seed, or might first have cleansed that, before He created us from it? —

God is that Being, for whose will no cause or reason is to be assigned, as a rule or standard by which it acts; seeing that, nothing is superior or equal to it, but it is itself the rule of all things. For if it acted by any rule or standard, or from any cause or reason, it would be no longer the *will of* God. Wherefore, what God wills, is not therefore right, because He ought or ever was bound so to will; but on the contrary, what takes place is therefore right, because He so wills. A cause and reason are assigned for the will of the creature, but not for the will of the Creator; unless you set up, over Him, another Creator.

Sect. LXXXIX.—By these arguments, I presume, the trope-inventing Diatribe, together with its trope, are sufficiently confuted. Let us, however, come to the text itself, for the purpose of seeing, what agreement there is between the text and the trope. For it is the way with all those who elude arguments by means of tropes, to hold the text itself in sovereign contempt, and to aim only, at picking out a certain term, and twisting and crucifying it upon the cross of their own opinion, without paying any regard whatever, either to circumstance, to consequence, to precedence, or to the intention or object of the author. Thus the Diatribe, in this passage, utterly disregarding the intention of Moses and the scope of his words, tears out of the text this term, "I will harden," and makes of it just what it will, according to its own lust: not at all considering, whether that can be again inserted so as to agree and square with the body of the text. And this is the reason why the Scripture was not sufficiently clear to those most received and most learned men of so many ages. And no wonder, for even the sun itself would not shine, if it should be assailed by such arts as these.

But (to say nothing about that, which I have already proved from the Scriptures, that Pharaoh cannot rightly be said to be hardened, 'because, being borne with by the long-suffering of God, he was not immediately punished,' seeing that, he was punished by so many plagues;) if *hardening* be 'bearing with divine long-suffering and not immediately punishing;' what need was there that God should so many times promise that He would then harden the heart of Pharaoh when the signs should be wrought, who now, before those signs were wrought, and before that hardening, was such, that, being inflated with his success, prosperity and wealth, and being borne with by the divine long-suffering and not punished, inflicted so many evils on the children of Israel? You see, therefore, that this trope of yours makes not at all to the purpose in this passage; seeing that, it applies generally unto *all*, as sinning *because* they are borne with by the divine long-suffering. And thus, we shall be compelled to say, that all are hardened, seeing that, there is no one who does not sin; and that, no one sins, but he who is borne with by the divine long-suffering. Wherefore, this hardening of Pharaoh, is another hardening, independent of that general hardening as produced by the long-suffering of the divine goodness.

Sect. XC.—The more immediate design of Moses then is, to announce, not so much the hardening of Pharaoh, as the veracity and mercy of God; that is, that the children of Israel might not distrust the promise of God, wherein He promised, that He would deliver them. (Ex. vi. 1). And since this was a matter of the greatest moment, He foretells them the difficulty, that they might not fall away from their faith; knowing, that all those things which were foretold must be accomplished in the order in which, He who had made the promise, had arranged them. As if He had said, I will deliver you, indeed, but you will with difficulty believe it; because, Pharaoh will so resist, and put off the deliverance. Nevertheless, believe ye; for the whole of his putting off shall, by My way of operation, only be the means of My working the more and greater miracles to your confirmation in faith, and to the display of My power; that henceforth, ye might the more steadily believe Me upon all other occasions.

In the same way does Christ also act, when, at the last supper, He promises His disciples a kingdom. He foretells them numberless difficulties, such as, His own death and their many tribulations; to the intent that, when it should come to pass, they might afterwards the more steadily believe.

And Moses by no means obscurely sets forth this meaning, where he saith, "But Pharaoh shall not send you away, that many wonders might be wrought in Egypt." And again, "For this purpose have I raised thee up, that I might shew in thee My power; that My name might be declared throughout all the earth." (Ex. ix. 16; Rom. ix. 17). Here, you see that Pharaoh was for this purpose hardened, that he might resist God and put off the redemption; in order that, there might be an occasion given for the working of signs, and for the display of the power of God, that He might be declared and believed on throughout all the earth. And what is this but shewing, that all these things were said and done to confirm faith, and to comfort the weak, that they might afterwards freely believe in God as true, faithful, powerful, and merciful? Just as though He had spoken to them in the kindest manner, as to little children, and had said, Be not terrified at the hardness of Pharaoh, for I work that very hardness Myself; and I, who deliver you, have it in My own hand. I will only use it, that I may thereby work many signs, and declare My Majesty, for the furtherance of your faith.

And this is the reason why Moses generally after each plague repeats, "And the heart of Pharaoh was hardened, so that he would not let the people go; as the Lord had spoken." (Ex. vii. 13, 22; viii. 15, 32; ix. 12, etc.). What is the intent of this, "as the Lord had spoken," but, that the Lord might appear true, who had foretold that he should be hardened? —Now, if there had been any *vertibility* or *liberty* of *will* in Pharaoh, which could turn either way, God could not with such certainty have foretold his hardening. But as He promised, who could neither be deceived nor lie, it of certainty and of necessity came to pass, that he was hardened: which could not have taken place, had not the hardening been totally apart from the power of man, and in the power of God alone, in the same manner as I said before; viz. from God being certain, that He should not omit the general operation of His Omnipotence in Pharaoh, or on Pharaoh's account; nay, that He could not omit it.

Moreover, God was equally certain, that the will of Pharaoh, being naturally evil and averse, could not consent to the word and work of God, which was contrary to it; and that, therefore, while the impetus of willing was preserved in Pharaoh by the Omnipotence of God, and while the hated word and work was continually set before his eyes without, nothing else could take place in Pharaoh, but offence and the hardening of his heart. For if God had then omitted the action of His Omnipotence in Pharaoh, when

He set before him the word of Moses which he hated, and the will of Pharaoh might be supposed to have acted alone by its own power, then, perhaps, there might have been room for a discussion, which way it had power to turn. But now, since it was led on and carried away by its own willing, no violence was done to its will, because it was not forced against its will, but was carried along, by the natural operation of God, to will naturally just as it was by nature, that is, evil; and therefore, it could not but run against the word, and thus become hardened. Hence we see, that this passage makes most forcibly against "Free-will"; and in this way—God who promised could not lie, and if He could not lie, then Pharaoh could not but be hardened.

Sect. XCI.—But let us also look into Paul, who takes up this passage of Moses, Rom. ix. How miserably is the Diatribe tortured with that part of the Scripture! Lest it should lose its hold of "Free-will," it puts on every shape. At one time it says, 'that there is a necessity of the consequence, but not a necessity of the thing consequent.' At another, 'that there is an ordinary will, or will of the sign, which may be resisted; and a will of decree, which cannot be resisted.' At another, 'that those passages adduced from Paul do not contend for, do not speak about, the salvation of man.' In one place it says 'that the prescience of God does impose necessity:' in another, 'that it does not impose necessity.' Again, in another place it asserts, 'that grace prevents the will that it might will, and then attends it as it proceeds and brings it to a happy issue.' Here it states, 'that the first cause does all things itself:' and directly afterwards, 'that it acts by second causes, remaining itself inactive.'

By these and the like sportings with words, it does nothing but fill up its time, and at the same time obscure the subject point from our sight, drawing us aside to something else. So stupid and doltish does it imagine us to be, that it thinks we feel no more interested in the cause than it feels itself. Or, as little children, when fearing the rod or at play, cover their eyes with their hands, and think, that as they see nobody themselves, nobody sees them; so the Diatribe, not being able to endure the brightness, nay the lightning of the most clear Scriptures, pretending by every kind of manoeuvre that it does not see, (which is in truth the case) wishes to persuade us that our eyes are also so covered that we cannot see. But all these manoeuvres, are but evidences of a convicted mind rashly struggling against invincible truth.

That figment about 'the necessity of the consequence, but not the necessity of the thing consequent,' has been before refuted. Let then Erasmus invent and invent again, cavil and cavil again, as much as he will—if God foreknew that Judas would be a traitor, Judas became a traitor of necessity; nor was it in the power of Judas nor of any other creature to alter it, or to change that will; though he did what he did willingly, not by compulsion; for that *willing* of his was his *own* work; which God, by the motion of His Omnipotence, moved on into action, as He does everything else.—God does not lie, nor is He deceived. This is a truth evident and invincible. There are no obscure or ambiguous words here, even though all the most learned men of all ages should be so blinded as to think and say to the contrary. How much soever, therefore, you may turn your back upon it, yet, the convicted conscience of yourself and all men is compelled to confess, that, IF GOD BE NOT DECEIVED IN THAT WHICH HE FOREKNOWS, THAT WHICH HE FOREKNOWS MUST, OF NECESSITY, TAKE PLACE. If it were not so, who could believe His promises, who would fear His threatenings, if what He promised or threatened did not of necessity take place! Or, how could He promise or threaten, if His prescience could be deceived or hindered by our mutability! This all-clear light of certain truth manifestly stops the mouths of all, puts an end to all questions, and for ever settles the victory over all evasive subtleties.

We know, indeed, that the prescience of man is fallible. We know that an eclipse does not therefore take place, because it is foreknown; but, that it is therefore foreknown, because it is to take place. But what have we to do with this prescience? We are disputing about the prescience of God! And if you do not ascribe to this, the necessity of the consequent foreknown, you take away faith and the fear of God, you destroy the force of all the divine promises and threatenings, and thus deny divinity itself. But, however, the Diatribe itself, after having held out for a long time and tried all things, and being pressed hard by the force of truth, at last confesses my sentiment: saying—

Sect. XCII.—"The question concerning the will and predestination of God, is somewhat difficult. For God wills those same things which He foreknows. And this is the substance of what Paul subjoins, "Who hath resisted His will," if He have mercy on whom He will, and harden whom He will? For if there were a king who could effect whatever he chose, and no one could resist him, he would be said to do whatsoever he willed. So the will of God, as it is the principal cause of all things which take place, seems to impose a necessity on our will."—Thus the Diatribe.

At last then I give thanks to God for a sound sentence in the Diatribe! Where now then is "Free-will"? —But again this slippery eel is twisted aside in a moment, saying,

—"But Paul does not explain this point, he only rebukes the disputer; "Who art thou, O man, that repliest against God! " (Rom. ix. 20.)—

O notable evasion! Is this the way to handle the Holy Scriptures, thus to make a declaration upon ones own authority, and out of ones own brain, without a Scripture, without a miracle, nay, to corrupt the most clear words of God? What! does not Paul explain that point? What does he then? 'He only rebukes the disputer,' says the Diatribe. And is not that rebuke the most complete explanation? For what was inquired into by that question concerning the will of God? Was it not this—whether or not it imposed a necessity on our will? Paul, then, answers that it is thus:—"He will have mercy on whom He will have mercy, and whom He will He hardeneth. It is not of him that willeth, nor of him that runneth, but of God that sheweth mercy." (Rom. ix. 15-16, 18). Moreover, not content with this explanation, he introduces those who murmur against this explanation in their defence of "Free-will," and prate that there is no merit allowed, that we are damned when the fault is not our own, and the like, and stops their murmuring and indignation: saying, "Thou wilt say then, Why doth He yet find fault? for who hath resisted His will? " (Rom. ix. 19.).

Do you not see that this is addressed to those, who, hearing that the will of God imposes necessity on us, say, "Why doth He yet find fault? " That is, Why does God thus insist, thus urge, thus exact, thus find fault? Why does He accuse, why does He reprove, as though we men could do what He requires if we would? He has no just cause for thus finding fault; let Him rather accuse His own will; let Him find fault with that; let Him press His requirement upon that; "For who hath resisted His will? " Who can obtain mercy if He wills not? Who can become softened if He wills to harden? It is not in our power to change His will, much less to resist it, where He wills us to be hardened; by that will, therefore, we are compelled to be hardened, whether we will or no.

If Paul had not explained this question, and had not stated to a certainty, that necessity is imposed on us by the prescience of God, what need was there for his introducing the murmurers and complainers saying, That His will cannot be resisted? For who would have murmured or been indignant, if he had not found necessity to be stated? Paul's words are not ambiguous where he speaks of resisting the will of God. Is there any thing ambiguous in what resisting is, or what His will is? Is it at all ambiguous concerning what he is speaking, when he speaks concerning the will of God? Let the myriads of the most approved doctors be blind; let them pretend, if they will, that the Scriptures are not quite clear, and that they tremble at a difficult question; we have words the most clear which plainly speak thus: "He will have mercy on whom He will have mercy, and whom He will He hardeneth:" and also, "Thou wilt say to me then, Why doth He yet complain, for who hath resisted His will? "

The question, therefore, is not difficult; nay, nothing can be more plain to common sense, than that this conclusion is certain, stable, and true:—if it be pre-established from the Scriptures, that God neither errs nor is deceived; then, whatever God *foreknows*, must, of *necessity*, take place. It would be a difficult question indeed, nay, an impossibility, I confess, if you should attempt to establish, both the *prescience* of God, and the *"Free-will"* of man. For what could be more difficult, nay a greater impossibility, than to attempt to prove, that contradictions do not clash; or that a number may, at the same time, be both nine and ten? There is no difficulty on our side of the question, but it is sought for and introduced, just as ambiguity and obscurity are sought for and violently introduced into the Scriptures.

The apostle, therefore, restrains the impious who are offended at these most clear words, by letting them know, that the divine will is accomplished, by necessity in us; and by letting them know also, that it is defined to a certainty, that they have nothing of liberty or "Free-will" left, but that all things depend upon the will of God alone. But he restrains them in this way:—by commanding them to be silent, and to revere the majesty of the divine power and will, over which we have no control, but which has over us a full control to do whatever it will. And yet it does us no injury, seeing that it is not indebted to us, it never received any thing from us, it never promised us any thing but what itself pleased and willed.

Sect. XCIII.—This, therefore, is not the place, this is not the time for adoring those Corcycian caverns, but for adoring the true Majesty in its to-be-feared, wonderful, and incomprehensible judgments; and saying, "Thy will be done in earth as it is in heaven." (Matt. vi. 10). Whereas, we are no where more irreverent and rash, than in trespassing and arguing upon these very inscrutable mysteries and judgments. And while we are pretending to a great reverence in searching the Holy Scriptures, those which God has commanded to be searched, we search not; but those which He has forbidden us to search into, those we search into and none other; and that with an unceasing temerity, not to say, blasphemy.

For is it not searching with temerity, when we attempt to make the all-free prescience of God to harmonize with our freedom, prepared to derogate prescience from God, rather than lose our own liberty? Is it not temerity, when He imposes necessity upon us, to say, with murmurings and blasphemies, "Why doth He yet find fault? for who hath resisted His will? " (Rom. ix. 19). Where is the God by nature most merciful? Where is He who "willeth not the death of a sinner? " Has He then created us for this purpose only, that He might delight Himself in the torments of men? And many things of the same kind, which will be howled forth by the damned in hell to all eternity.

But however, natural Reason herself is compelled to confess, that the living and true God must be such an one as, by His own liberty, to impose necessity on us. For He must be a ridiculous God, or idol rather, who did not, to a certainty, foreknow the future, or was liable to be deceived in events, when even the Gentiles ascribed to their gods 'fate inevitable.' And He would be equally ridiculous, if He could not do and did not all things, or if any thing could be done without Him. If then the prescience and omnipotence of God be granted, it, naturally follows, as an irrefragable consequence that we neither were made by ourselves, nor live by ourselves, nor do any thing by ourselves, but by His Omnipotence. And since He at the first foreknew that we should be such, and since He has made us such, and moves and rules over us as such, how, I ask, can it be pretended, that there is any liberty in us to do, in any respect, otherwise than He at first foreknew and now proceeds in action!

Wherefore, the prescience and Omnipotence of God, are diametrically opposite to our "Free-will." And it must be, that either God is deceived in His prescience and errs in His action, (which is impossible) or we act, and are acted upon, according to His prescience and action.—But by the Omnipotence of God, I mean, not that power by which He *does not* many things that He *could do*, but that *actual power* by which He powerfully *works all in all*, in which sense the Scripture calls Him Omnipotent. This Omnipotence and prescience of God, I say, utterly abolishes the doctrine of "Free-will." No pretext can here be framed about the obscurity of the Scripture, or the difficulty of the subject-point: the words are most clear, and known to every school-boy; and the point is plain and easy and stands proved by judgment of common sense; so that the series of ages, of times, or of persons, either writing or teaching to the contrary, be it as great as it may, amounts to nothing at all.

Sect. XCIV.—But it is this, that seems to give the greatest offence to common sense or natural reason,—that the God, who is set forth as being so full of mercy and goodness, should, of His mere will, leave men, harden them, and damn them, as though He delighted in the sins, and in the great and eternal torments of the miserable. To think thus of God, seems iniquitous, cruel, intolerable; and it is this that has given offence to so many and great men of so many ages.

And who would not be offended? I myself have been offended more than once, even unto the deepest abyss of desperation; nay, so far, as even to wish that I had never been born a man; that is, before I was brought to know how healthful that desperation was, and how near it was unto grace. Here it is, that there has been so much toiling and labouring, to excuse the goodness of God, and to accuse the will of man. Here it is, that distinctions have been invented between the *ordinary* will of God and the *absolute* will of God: between the necessity of the consequence, and the necessity of the thing consequent: and many other inventions of the same kind. By which, nothing has ever been effected but an imposition upon the un-learned, by vanities of words, and by "oppositions of science falsely so called." For after all, a conscious conviction has been left deeply rooted in the heart both of the learned and the unlearned, if ever they have come to an experience of these things; and a knowledge, that our necessity, is a consequence that must follow upon the belief of the prescience and Omnipotence of God.

And even natural Reason herself, who is so offended at this necessity, and who invents so many contrivances to take it out of the way, is compelled to grant it upon her own conviction from her own judgment, even though there were no Scripture at all. For all men find these sentiments written in their hearts, and they acknowledge and approve them (though against their will) whenever they hear them treated on.—First, that God is Omnipotent, not only in power but in action (as I said before): and that, if it were not so, He would be a ridiculous God.—And next, that He knows and foreknows all things, and neither can err nor be deceived. These two points then being granted by the hearts and minds of all, they are at once compelled, from an inevitable consequence, to admit,—that we are not made from our own will, but from necessity: and moreover, that we do not what we will according to the law of "Free-will," but as God foreknew and proceeds in action, according to His infallible and immutable counsel and power. Wherefore, it is found written alike in the hearts of all men, that there is no such thing as "Free-will"; though that writing be obscured by so many contending disputations, and by the great authority of so many men who have, through so many ages, taught otherwise. Even as every other law also, which, according to the testimony of Paul, is written in our hearts, is then acknowledged when it is rightly set forth, and then obscured, when it is confused by wicked teachers, and drawn aside by other opinions.

Sect. XCV.—I now return to Paul. If he does not, Rom. ix., explain this point, nor clearly state our necessity from the prescience and will of God; what need was there for him to introduce the similitude of the "potter," who, of the "same lump" of clay, makes "one vessel unto honour and another unto dishonour?" (Rom. ix. 21). What need was there for him to observe, that the thing formed does not say to him that formed it, "Why hast thou made me thus?" (20). He is there speaking of men; and he compares them to clay, and God to a potter. This similitude, therefore, stands coldly useless, nay, is introduced ridiculously and in vain, if it be not his sentiment, that we have no liberty whatever. Nay, the whole of the argument of Paul, wherein he defends grace, is in vain. For the design of the whole epistle is to shew, that we can do nothing, even when we seem to do well; as he in the same epistle testifies, where he says, that Israel which followed after righteousness, did not attain unto righteousness; but that the Gentiles which followed not after it did attain unto it. (Rom. ix. 30-31). Concerning which I shall speak more at large hearafter, when I produce my forces.

The fact is, the Diatribe designedly keeps back the body of Paul's argument and its scope, and comfortably satisfies itself with prating upon a few detached and corrupted terms. Nor does the exhortation which Paul afterwards gives, Rom. xi., at all help the Diatribe; where he saith, "Thou standest by faith, be not high-minded;" (20), again, "and they also, if they shall believe, shall be grafted in, &c. (23);" for he says nothing there about the ability of man, but brings forth imperative and conditional expressions; and what effect they are intended to produce, has been fully shewn already. Moreover, Paul, there anticipating the boasters of "Free-will," does not say, they *can* believe, but he saith, "God is able to graft them in again." (23).

To be brief: The Diatribe moves along with so much hesitation, and so lingeringly, in handling these passages of Paul, that its conscience seems to give the lie to all that it writes. For just at the point where it ought to have gone on to the proof, it for the most part, stops short with a 'But of this enough;' 'But I shall not now proceed with this;' 'But this is not my present purpose;' 'But here they should have said so and so;' and many evasions of the same kind; and it leaves off the subject just in the middle; so that, you are left in uncertainty whether it wished to be understood as speaking on "Free-will " or whether it was only evading the sense of Paul by means of vanities of words. And all this is being just in its character, as not having a serious thought upon the cause in which it is engaged. But as for me I dare not be thus cold, thus always on the tip-toe of policy, or thus move to and fro as a reed shaken with the wind. I must assert with certainty, with constancy, and with ardour; and prove what I assert solidly, appropriately, and fully.

Sect. XCVI.—And now, how excellently does the Diatribe preserve *liberty* in harmony with *necessity*, where it says—"Nor does all necessity exclude "Free-will." For instance: God the Father begets a son, of necessity; but yet, He begets him willingly and freely, seeing that, He is not forced."—

Am I here, I pray you, disputing about *compulsion* and *force*? Have I not said in all my books again and again, that my dispute, on this subject, is about *the necessity of immutability*? I know that the Father begets willingly, and that Judas willingly betrayed Christ. But I say, this willing, in the person of Judas, was decreed to take place from immutability and certainty, if God foreknew it. Or, if men do not yet understand what I mean,—I make two necessities: the one a *necessity of force*, in reference to *the act*; the other a *necessity of immutability* in reference to *the time*. Let him, therefore, who wishes to hear what I have to say, understand, that I here speak of the *latter*, not of the *former*: that is, I do not dispute whether Judas became a traitor willingly or unwillingly, but whether or not, it was decreed to come to pass, that Judas *should will* to betray Christ *at a certain time* infallibly predetermined of God!

But only listen to what the Diatribe says upon this point—"With reference to the immutable prescience of God, Judas was of necessity to become a traitor; nevertheless, Judas had it in his power to change his own will."—

Dost thou understand, friend Diatribe, what thou sayest? (To say nothing of that which has been already proved, that the will cannot will any thing but evil.) How could Judas change his own will, if the immutable prescience of God stand granted! Could he change the prescience of God and render it fallible!

Here the Diatribe gives it up, and, leaving its standard, and throwing down its arms, runs from its post, and hands over the discussion to the subtleties of the schools concerning the necessity of the consequence and of the thing consequent: pretending—'that it does not wish to engage in the discussion of points so nice.'—

A step of policy truly, friend Diatribe! —When you have brought the subject-point into the midst of the field, and just when the champion-disputant was required, then you shew your back, and leave to others the business of answering and defining. But you should have taken this step at the first, and abstained from writing altogether. 'He who ne'er proved the training-field of arms, let him ne'er in the battle's brunt appear.' For it never was expected of Erasmus that he should remove that difficulty which lies in God's foreknowing all things, and our, nevertheless, doing all things by contingency: this difficulty existed in the world long before ever the Diatribe saw the light: but yet, it was expected that he should make some kind of answer, and give some kind of definition. Whereas he, by using a rhetorical transition, drags away us, knowing nothing of rhetoric, along with himself, as though we were here contending for a thing of nought, and were engaged in quibbling about insignificant niceties; and thus, nobly betakes himself out of the midst of the field, bearing the crowns both of the scholar and the conqueror.

But not so, brother! There is no rhetoric of sufficient force to cheat an honest conscience. The voice of conscience is proof against all powers and figures of eloquence. I cannot here suffer a rhetorician to pass on under the cloak of dissimulation. This is not a time for such manoeuvring. This is that part of the discussion, where matters come to the turning point. Here is the hinge upon which the whole turns. Here, therefore, "Free-will" must be completely vanquished, or completely triumph. But here you, seeing your danger, nay, the certainty of the victory over "Free-will," pretend that you see nothing but argumentative niceties. Is this to act the part of a faithful theologian? Can you feel a serious interest in your cause, who thus leave your auditors in suspense, and your arguments in a state that confuses and exasperates them, while you, nevertheless, wish to appear to have given honest satisfaction and open explanation? This craft and cunning might, perhaps, be borne with in profane subjects, but in a theological subject, where simple and open truth is the object required, for the salvation of souls, it is utterly hateful and intolerable!

Sect. XCVII.—The Sophists also felt the invincible and insupportable force of this argument, and therefore they invented the *necessity* of the *consequence* and of the *thing consequent*. But to what little purpose this figment is, I have shewn already. For they do not all the while observe, what they are saying, and what conclusions they are admitting against themselves. For if you grant the necessity of the consequence, "Free-will" lies vanquished and prostrate, nor does either the necessity, or the contingency of the thing consequent, profit it anything. What is it to me if "Free-will" be not compelled, but do what it does willingly? It is enough for me, that you grant, that it is of necessity, that it does willingly what it does; and that, it cannot do otherwise if God foreknew it would be so.

If God foreknew, either that Judas would be a traitor, or that he would change his willing to be a traitor, whichsoever of the two God foreknew, must, of necessity, take place, or God will be deceived in His prescience and prediction, which is impossible. This is the effect of the necessity of the consequence, that is, if God foreknows a thing, that thing must of necessity take place; that is, there is no such thing as "Free-will." This necessity of the consequence, therefore, is not 'obscure or ambiguous;' so that, even if the doctors of all ages were blinded, yet they must admit it, because it is so manifest and plain, as to be actually palpable. And as to the necessity of the thing consequent, with which they comfort themselves, that is a mere phantom, and is in diametrical opposition to the necessity of the consequence.

For example: The necessity of the consequence is, (so to set it forth,) God foreknows that Judas will be a traitor—therefore it will certainly and infallibly come to pass, that Judas shall be a traitor. Against this necessity of the consequence, you comfort yourself thus:—But since Judas can change his willing to betray, therefore, there is no necessity of the thing consequent. How, I ask you, will these two positions harmonize, Judas *is able to will not* to betray, and, Judas *must of necessity will* to betray? Do not these two directly contradict and militate against each other? But he will not be compelled, you say, to betray against his will. What is that to the purpose? You were speaking of the necessity of the thing consequent; and saying, that that need not, of necessity, follow, from the necessity of the consequence; you were not speaking of the *compulsive* necessity of the thing consequent. The question was, concerning the *necessity* of the thing consequent, and you produce an example concerning the *compulsive necessity* of the thing consequent. I ask one thing, and you answer another. But this arises from that yawning sleepiness, under which you do not observe, what nothingness that figment amounts to, concerning the necessity of the thing consequent.

Suffice it to have spoken thus to the *former part* of this SECOND PART, which has been concerning the *hardening of Pharaoh*, and which involves, indeed, all the Scriptures, and all our forces, and those invincible. Now let us proceed to the remaining part concerning *Jacob and Esau*, who are spoken of as being "not yet born." (Rom. ix. 11).

Sect. XCVIII.–This place the Diatribe evades by saying–'that it does not properly pertain to the salvation of man. For God (it says) may will that a man shall be a servant, or a poor man; and yet, not reject him from eternal salvation.'–

Only observe, I pray you, how many evasions and ways of escape a slippery mind will invent, which would flee from the truth, and yet cannot get away from it after all. Be it so, that this passage does not pertain to the salvation of man, (to which point I shall speak hereafter), are we to suppose, then, that Paul who adduces it, does so, for no purpose whatever? Shall we make Paul to be ridiculous, or a vain trifler, in a discussion so serious?

But all this breathes nothing but Jerome, who dares to say, in more places than one, with a supercilious brow and a sacrilegious mouth, 'that those things are made to be of force in Paul, which, in their own places, are of no force.' This is no less than saying, that Paul, where he lays the foundation of the Christian doctrine, does nothing but corrupt the Holy Scriptures, and delude believing souls with sentiments hatched out of his own brain, and violently thrust into the Scriptures.–Is this honouring the Holy Spirit in Paul, that sanctified and elect instrument of God! Thus, when Jerome ought to be read with judgment, and this saying of his to be numbered among those many things which that man impiously wrote, (such was his yawning inconsiderateness, and his stupidity in understanding the Scriptures), the Diatribe drags him in without any judgment; and not thinking it right, that his authority should be lessened by any mitigating gloss whatever, takes him as a most certain oracle, whereby to judge of, and attemper the Scriptures. And thus it is; we take the impious sayings of men as rules and guides in the Holy Scripture, and then wonder that it should become 'obscure and ambiguous,' and that so many fathers should be blind in it; whereas, the whole proceeds from this impious and sacrilegious Reason.

Sect. XCIX.–Let him, then, be anathema who shall say, 'that those things which are of no force in their own places are made to be of force in Paul.' This, however, is only said, it is not proved. And it is said by those, who understand neither Paul, nor the passages adduced by him, but are deceived by terms; that is, by their own impious interpretations of them. And if it be allowed that this passage, Gen. xxv. 21-23 is to be understood in a temporal sense (which is not the true sense) yet it is rightly and effectually adduced by Paul, when he proves from it, that it was not of the "merits" of Jacob and Esau, "but of Him that calleth," that it was said unto Rebecca, "the elder shall serve the younger." (Rom. ix. 11-16).

Paul is argumentatively considering, whether or not they attained unto that which was said of them, by the power or merits of "Free-will"; and he proves, that they did not; but that Jacob attained unto that, unto which Esau attained not, solely by the grace "of Him that calleth." And he proves that, by the incontrovertible words of the Scripture: that is, that they were "not yet born:" and also, that they had "done neither good nor evil." This proof contains the weighty sum of his whole subject point: and by the same proof, our subject point is settled also.

The Diatribe, however, having dissemblingly passed over all these particulars, with an excellent rhetorical fetch, does not here argue at all upon merit, (which, nevertheless, it undertook to do, and which this subject point of Paul requires), but cavils about temporal bondage, as though that were at all to the purpose;—but it is merely that it might not seem to be overthrown by the all-forcible words of Paul. For what had it, which it could yelp against Paul in support of "Free-will"? What did "Free-will" do *for* Jacob, or what did it do *against* Esau, when it was already determined, by the prescience and predestination of God, before either of them was born, what should be the portion of each; that is, that the one should serve, and the other rule? Thus the rewards were decreed, before the workmen wrought, or were born. It is to this that the Diatribe ought to have answered. Paul contends for this:—that neither had done either good or evil: and yet, that by the divine sentence, the one was decreed to be servant, the other lord. The question here, is not, whether that servitude pertained unto salvation, but from what *merit* it was imposed on him who had not deserved it. But it is wearisome to contend with these depraved attempts to pervert and evade the Scripture.

Sect. C.—But however, that Moses does not intend their servitude only, and that Paul is perfectly right in understanding it concerning eternal salvation, is manifest from the text itself. And although this is somewhat wide of our present purpose, yet I will not suffer Paul to be contaminated with the calumnies of the sacrilegious. The oracle in Moses is thus—"Two manner of people shall be separated from thy bowels, and the one people shall be stronger than the other people; and the elder shall serve the younger." (Gen. xxv. 23).

Here, manifestly, are two people distinctly mentioned. The one, though the younger, is received into the grace of God; to the intent that, he might overcome the other; not by his own strength, indeed, but by a favouring God: for how could the younger overcome the elder unless God were with him!

Since, therefore, the younger was to be the people of God, it is not only the external rule or servitude which is there spoken of, but all that pertains to the spirit of God; that is, the blessing, the word, the Spirit, the promise of Christ, and the everlasting kingdom. And this the Scripture more fully confirms afterwards, where it describes Jacob as being blessed, and receiving the promises and the kingdom.

All this Paul briefly intimates, where he saith, "The elder shall serve the younger:" and he sends us to Moses, who treats upon the particulars more fully. So that you may say, in reply to the sacrilegious sentiment of Jerome and the Diatribe, that these passages which Paul adduces have more force in their own place than they have in his Epistle. And this is true also, not of Paul only, but of all the Apostles; who adduce Scriptures as testimonies and assertions of their own sentiments. But it would be ridiculous to adduce that as a testimony, which testifies nothing, and does not make at all to the purpose. And even if there were some among the philosophers so ridiculous as to prove that which was unknown, by that which was less known still, or by that which was totally irrelevant to the subject, with what face can we attribute such kind of proceeding to the greatest champions and authors of the Christian doctrines, especially, since they teach those things which are the essential articles of faith, and on which the salvation of souls depends? But such a face becomes those who, in the Holy Scriptures, feel no serious interest whatever.

Sect. CI.—And with respect to that of Malachi which Paul annexes, "Jacob have I loved, but Esau have I hated;" (Mal. i. 2-3). that, the Diatribe perverts by a threefold contrivance. The first is—"If (it says) you stick to the letter, God does not love as we love, nor does He hate any one: because, passions of this kind do not pertain unto God."—

What do I hear! Are we now inquiring *whether or not* God loves and hates, and not rather *why* He loves and hates? Our inquiry is, from what merit it is in us that He loves or hates. We know well enough, that God does not love or hate as we do; because, we love and hate mutably, but He loves and hates from an eternal and immutable nature; and hence it is, that accidents and passions do not pertain unto Him.

And it is this very state of the truth, that of necessity proves "Free-will" to be nothing at all; seeing that, the love and hatred of God towards men is immutable and eternal; existing, not only before there was any merit or work of "Free-will," but before the worlds were made; and that, all things take place in us from necessity, accordingly as He loved or loved not from all eternity. So that, not the love of God only, but even the *manner* of His love imposes on us necessity. Here then it may be seen, how much its invented ways of escape profit the Diatribe; for the more it attempts to get away from the truth, the more it runs upon it; with so little success does it fight against it!

But be it so, that your trope stands good—that the love of God is the *effect* of love, and the hatred of God the *effect* of hatred. Does, then, that effect take place without, and independent of, the *will* of God? Will you here say also, that God does not *will* as we do, and that the passion of *willing* does not pertain to Him? If then those effects take place, they do not take place but according to the *will* of God. Hence, therefore, what God wills, that He loves and hates. Now then, tell me, for what merit did God love Jacob or hate Esau, before they wrought, or were born? Wherefore it stands manifest, that Paul most rightly adduces Malachi in support of the passage from Moses: that is, that God therefore called Jacob before he was born, because He loved him; but that He was not first loved by Jacob, nor moved to love him from any merit in him. So that, in the cases of Jacob and Esau, it is shewn—what ability there is in our "Free-will"!

Sect. CII.—The second contrivance is this:—'that Malachi does not seem to speak of that hatred by which we are damned to all eternity, but of temporal affliction: seeing that, those are reproved who wished to destroy Edom.'—

This, again, is advanced in contempt of Paul, as though he had done violence to the Scriptures. Thus, we hold in no reverence whatever, the majesty of the Holy Spirit, and only aim at establishing our own sentiments. But let us bear with this contempt for a moment, and see what it effects. Malachi, then, speaks of temporal affliction. And what if he do? What is that to your purpose? Paul proves out of Malachi, that that affliction was laid on Esau without any desert, by the hatred of God only: and this he does, that he might thence conclude, that there is no such thing as "Free-will." This is the point that makes against you, and it is to this you ought to have answered. I am arguing about merit, and you are all the while talking about reward; and yet, you so talk about it, as not to evade that which you wish to evade; nay, in your very talking about reward, you acknowledge merit; and yet, pretend you do not see it. Tell me, then, what moved God to love Jacob, and to hate Esau, even before they were born?

But however, the assertion, that Malachi is speaking of temporal affliction only, is false: nor is he speaking of the destroying of Edom: you entirely pervert the sense of the prophet by this contrivance. The prophet shews what he means, in words the most clear.—He upbraids the Israelites with ingratitude: because, after God had loved them, they did not, in return, either love Him as their Father, or fear Him as their Lord. (Mal. i. 6.).

That God had loved them, he proves, both by the Scriptures, and by facts: viz. in this:—that although Jacob and Esau were brothers, as Moses records Gen. xxv. 21-28, yet He loved Jacob and chose him before he was born, as we have heard from Paul aready; but that, He so hated Esau, that He removed away his dwelling into the desert; that moreover, he so continued and pursued that hatred, that when He brought back Jacob from captivity and restored him, He would not suffer the Edomites to be restored; and that, even if they at any time said they wished to build, He threatened them with destruction. If this be not the plain meaning of the prophet's text, let the whole world prove me a liar.—Therefore the temerity of the Edomites is not here reproved, but, as I said before, the ingratitude of the sons of Jacob; who do not see what God has done, for them, and against their brethren the Edomites; and for no other reason, than because, He hated the one, and loved the other.

How then will your assertion stand good, that the prophet is here speaking of temporal affliction, when he testifies, in the plainest words, that he is speaking of the two people as proceeding from the two patriarchs, the one received to be a people and saved, and the other left and at last destroyed? To be received as a people, and not to be received as a people, does not pertain to temporal good and evil only, but unto all things. For our God is not the God of temporal things only, but of all things. Nor does God will to be thy God so as to be worshipped with one shoulder, or with a lame foot, but with all thy might, and with all thy heart, that He may be thy God as well here, as hereafter, in all things, times, and works.

Sect. CIII.—The third contrivance is—'that, according to the trope interpretation of the passage, God neither loves all the Gentiles, nor hates all the Jews; but, out of each people, some. And that, by this use of the trope, the Scripture testimony in question, does not at all go to prove necessity, but to beat down the arrogance of the Jews.'—The Diatribe having opened this way of escape, then comes to this—'that God is said to hate men before they are born, because, He foreknows that they will do that which will merit hatred: and that thus, the hatred and love of God do not at all militate against "Free-will" '—And at last, it draws this conclusion—'that the Jews were cut off from the olive tree on account of the merit of unbelief, and the Gentiles grafted in on account of the merit of faith, according to the authority of Paul; and that, a trope is held out to those who are cut off, of being grafted in again, and a warning given to those who are grafted in, that they fall not off.'—

May I perish if the Diatribe itself knows what it is talking about. But, perhaps, this is also a rhetorical fetch; which teaches you, when any danger seems to be at hand, always to render your sense obscure, lest you should be taken in your own words. I, for my part, can see no place whatever in this passage for those trope-interpretations, of which the Diatribe dreams, but which it cannot establish by proof. Therefore, it is no wonder that this testimony does not make against it, in the trope-interpreted sense, because, it has no such sense.

Moreover, we are not disputing about cutting off and grafting in, of which Paul here speaks in his exhortations. I know that men are grafted in by faith, and cut off by unbelief; and that they are to be exhorted to believe that they be not cut off. But it does not follow, nor is it proved from this, that they *can* believe or fall away *by the power of* "*Free-will*," which is now the point in question. We are not disputing about, who are the believing and who are not; who are Jews and who are Gentiles; and what is the consequence of believing and falling away; that pertains unto exhortation. Our point in dispute is, *by what merit* or *work* they attain unto that faith by which they are grafted in, or unto that unbelief by which they are cut off. This is the point that belongs to you as the teacher of "Free-will." And pray, describe to me this merit.

Paul teaches us, that this comes to them by no work of theirs, but only according to the love or the hatred of God: and when it is come to them, he exhorts them to persevere, that they be not cut off. But this exhortation does not prove what we *can do*, but what we *ought to do*.

I am compelled thus to hedge in my adversary with many words, lest he should slip away from, and leave the subject point, and take up any thing but that: and in fact, to hold him thus to the point, is to vanquish him. For all that he aims at, is to slide away from the point, withdraw himself out of sight, and take up any thing but that, which he first laid down as his subject design.

Sect. CIV.—The next passage which the Diatribe takes up is that of Isaiah xlv. 9, "Shall the clay say to Him that fashioneth it, what makest Thou? " And that of Jeremiah xviii. 6, "Behold as the clay is in the potter's hand, so are ye in Mine hand." Here the Diatribe says again—"these passages are made to have more force in Paul, than they have in the places of the prophets from which they are taken; because, in the prophets they speak of temporal affliction, but Paul uses them, with reference to eternal election and reprobation."—So that, here again, temerity or ignorance in Paul, is insinuated.

But before we see how the Diatribe proves, that neither of these passages excludes "Free-will," I will make this remark:—that Paul does not appear to have taken this passage out of the Scriptures, nor does the Diatribe prove that he has. For Paul usually mentions the name of his author, or declares that he has taken a certain part from the Scriptures; whereas, here, he does neither. It is most probable, therefore, that Paul uses this general similitude according to *his* spirit in support of his own cause, as others have used it in support of theirs. It is in the same way that he uses this similitude. "A little leaven leaveneth the whole lump:" which, I Cor. v. 6, he uses to represent corrupt morals: and applies it in another place (Gal. v. 9) to those who corrupt the Word of God: so Christ also speaks of the "leaven of Herod" and "of the Pharisees." (Mark viii. 15; Matt. xvi. 6).

Supposing, therefore, that the prophets use this similitude, when speaking more particularly of temporal punishment; (upon which I shall not now dwell, lest I should be too much occupied about irrelevant questions, and kept away from the subject point,) yet Paul uses it, in his spirit, against "Free-will." And as to saying that the liberty of the will is not destroyed by our being as clay in the hand of an afflicting God, I know not what it means, nor why the Diatribe contends for such a point: for, without doubt, afflictions come upon us from God against our will, and impose upon us the necessity of bearing them, whether we will or no: nor is it in our power to avert them: though we are exhorted to bear them with a willing mind.

Sect. CV.—But it is worth while to hear the Diatribe make out, how it is that the argument of Paul does not exclude "Free-will" by that similitude: for it brings forward two absurd objections: the one taken from the Scriptures, the other from Reason. From the Scriptures it collects this objection.

—When Paul, 2 Tim. ii. 20, had said, that "in a great house there are vessels of gold and silver, wood and earth, some to honour and some to dishonour," he immediately adds, "If a man therefore purge himself from these, he shall be a vessel unto honour, &c." (21.)—Then the Diatribe goes on to argue thus:—"What could be more ridiculous than for any one to say to an earthen chamber-convenience, If thou shalt purify thyself, thou shalt be a vessel unto honour? But this would be rightly said to a rational earthen vessel, which can, when admonished, form itself according to the will of the Lord."—By these observations it means to say, that the similitude is not in all respects applicable, and is so mistaken, that it effects nothing at all.

I answer: (not to cavil upon this point:)—that Paul does not say, if any one shall purify himself from his own filth, but "from these;" that is, from the vessels unto dishonour: so that the sense is, if any one shall remain separate, and shall not mingle himself with wicked teachers, he shall be a vessel unto honour. Let us grant also that this passage of Paul makes for the Diatribe just as it wishes: that is, that the similitude is not effective. But how will it prove, that Paul is here speaking on the same subject as he is in Rom. ix. 11-23, which is the passage in dispute? Is it enough to cite a different passage without at all regarding whether it have the same or a different tendency? There is not (as I have often shewn) a more easy or more frequent fall in the Scriptures, than the bringing together different Scripture passages as being of the same meaning. Hence, the similitude in those passages, of which the Diatribe boasts, makes less to its purpose than our similitude which it would refute.

But (not to be contentious), let us grant, that each passage of Paul is of the same tendency; and that a similitude does not always apply in all respects; (which is without controversy true; for otherwise, it would not be a similitude, nor a translation, but the thing itself; according to the proverb, 'A similitude halts, and does not always go upon four feet;') yet the Diatribe errs and transgresses in this:—neglecting the scope of the similitude, which is to be most particularly observed, it contentiously catches at certain words of it: whereas, 'the knowledge of what is said, (as Hilary observes,) is to be gained from the scope of what is said, not from certain detached words only.' Thus, the efficacy of a similitude depends upon the cause of the similitude. Why then does the Diatribe disregard that, for the purpose of which Paul uses this similitude, and catch at that, which he says is unconnected with the purport of the similitude? That is to say, it is an exhortation where he saith, "If a man purge himself from these;" but a point of doctrine where he saith, "In a great house, there are vessels of gold, &c." So that, from all the circumstances of the words and mind of Paul, you may understand that he is establishing the doctrine concerning the diversity and use of vessels.

The sense, therefore, is this:—seeing that so many depart from the faith, there is no comfort for us but the being certain that "the foundation of God standeth sure, having this seal, The Lord knoweth them that are His. And let every one that calleth upon the name of the Lord depart from evil." (2 Tim. ii. 19). This then is the cause and efficacy of the similitude—that God knows His own! Then follows the similitude—that there are different vessels, some to honour and some to dishonour. By this it is proved at once, that the vessels do not prepare themselves, but that the Master prepares them. And this is what Paul means, where he saith, "Hath not the potter power over the clay, &c." (Rom. ix. 21). Thus, the similitude of Paul stands most effective: and that to prove, that there is no such thing as "Free-will" in the sight of God.

After this, follows the exhortation: "If a man purify himself from these," &c. and for what purpose this is, may be clearly collected from what we have said already. It does not follow from this, that the man can purify himself. Nay, if any thing be proved hereby it is this:—that "Free-will" can purify itself without grace. For he does not say, if grace purify a man; but, "if a man purify himself." But concerning imperative and conditional passages, we have said enough. Moreover, the similitude is not set forth in conditional, but in indicative verbs—that the elect and the reprobate, are as vessels of honour and of dishonour. In a word, if this fetch stand good, the whole argument of Paul comes to nothing. For in vain does he introduce vessels murmuring against God as the potter, if the fault plainly appear to be in the vessel, and not in the potter. For who would murmur at hearing him damned, who *merited* damnation!

Sect. CVI.—The other absurd objection, the Diatribe gathers from Madam Reason; who is called, Human Reason—that the fault is not to be laid on the vessel, but on the potter: especially, since He is such a potter, who *creates* the clay as well as *attempers* it.—"Whereas, (says the Diatribe) here the vessel is cast into eternal fire, which merited nothing: except that it had no power of its own."—

In no one place does the Diatribe more openly betray itself, than in this. For it is here heard to say, in other words indeed, but in the same meaning, that which Paul makes the impious to say, "Why doth He yet complain? for who hath resisted His will?" (Rom. ix. 19). This is that which Reason cannot receive, and cannot bear. This is that, which has offended so many men renowned for talent, who have been received through so many ages. Here they require, that God should act according to human laws, and do what seems right unto men, or cease to be God! 'His secrets of Majesty, say they, do not better His character in our estimation. Let Him render a reason why He is God, or why He wills and does that, which has no appearance of justice in it. It is as if one should ask a cobbler or a collar-maker to take the seat of judgment.'

Thus, flesh does not think God worthy of so great glory, that it should believe Him to be just and good, while He says and does those things which are above that, which the volume of Justin and the fifth book of Aristotle's Ethics, have defined to be justice. That Majesty which is the Creating Cause of all things, must bow to one of the dregs of His creation: and that Corycian cavern must, *vice versa*, fear its spectators. It is absurd that He should condemn him, who cannot avoid the merit of damnation. And, on account of this absurdity, it must be false, that "God has mercy on whom He will have mercy, and hardens whom He will." (Rom. ix. 18). He must be brought to order. He must have certain laws prescribed to Him, that he damn not any one but him, who, according to our judgment, deserves to be damned.

And thus, an effectual answer is given to Paul and his similitude. He must recall it, and allow it to be utterly ineffective: and must so attemper it, that this potter (according to the Diatribe's interpretation) make the vessel to dishonour from *merit preceding*: in the same manner in which He rejected some Jews on account of unbelief, and received Gentiles on account of faith. But if God work thus, and have respect unto merit, why do those impious ones murmur and expostulate? Why do they say, "Why doth He find fault? for who hath resisted His will? " (Rom. ix. 19). And what need was there for Paul to restrain them? For who wonders even, much less is indignant and expostulates, when any one is damned who merited damnation? Moreover where remains the power of the potter to make what vessel He will, if, being subject to merit and laws, He is not permitted to make what He *will*, but is required to make what He *ought*? The respect of merit militates against the power and liberty of making what He will: as is proved by that "good man of the house," who, when the workmen murmured and expostulated concerning their right, objected in answer, "Is it not lawful for me to do what I will with mine own? "—These are the arguments, which will not permit the gloss of the Diatribe to be of any avail.

Sect. CVII.—But let us, I pray you, suppose that God *ought to be* such an one, who should have respect unto *merit* in those who are to be *damned*. Must we not, in like manner, also require and grant, that He ought to have respect unto merit in those who are to be *saved*? For if we are to follow Reason, it is equally unjust, that the undeserving should be crowned, as that the undeserving should be damned. We will conclude, therefore, that God ought to justify from *merit preceding*, or we will declare Him to be unjust, as being one who delights in evil and wicked men, and who invites and crowns their impiety by rewards.—And then, woe unto you, sensibly miserable sinners, under that God! For who among you can be saved!

Behold, therefore, the iniquity of the human heart! When God saves the undeserving without merit, nay, justifies the impious with all their demerit, it does not accuse Him of iniquity, it does not expostulate with Him why He does it, although it is, in its own judgment, most iniquitous; but because it is to its own profit, and plausible, it considers it just and good. But when He damns the undeserving, this, because it is not to its own profit, is iniquitous; this is intolerable; here it expostulates, here it murmurs, here it blasphemes!

You see, therefore, that the Diatribe, together with its friends, do not, in this cause, judge according to equity, but according to the feeling sense of their own profit. For, if they regarded equity, they would expostulate with God when He crowned the undeserving, as they expostulate with Him when He damns the undeserving. And also, they would equally praise and proclaim God when He damns the undeserving, as they do when He saves the undeserving; for the iniquity in either instance is the same, if our own opinion be regarded:—unless they mean to say, that the iniquity is not equal, whether you laud Cain for his fratricide and make him a king, or cast the innocent Abel into prison and murder him!

Since, therefore, Reason praises God when He saves the undeserving, but accuses Him when He damns the undeserving; it stands convicted of not praising God as God, but as a certain one who serves its own profit; that is, it seeks, in God, itself and the things of itself, but seeks not God and the things of God. But if it be pleased with a God who crowns the undeserving, it ought not to be displeased with a God who damns the undeserving. For if He be just in the one instance, how shall He not be just in the other? seeing that, in the one instance, He pours forth grace and mercy upon the undeserving, and in the other, pours forth wrath and severity upon the undeserving? —He is, however, in both instances, monstrous and iniquitous in the sight of men, yet just and true in Himself. But, *how* it is just, that He should crown the undeserving, is incomprehensible now, but we shall see when we come there, where it will be no longer believed, but seen in revelation face to face. So also, *how* it is just, that He should damn the undeserving, is incomprehensible now, yet, we believe it, until the Son of Man shall be revealed!

Sect. CVIII.—The Diatribe, however, being itself bitterly offended at this similitude of the "potter" and the "clay," is not a little indignant, that it should be so pestered with it. And at last it comes to this. Having collected together different passages of Scripture, some of which seem to attribute all to man, and others all to grace, it angrily contends—'that the Scriptures on both sides should be understood according to *a sound interpretation*, and not received simply as they stand: and that, otherwise, if we still so press upon it that similitude, it is prepared to press upon us, in retaliation, those subjunctive and conditional passages; and especially, that of Paul, "If a man purify himself from these." This passage (it says) makes Paul to contradict himself, and to attribute all to man, unless a sound interpretation be brought in to make it clear. And if an interpretation be admitted here, in order to clear up the cause of grace, why should not an interpretation be admitted in the similitude of the potter also, to clear up the cause of "Free-will? "—

I answer: It matters not with me, whether you receive the passages in a simple sense, a twofold sense, or a hundred-fold sense. What I say is this: that by this sound interpretation of yours, nothing that you desire is either effected or proved. For that which is required to be proved, according to your design is, that "Free-will" cannot will good. Whereas, by this passage, "If a man purify himself from these," as it is a conditional sentence, neither any thing nor nothing is proved, for it is only an exhortation of Paul. Or, if you add the conclusion of the Diatribe, and say, 'the exhortation is in vain, if a man cannot purify himself;' then it proves, that "Free-will" can do all things without grace. And thus the Diatribe explodes itself.

We are waiting, therefore, for some passage of the Scripture, to shew us that this interpretation is right; we give no credit to those who hatch it out of their own brain. For, we deny, that any passage can be found which attributes all to man. We deny that Paul contradicts himself, where he says, "If a man shall purify himself from these." And we aver, that both the contradiction and the interpretation which exhorts it, are fictions; that they are both thought of, but neither of them proved. This, indeed, we confess, that, if we were permitted to augment the Scriptures by the conclusions and additions of the Diatribe, and to say, 'if we are not able to perform the things which are commanded, the precepts are given in vain;' then, in truth, Paul would militate against himself, as would the whole Scripture also: for then, the Scripture would be different from what it was before, and would prove that "Free-will" can do all things. What wonder, however, if he should then contradict himself again, where he saith, in another place, that "God worketh all in all! " (1 Cor. xii. 6).

But, however, the Scripture in question, thus augmented, makes not only against us, but against the Diatribe itself, which defined "Free-will" to be that, 'which cannot will any thing good.' Let, therefore, the Diatribe clear itself first, and say, how these two assertions agree with Paul:—'Free-will cannot will any thing good,' and also, 'If a man purify himself from these: therefore, man can purify himself, or it is said in vain.'—You see, therefore, that the Diatribe, being entangled and overcome by that similitude of the potter, only aims at evading it; not at all considering in the meantime, how its interpretation militates against its subject point, and how it is refuting and laughing at itself.

Sect. CIX.—But as to myself, as I said before, I never aimed at any kind of invented interpretation. Nor did I ever speak thus: 'Stretch forth thine hand; that is, grace shall stretch it forth.' All these things, are the Diatribe's own inventions concerning me, to the furtherance of its own cause. What I said was this:—that there is no contradiction in the words of the Scripture, nor any need of an invented interpretation to clear up a difficulty. But that the assertors of "Free-will" wilfully stumbled upon plain ground, and dream of contradictions where there are none.

For example: There is no contradiction in these Scriptures, "If a man purify himself," and, "God worketh all in all." Nor is it necessary to say, in order to explain this difficulty, God does something and man does something. Because, the former Scripture is conditional, which neither affirms or denies any work or power in man, but simply shews what work or power there *ought to be* in man. There is nothing figurative here; nothing that requires an invented interpretation; the words are plain, the sense is plain; that is, if you do not add conclusions and corruptions, after the manner of the Diatribe: for then, the sense would not be plain: not, however, by its own fault, but by the fault of the corruptor.

But the latter Scripture, "God worketh all in all," (1 Cor. xii. 6), is an indicative passage; declaring, that all works and all power are of God. How then do these two passages, the one of which says nothing of the power of man, and the other of which attributes all to God, contradict each other, and not rather sweetly harmonize. But the Diatribe is so drowned, suffocated in, and corrupted with, that sense of the carnal interpretation, 'that impossibilities are commanded in vain,' that it has no power over itself; but as soon as it hears an imperative or conditional word, it immediately tacks to it its indicative conclusions:—a certain thing is commanded: therefore, we are able to do it, and do do it, or the command is ridiculous.

On this side it bursts forth and boasts of its complete victory: as though it held it as a settled point, that these conclusions, as soon as hatched in thought, were established as firmly as the Divine Authority. And hence, it pronounces with all confidence, that in some places of the Scripture all is attributed to man: and that, therefore, there is a contradiction that requires interpretation. But it does not see, that all this is the figment of its own brain, no where confirmed by one iota of Scripture. And not only so, but that it is of such a nature, that if it were admitted, it would confute no one more directly than itself: because, if it proved any thing, it would prove that "Free-will" can do all things: whereas, it undertook to prove the directly contrary.

Sect. CX.—In the same way also it so continually repeats this:—"If man do nothing, there is no place for merit, and where there is no place for merit, there can be no place either for punishment or for reward."—

Here again, it does not see, that by these carnal arguments, it refutes itself more directly than it refutes us. For what do these conclusions prove, but that all merit is in the power of "Free-will? " And then, where is any room for grace? Moreover, supposing "Free-will" to merit a certain little, and grace the rest, why does "Free-will" receive the whole reward? Or, shall we suppose it to receive but a certain small portion of reward? Then, if there be a place for merit, in order that there might be a place for reward, the merit must be as great as the reward.

But why do I thus lose both words and time upon a thing of nought? For, even supposing the whole were established at which the Diatribe is aiming, and that merit is partly the work of man, and partly the work of God; yet it cannot define that work itself, what it is, of what kind it is, or how far it is to extend; therefore, its disputation is about nothing at all. Since, therefore, it cannot prove any one thing which it asserts, nor establish its interpretation nor contradiction, nor bring forward a passage that attributes all to man; and since all are the phantoms of its own cogitation, Paul's similitude of the "potter" and the "clay," stands unshaken and invincible—that it is not according to our "Free-will," what kind of vessels we are made. And as to the exhortations of Paul, "If a man purify himself from these," and the like, they are certain models, according to which, we ought to be formed; but they are not proofs of our working power, or of our desire.—Suffice it to have spoken thus upon these points, the HARDENING OF PHARAOH, the CASE OF ESAU, and the SIMILITUDE OF THE POTTER.

Sect. CXI.—The Diatribe at length comes to THE PASSAGES CITED BY LUTHER AGAINST "FREE-WILL," WITH THE INTENT TO REFUTE THEM.

The first passage, is that of Gen. vi. 3, "My Spirit shall not always remain in man; seeing that he is flesh." This passage it confutes variously. First, it says, 'that flesh, here, does not signify vile affection, but infirmity.' Then it augments the text of Moses, 'that this saying of his, refers to the men of that age, and not to the whole race of men: as if he had said, in these men.' And moreover, 'that it does not refer to all the men, even of that age; because, Noah was excepted,' And at last it says, 'that this word has, in the Hebrew, another signification; that it signifies the mercy, and not the severity, of God; according to the authority of Jerome.' By this it would, perhaps, persuade us, that since that saying did not apply to Noah but to the wicked, it was not the mercy, but the severity of God that was shewn to Noah, and the mercy, not the severity of God that was shewn to the wicked.

But let us away with these ridiculing vanities of the Diatribe: for there is nothing which it advances, which does not evince that it looks upon the Scriptures as mere fables. What Jerome here triflingly talks about, is nothing at all to me; for it is certain that he cannot prove any thing that he says. Nor is our dispute concerning the sense of Jerome, but concerning the sense of the Scripture. Let that perverter of the Scriptures attempt to make it appear, that the Spirit of God signifies indignation.—I say, that he is deficient in both parts of the necessary two-fold proof. First, he cannot produce one passage of the Scripture, in which the Spirit of God is understood as signifying indignation: for, on the contrary, kindness and sweetness are every where ascribed to the Spirit. And next, if he should prove that it is understood in any place as signifying indignation, yet, he cannot easily prove, that it follows of necessity, that it is so to be received in this place.

So also, let him attempt to make it appear, that "flesh," is here to be understood as signifying infirmity; yet, he is as deficient as ever in proof. For where Paul calls the Corinthians "carnal," he does not signify infirmity, but corrupt affection, because, he charges them with "strife and divisions;" which is not infirmity, or incapacity to receive "stronger" doctrine, but malice and that "old leaven," which he commands them to "purge out." (1 Cor. iii. 3; v. 7.) But let us examine the Hebrew.

Sect. CXII.—"My Spirit shall not always judge in man; for he is flesh." These are, verbatim, the words of Moses: and if we would away with our own dreams, the words as they there stand, are, I think, sufficiently plain and clear. And that they are the words of an angry God, is fully manifest, both from what precedes, and from what follows, together with the effect—the flood! The cause of their being spoken, was, the sons of men taking unto them wives from the mere lust of the flesh, and then, so filling the earth with violence, as to cause God to hasten the flood, and scarcely to delay that for "an hundred and twenty years," (Gen. vi. 1-3,) which, but for them, He would never have brought upon the earth at all. Read and study Moses, and you will plainly see that this is his meaning.

But it is no wonder that the Scriptures should be obscure, or that you should be enabled to establish from them, not only a *free*, but a *divine* will, where you are allowed so to trifle with them, as to seek to make out of them a Virgilian patch-work. And this is what you call, clearing up difficulties, and putting an end to all dispute by means of an interpretation! But it is with these trifling vanities that Jerome and Origen have filled the world: and have been the original cause of that pestilent practice—the not attending to the simplicity of the Scriptures.

It is enough for me to prove, that in this passage, the divine authority calls men "flesh;" and flesh, in that sense, that the Spirit of God could not continue among them, but was, at a decreed time, to be taken from them. And what God meant when He declared that His Spirit should not "always judge among men," is explained immediately afterwards, where He determines "an hundred and twenty years" as the time that He would still continue to judge.

Here He contrasts "spirit" with "flesh:" shewing that men being flesh, receive not the Spirit: and He, as being a Spirit, cannot approve of flesh: wherefore it is, that the Spirit, after "an hundred and twenty years," is to be withdrawn. Hence you may understand the passage of Moses thus—My Spirit, which is in Noah and in the other holy men, rebukes those impious ones, by the word of their preaching, and by their holy lives, (for to "judge among men," is to act among them in the office of the word; to reprove, to rebuke, to beseech them, opportunely and importunely,) but in vain: for they, being blinded and hardened by the flesh, only become the worse the more they are judged.—And so it ever is, that wherever the Word of God comes forth in the world, these men become the worse, the more they hear of it. And this is the reason why wrath is hastened, even as the flood was hastened at that time: because, they now, not only sin, but even despise grace: as Christ saith, "Light is come into the world, and men hate the light." (John iii. 19.)

Since, therefore, men, according to the testimony of God Himself, are "flesh," they can savour of nothing but flesh; so far is it from possibility that "Free-will" should do any thing but sin. And if, even while the Spirit of God is among them calling and teaching, they only become worse, what will they do when left to themselves without the Spirit of God!

Sect. CXIII.—Nor is it at all to the purpose, your saying,—'that Moses is speaking with reference to the men of that age'—for the same applies unto all men; because, all are flesh; as Christ saith, "That which is born of the flesh is flesh." (John iii. 6.) And how deep a corruption that is, He Himself shews in the same chapter, where He saith, "Except a man be born again, he cannot enter the kingdom of God." Let, therefore, the Christian know, that Origen and Jerome, together with all their train, perniciously err, when they say, that "flesh" ought not, in these passages, to be understood as meaning 'corrupt affection:' because, that of 1 Cor. iii. 3, "For ye are yet carnal," signifies ungodliness. For Paul means, that there are some among them still ungodly: and moreover, that even the saints, in as far as they savour of carnal things, are "carnal," though justified by the Spirit.

In a word; you may take this as a general observation upon the Scriptures.—Wherever mention is made of "flesh" in contradistinction to "spirit," you may there, by "flesh," understand every thing that is contrary to spirit: as in this passage, "The flesh profiteth nothing." (John vi. 63.) But where it is used abstractedly, there you may understand the corporal state and nature: as "They twain shall be one flesh," (Matt. xix. 5,) "My flesh is meat indeed," (John vi. 55,) "The Word was made flesh," (John i. 14.) In such passages, you may make a figurative alteration in the Hebrew, and for 'flesh,' say 'body'. For in the Hebrew tongue, the one term "flesh" embraces in signification our two terms, 'flesh' and 'body.' And I could wish that these two terms had been distinctively used throughout the Canon of the Scripture.—Thus then, I presume, my passage Gen. vi. still stands directly against "Free-will:" since "flesh" is proved to be that which Paul declares, Rom. viii. 5-8, cannot be subject to God, as we may there see; and since the Diatribe itself asserts, 'that it cannot will any thing good.'

Sect. CXIV.—Another passage is that of Gen. viii. 21, "The thought and imagination of man's heart, is evil from his youth." And that also Gen. vi. 5, "Every imagination of man's heart is only evil continually." These passages it evades thus:—"The proneness to evil which is in most men, does not, wholly, take away the freedom of the will."—

Does God, I pray you, here speak of 'most men,' and not rather of all men, when, after the flood, as it were repenting, He promises to those who were then remaining, and to those who were to come, that He would no more bring a flood upon the earth "for man's sake:" assigning this as the reason:—because man is prone to evil! As though He had said, If I should act according to the wickedness of man, I should never cease from bringing a flood. Wherefore, henceforth, I will not act according to *that which he deserves, &c.* You see, therefore, that God, both before and after the flood, declares that man is evil: so that what the Diatribe says about 'most men,' amounts to nothing at all.

Moreover, a proneness or inclination to evil, appears to the Diatribe, to be a matter of little moment; as though it were in our own power to keep ourselves upright, or to restrain it: whereas the Scripture, by that proneness, signifies the continual bent and impetus of the will, to evil. Why does not the Diatribe here appeal to the Hebrew? Moses says nothing there about proneness. But, that you may have no room for cavillation, the Hebrew, (Gen. vi. 5), runs thus:—"CHOL IETZER MAHESCHEBOTH LIBBO RAK RA CHOL HAIOM:" that is, "Every imagination of the thought of the heart is only evil all days." He does not say, that he is intent or prone to evil; but that, evil altogether, and nothing but evil, is thought or imagined by man throughout his whole life. The nature of his evil is described to be that, which neither does nor can do any thing but evil, as being evil itself: for, according to the testimony of Christ, an evil tree can bring forth none other than evil fruit. (Matt. vii. 17-18).

And as to the Diatribe's pertly objecting—"Why was time given for repentance, then, if no part of repentance depend on Free-will, and all things be conducted according to the law of necessity."—

I answer: You may make the same objection to all the precepts of God; and say, Why does He command at all, if all things take place of necessity? He commands, in order to instruct and admonish, that men, being humbled under the knowledge of their evil, might come to grace, as I have fully shewn already.—This passage, therefore, still remains invincible against the freedom of the will!

Sect. CXV.—The third passage is that in Isaiah xl. 2.—"She hath received at the Lord's hand double for all her sins."—"Jerome (says the Diatribe) interprets this concerning the divine vengeance, not concerning His grace given in return for evil deeds."—

I hear you.—Jerome says so: therefore, it is true! —I am disputing about Isaiah, who here speaks in the clearest words, and Jerome is cast in my teeth; a man, (to say no worse of him) of neither judgment nor application. Where now is that promise of ours, by which we agreed at the outset, 'that we would go according to the Scriptures, and not according to the commentaries of men?' The whole of this chapter of Isaiah, according to the testimony of the evangelists, where they mention it as referring to John the Baptist, "the voice of one crying," speaks of the remission of sins proclaimed by the Gospel. But we will allow Jerome, after his manner, to thrust in the blindness of the Jews for an historical sense, and his own trifling vanities for an allegory; and, turning all grammar upside down, we will understand this passage as speaking of vengeance, which speaks of the remission of sins.—But, I pray you, what vengeance is fulfilled in the preaching of Christ? Let us, however, see how the words run in the Hebrew.

"Comfort ye, comfort ye My people, (in the vocative) or, My people (in the objective) saith your God."—He, I presume, who commands to "comfort," is not executing vengeance! It then follows.

"Speak ye to the heart of Jerusalem, and cry unto her." (Isa. xl. 1-2).—"Speak ye to the heart" is a Hebraism; and signifies to speak good things, sweet things, and alluring things. Thus, Shechem, Gen. xxxiv. 3, speaks to the heart of Dinah, whom he defiled: that is, when she was heavy-hearted, he comforted her with tender words, as our translator has rendered it. And what those good and sweet things are, which are commanded to be proclaimed to their comfort, the prophet explains directly afterwards: saying,

"That her warfare is accomplished, her iniquity is pardoned; for she hath received of the Lord's hand double for all her sins."—"Her warfare," (militia,) which our translators have rendered "her evil," (malitia), is considered by the Jews, those audacious grammarians, to signify an appointed time. For thus they understand that passage Job vii. 1. "Is there not an appointed time to man upon earth? " that is, his time is determinately appointed. But I receive it simply, and according to grammatical propriety, as signifying "warfare." Wherefore, you may understand Isaiah, as speaking with reference to the race and labour of the people under the law, who are, as it were, fighting on a platform. Hence

Paul compares both the preachers and the hearers of the word to soldiers: as in the case of Timothy, 2 Tim. ii. 3, whom he commands to be "a good soldier," and to "fight the good fight." And, 1 Cor. ix. 24, he represents them as running "in a race:" and observes also, that "no one is crowned except he strive lawfully." He equips the Ephesians and Thessalonians with arms, Ephes. vi. 10-18. And he glories, himself, that he had "fought the good fight," 2 Tim. iv. 7.: with many like instances in other places. So also at 1 Samuel ii. 22, it is in the Hebrew, "And the sons of Eli slept with the women who fought (*militantibus*) at the door of the tabernacle of the congregation:" of whose fighting, Moses makes mention in Exodus. And hence it is, that the God of that people is called the "Lord of Sabaoth:" that is, the Lord of warfare and of armies.

Isaiah, therefore, is proclaiming, that the warfare of the people under the law, who are pressed down under the law as a burthen intolerable, as Peter saith, Acts xv. 7-10, is to be at an end; and that they being freed from the law, are to be translated into the new warfare of the Spirit. Moreover, this end of their most hard warfare, and this translation to the new and all-free warfare, is not given unto them on account of their merit, seeing that, they could not endure it; nay, it is rather given unto them on account of their demerit; for their warfare is ended, by their iniquities being freely forgiven them.

The words are not 'obscure or ambiguous' here. He saith, that their warfare was ended, by their iniquities being forgiven them: manifestly signifying, that the soldiers under the law, did not fulfil the law, and could not fulfil it: and that they only carried on a warfare of sin, and were soldier-sinners. As though God had said, I am compelled to forgive them their sins, if I would have My law fulfilled by them; nay, I must take away My law entirely when I forgive them; for I see they cannot but sin, and the more so the more they fight; that is, the more they strive to fulfil the law by their own powers. For in the Hebrew, "her iniquity is pardoned" signifies, its being done in gratuitous good-will. And it is thus that the iniquity is pardoned; without any merit, nay, under all demerit; as is shewn in what follows, "for she hath received at the Lord's hand double for all her sins."—That is, as I said before, not only the remission of sins, but an end of the warfare: which is nothing more or less than this:—the law being taken out of the way, which is "the strength of sin," and their sin being pardoned, which is "the sting of death," they reign in a two-fold liberty by the victory of Jesus Christ: which is what Isaiah means when he says, "from the hand of the Lord:" for they do not obtain it by their own powers, or on account of their own merit, but they receive it from the conqueror and giver, Jesus Christ.

And that which is, according to the Hebrew, "*in* all her sins," is, according to the Latin, "*for* all her sins," or, "*on account of* all her sins." As in Hosea xii. 12, "Israel served *in* a wife:" that is, "*for* a wife." And so also in Psalm lix. 3, "They lay in wait *in* my soul;" that is, "*for* my soul." Isaiah therefore is here pointing out to us those merits of ours, by which we imagine we are to obtain the two-fold liberty; that of the end of the law-warfare, and that of the pardon of sin; making it appear to us, that they were nothing but sins, nay, all sins.

Could I, therefore, suffer this most beautiful passage, which stands invincible against "Free-will," to be thus bedaubed with Jewish filth cast upon it by Jerome and the Diatribe? —God forbid! No! My Isaiah stands victor over "Free-will"; and clearly shews, that grace is given, not to merits or to the endeavours of "Free-will," but to sins and demerits; and that "Free-will" with all its powers, can do nothing but carry on a warfare of sin; so that, the very law which it imagines to be given as a help, becomes intolerable to it, and makes it the greater sinner, the longer it is under its warfare.

Sect. CXVI.—But as to the Diatribe disputing thus—"Although sin abound by the law, and where sin has abounded, grace much more abound; yet it does not therefore follow, that man, doing by God's help what is pleasing to Him, cannot by works morally good, prepare himself for the favour of God."—

Wonderful! Surely the Diatribe does not speak this out of its own head, but has taken it out of some paper or other, sent or received from another quarter, and inserted it in its book! For it certainly can neither see nor hear the meaning of these words! If sin abound by the law, how is it possible that a man can prepare himself by moral works, for the favour of God? How can works avail any thing, when the law avails nothing? Or, what else is it for sin to abound by the law, but for all the works, done according to the law, to become sins? —But of this elsewhere. But what does it mean when it says, that man, assisted by the help of God, can prepare himself by moral works? Are we here disputing concerning the divine assistance, or concerning "Free-will"? For what is not possible through the divine assistance? But the fact is, as I said before, the Diatribe cares nothing for the cause it has taken up, and therefore it snores and yawns forth such words as these.

But however, it adduces Cornelius the centurion, Acts x. 31, as an example: observing—'that his prayers and alms pleased God before he was baptized, and before he was inspired by the Holy Spirit.'

I have read Luke upon the Acts too, and yet I never perceived from one single syllable, that the works of Cornelius were morally good without the Holy Spirit, as the Diatribe dreams. But on the contrary, I find that he was "a just man and one that feared God:" for thus Luke calls him. But to call a man without the Holy Spirit, "a just man and one that feared God," is the same thing as calling Baal, Christ!

Moreover, the whole context shews, that Cornelius was "clean" before God, even upon the testimony of the vision which was sent down from heaven to Peter, and which reproved him. Are then the righteousness and faith of Cornelius set forth by Luke in such words and attending circumstances, and do the Diatribe and its Sophists remain blind with open eyes, or see the contrary, in a light of words and an evidence of circumstances so clear? Such is their want of diligence in reading and contemplating the Scriptures: and yet, they must brand them with the assertion that they are 'obscure and ambiguous.' But grant it, that he was not as yet baptized, nor had as yet heard the word concerning Christ risen from the dead:—does it therefore follow, that He was without the Holy Spirit? According to this, you will say that John the Baptist and his parents, the mother of Christ, and Simeon, were without the Holy Spirit! —But let us take leave of such thick darkness!

Sect. CXVII.—The fourth passage is that of Isaiah in the same chapter. "All flesh is grass, and all the glory of it as the flower of grass: the grass is withered, the flower of grass is fallen: because the Spirit of the Lord hath blown upon it." (Isa. xl. 6-7).—

This Scripture appears to my friend Diatribe, to be treated with violence, by being dragged in as applicable to the causes of grace, and "Free-will." Why so, I pray? 'Because, (it says), Jerome understands "spirit" to signify indignation, and "flesh" to signify the infirm condition of man, which cannot stand against God.' Here again the trifling vanities of Jerome are cast in my teeth instead of Isaiah. And I find I have more to do in fighting against that wearisomeness, with which the Diatribe with so much diligence (to use no harsher term) wears me out, than I have in fighting against the Diatribe itself. But I have given my opinion upon the sentiment of Jerome already.

Let me beg permission of the Diatribe to compare this gentleman with himself. He says 'that "flesh," signifies the infirm condition of man; and "spirit," the divine indignation.'

Has then the divine indignation nothing else to "wither" but that miserable infirm condition of man, which it ought rather to raise up?

This, however, is more excellent still. 'The "flower of grass," is the glory which arises from the prosperity of corporal things.'

The Jews gloried in their temple, their circumcision, and their sacrifices, and the Greeks in their wisdom. Therefore, the "flower of grass," is the glory of the flesh, the righteousness of works, and the wisdom of the world.—How then are righteousness and wisdom called by the Diatribe, 'corporal things?' And after all, what have these to do with Isaiah, who interprets his own meaning in his own words, saying, "Surely the people is grass? " He does not say; Surely the infirm condition of man is grass, but "the people;" and affirms it with an asseveration. And what is the people? Is it the infirm condition of man only? But whether Jerome, by 'the infirm condition of man' means the whole creation together, or the miserable lot and state of man only, I am sure I know not. Be it, however, which it may, he certainly makes the divine indignation to gain a glorious renown and a noble spoil, from withering a miserable creation or a race of wretched men, and not rather, from scattering the proud, pulling down the mighty from their seat, and sending the rich empty away: as Mary sings! (Luke i. 51-53).

Sect. CXVIII.—But let us dispatch these hobgoblins of glosses, and take Isaiah's words as they are. "The people (he saith) is grass." "People" does not signify flesh merely, or the infirm condition of human nature, but it comprehends every thing that there is in people—the rich, the wise, the just, the saints. Unless you mean to say, that the pharisees, the elders, the princes, the nobles, and the rich men, were not of the people of the Jews! The "flower of grass" is rightly called their glory, because it was in their kingdom, their government, and above all, in the law, in God, in righteousness, and in wisdom, that they gloried: as Paul shews, Rom. ii. iii and ix.

When, therefore, Isaiah saith, "All flesh," what else does he mean but all "grass," or, all "people? " For he does not say "flesh" only, but "all flesh." And to "people" belong soul, body, mind, reason, judgment, and whatever is called or found to be most excellent in man. For when he says "all flesh is grass," he excepts nothing but the spirit which withereth it. Nor does he omit any thing when he says, "the people is grass." Speak, therefore, of "Free-will," speak of anything that can be called the highest or the lowest in the people,—Isaiah calls the whole "flesh" and grass! " Because, those three terms "flesh," "grass," and "people," according to his interpretation who is himself the writer of the book, signify in that place, the same thing.

Moreover, you yourself affirm, that the wisdom of the Greeks and the righteousness of the Jews which were withered by the Gospel, were "grass" and "the flower of grass." Do you then think, that the wisdom which the Greeks had was not the most excellent? and that the righteousness which the Jews wrought was not the most excellent? If you do, shew us what was more excellent. With what assurance then is it, that you, Philip-like, flout and say,

—"If any one shall contend, that that which is most excellent in the nature of man, is nothing else but "flesh;" that is, that it is impious, I will agree with him, when he shall have proved his assertion by testimonies from the Holy Scripture? "—

You have here Isaiah, who cries with a loud voice that the people, devoid of the Spirit of the Lord, is "flesh;" although you will not understand him thus. You have also your own confession, where you said, (though unwittingly perhaps), that the wisdom of the Greeks was "grass," or the glory of grass; which is the same thing as saying, it was "flesh."—Unless you mean to say, that the wisdom of the Greeks did not pertain to reason, or to the EGEMONICON, as you say, that is, *the principal part of man*. If, therefore, you will not deign to listen to me, listen to yourself; where, being caught in the powerful trap of truth, you speak the truth.

You have moreover the testimony of John, "That which is born of the flesh is flesh, and that which is born of the Spirit is spirit." (John iii. 6). You have, I say, this passage, which makes it evidently manifest, that what is not born of the Spirit, is flesh: for if it be not so, the distinction of Christ could not subsist, who divides all men into two distinct divisions, "flesh" and "spirit." This passage you floutingly pass by, as if it did not give you the information you want, and betake yourself somewhere else, as usual; just dropping as you go along an observation, that John is here saying, that those who believe are born of God, and are made the sons of God, nay, that they are gods, and new creatures. You pay no regard, therefore, to the conclusion that is to be drawn from this division, but merely tell us at your ease, what persons are on one side of the division: thus confidently relying upon your rhetorical manoeuvre, as though there were no one likely to discover an evasion and dissimulation so subtlely managed.

Sect. CXIX.–It is difficult to refrain from concluding, that you are, in this passage, crafty and double-dealing. For he who treats of the Scriptures with that prevarication and hypocrisy which you practise in treating of them, may have face enough to pretend, that he is not as yet fully acquainted with the Scriptures, and is willing to be taught; when, at the same time, he wills nothing less, and merely prates thus, in order to cast a reproach upon the all-clear light of the Scriptures, and to cover with the best cloak his determinate perseverance in his own opinions. Thus the Jews, even to this day, pretend, that what Christ, the Apostles, and the whole church have taught, is not to be proved by the Scriptures. The papists too pretend, that they do not yet fully understand the Scriptures; although the very stones speak aloud the truth. But perhaps you are waiting for a passage to be produced from the Scriptures, which shall contain these letters and syllables, 'The principal part of man is flesh:' or, 'That which is most excellent in man is flesh:' otherwise, you will declare yourself an invincible victor. Just as though the Jews should require, that a portion be produced from the prophets, which shall consist of these letters, 'Jesus the son of the carpenter, who was born of the Virgin Mary in Bethlehem, is the Messiah the Son of God! '

Here, where you are closely put to it by a plain sentence, you challenge us to produce letters and syllables. In another place, where you are overcome both by the sentence and by the letters too, you have recourse to 'tropes,' to 'difficulties,' and to 'sound interpretations.' And there is no place, in which you do not invent something whereby to contradict the Scriptures. At one time, you fly to the interpretations of the Fathers: at another, to absurdities of Reason: and when neither of these will serve your turn, you dwell on that which is irrelevant or contingent: yet with an especial care, that you are not caught by the passage immediately in point. But what shall I call you? Proteus is not half a Proteus compared with you! Yet after all you cannot get off. What victories did the Arians boast of, because these syllables and letters, HOMOOUSIOS, were not to be found in the Scriptures? Considering it nothing to the purpose, that the same thing could be most effectually proved in other words. But whether or not this be a sign of a good, (not to say pious,) mind, and a mind desiring to be taught, let impiety or iniquity itself be judge.

Take your victory, then; while we, as the vanquished confess, that these characters and syllables, 'That, which is most excellent in man is nothing but flesh,' is not to be found in the Scriptures. But just behold what a victory you have gained, when we most abundantly prove, that though it is not found in the Scriptures, that one detached portion, or 'that which is most excellent,' or the 'principal part,' of man is flesh, but that the whole of man is flesh! And not only so, but that the whole people is flesh! And further still, that the whole human race is flesh! For Christ saith, "That which is born of the flesh is flesh." Do you here set about your difficulty-solving, your trope-inventing, and searching for the interpretations of the Fathers; or, turning quite another way, enter upon a dissertation on the Trojan war, in order to avoid seeing and hearing this passage now adduced.

We do not believe only, but we see and experience, that the whole human race is "*born* of the flesh;" and therefore, we are compelled to believe upon the word of Christ, that which we do not see; that the whole human race "*is* flesh." Do we now then give the Sophists any room to doubt and dispute, whether or not the principal (*egemonica*) part of man be comprehended in the whole man, in the whole people, in the whole race of men? We know, however, that in the whole human race, both the body and soul are comprehended, together with all their powers and works, with all their vices and virtues, with all their wisdom and folly, with all their righteousness and unrighteousness! All things are "flesh;" because, all things savour of the flesh, that is, of their own; and are, as Paul saith, Without the glory of God, and the Spirit of God! (Rom. iii. 23; viii. 5-9).

Sect. CXX.—And as to your saying—"Yet *every* affection of man is not flesh. There is an affection called, soul: there is an affection called, spirit: by which, we aspire to what is meritoriously good, as the philosophers aspired: who taught, that we should rather die a thousand deaths than commit one base action, even though we were assured that men would never know it, and that God would pardon it."—

I answer: He who believes nothing certainly, may easily believe and say any thing. I will not ask you, but let your friend Lucian ask you, whether you can bring forward any one out of the whole human race, let him be two-fold or seven-fold greater than Socrates himself, whoever performed this of which you speak, and which you say they taught. Why then do you thus babble in vanities of words? Could they ever aspire to that which is meritoriously good, who did not even know what good is?

If I should ask you for some of the brightest examples of your meritorious good, you would say, perhaps, that it was meritoriously good when men died for their country, for their wives and children, and for their parents; or when they refrained from lying, or from treachery; or when they endured exquisite torments, as did Q. Scevola, M. Regulus, and others. But what can you point out in all those men, but an external shew of works. For did you ever see their hearts? Nay, it was manifest from the very appearance of their works, that they did all these things for their own glory; so much so, that they were not even ashamed to confess, and to boast, that they sought their own glory. For the Romans, according to their own testimonies, did whatever they did of virtue or valour, from a thirst after glory. The same did the Greeks, the same did the Jews, the same do all the race of men.

But though this be meritoriously good before men, yet, before God, nothing is less meritoriously good than all this; nay, it is most impious, and the greatest of sacrilege; because, they did it not for the glory of God, nor that they might glorify God, but with the most impious of all robbery. For as they were robbing God of His glory and taking it to themselves, they never were farther from meritorious good, never more base, than when they were shining in their most exalted virtues. How could they do what they did for the glory of God, when they neither knew God nor His glory? Not, however, because it did not appear, but because the "flesh" did not permit them to see the glory of God, from their fury and madness after their own glory. This, therefore, is that right-ruling 'spirit,' that 'principal part of man, which aspires to what is meritoriously good'—it is a plunderer of the divine glory, and an usurper of the divine Majesty! and then the most so, when men are at the highest of their meritorious good, and the most glittering in their brightest virtues! Deny, therefore, if you can, that these are "flesh" and carried away by an impious affection.

But I do not believe that the Diatribe can be so much offended at the expression, where man is said to be, either "flesh" or "spirit;" because a Latin would here say, Man is either carnal or spiritual. For this particularity, as well as many others, must be granted to the Hebrew tongue, that when it says, Man is "flesh" or "spirit," its signification is the same as ours is, when we say, Man is carnal or spiritual. The same signification which the Latins also convey, when they say, 'The wolf is destructive to the folds,' 'Moisture is favourable to the young corn:' or when they say, 'This fellow is iniquity and evil itself.' So also the Holy Scripture, by a force of expression, calls man "flesh;" that is, carnality itself; because it savours too much of, nay, of nothing but, those things which are of the flesh: and "spirit," because he savours of, seeks, does, and can endure, nothing but those things which are of the spirit.

Unless, perhaps, the Diatribe should still make this remaining query—Supposing the whole of man to be "flesh," and that which is most excellent in man to be called "flesh," must therefore that which is called "flesh" be at once called ungodly? —I call him ungodly who is without the Spirit of God. For the Scripture saith, that the Spirit was therefore given, that He might justify the ungodly. And as Christ makes a distinction between the spirit and the flesh, saying, "That which is born of the flesh is flesh," and adds, that that which is born of the flesh "cannot see the kingdom of God" (John iii.

3-6), it evidently follows, that whatsoever is flesh is ungodly, under the wrath of God, and a stranger to the kingdom of God. And if it be a stranger to the kingdom of God, it necessarily follows, that it is under the kingdom and spirit of Satan. For there is no *medium* between the kingdom of God and the kingdom of Satan; they are mutually and eternally opposed to each other.

These are the arguments that prove, that the most exalted virtues among the nations, the highest perfections of the philosophers, and the greatest excellencies among men, appear indeed, in the sight of men, to be meritoriously virtuous and good, and are so called; but that, in the sight of God, they are in truth "flesh," and subservient to the kingdom of Satan: that is, ungodly, sacrilegious, and, in every respect, evil!

Sect. CXXI.—But pray let us suppose the sentiment of the Diatribe to stand good—'that every affection is not "flesh;" that is, ungodly; but is that which is called good and sound spirit.'—Only observe what absurdity must hence follow; not only with respect to human reason, but with respect to the Christian religion, and the most important Articles of Faith. For if that which is most excellent in man be not ungodly, nor utterly depraved, nor damnable, but that which is flesh only, that is the grosser and viler affections, what sort of a Redeemer shall we make Christ? Shall we rate the price of His blood so low as to say, that it redeemed that part of man only which is the most vile, and that the most excellent part of man has power to work its own salvation, and does not want Christ? Henceforth then, I must preach Christ as the Redeemer, not of the whole man, but of his vilest part; that is, of his flesh; but that the man himself is his own redeemer, in his better part!

Have it, therefore, which way you will. If the better part of man be sound, it does not want Christ as a Redeemer. And if it does not want Christ, it triumphs in a glory above that of Christ: for it takes care of the redemption of the better part itself, whereas Christ only takes care of that of the vile part. And then, moreover, the kingdom of Satan will come to nothing at all, for it will reign only in the viler part of man, because the man himself will rule over the better part.

So that, by this doctrine of yours, concerning 'the principal part of man,' it will come to pass, that man will be exalted above Christ and the devil both: that is, he will be made God of gods, and Lord of lords! —Where is now that 'probable opinion' which asserted 'that "Free-will" cannot will anything good? ' It here contends, that it is a principal part, meritoriously good, and sound; and that, it does not even want Christ, but can do more than God Himself and the devil can do, put together!

I say this, that you may again see, how eminently perilous a matter it is to attempt sacred and divine things, without the Spirit of God, in the temerity of human reason. If, therefore, Christ be the Lamb of God that taketh away the sins of the world, it follows, that the whole world is under sin, damnation, and the devil. Hence your distinction between the *principal parts*, and the parts *not principal*, profits you nothing: for the *world*, signifies *men, savouring of nothing but the things of the world, throughout all their faculties*.

Sect. CXXII.—"If the whole man, (says the Diatribe) even when regenerated by faith, is nothing else but "flesh," where is the "spirit" born of the Spirit? Where is the child of God? Where is the new-creature? I want information upon these points."—Thus the Diatribe

Where now! Where now! my very dear friend, Diatribe! What dream now! You demand to be informed, how the "spirit" born of the Spirit can be "flesh." Oh how elated, how secure of victory do you insultingly put this question to me, as though it were impossible for me to stand my ground here.—All this while, you are abusing the authority of the Ancients: for they say 'that there are certain *seeds of good* implanted in the minds of men. But, however, whether you use, or whether abuse, the authority of the Ancients, it is all one to me: you will see by and by what you believe, when you believe men prating out of their own brain, without the Word of God. Though perhaps your care about religion does not give you much concern, as to what any one believes; since you so easily believe men, without at all regarding, whether or not that which they say, be certain or uncertain in the sight of God. And I also wish to be informed, when I ever taught that, with which you so freely and publicly charge me. Who would be so mad as to say, that he who is "born of the Spirit," is nothing but "flesh? "

I make a manifest distinction between "flesh" and "spirit," as things that directly militate against each other; and I say, according to the divine oracles, that the man who is not regenerated by faith "is flesh;" but I say, that he who is thus regenerated, is no longer flesh, excepting as to the remnants of the flesh, which war against the first fruits of the Spirit received. Nor do I suppose you wish to attempt to charge me, invidiously, with any thing wrong here; if you do, there is no charge that you could more iniquitously bring against me.

But you either understand nothing of my side of the subject, or else you find yourself unequal to the magnitude of the cause; by which you are, perhaps, so overwhelmed and confounded, that you do not rightly know what you say against me, or for yourself. For where you declare it to be your belief, upon the authority of the ancients, 'that there are certain seeds of good implanted in the minds of men, you must surely quite forget yourself; because, you before asserted, 'that "Free-will" cannot will any thing good.' And how 'cannot will any thing good,' and 'certain seeds of good' can stand in harmony together, I know not. Thus am I perpetually compelled to remind you of the subject-design with which you set out; from which you with perpetual forgetfulness depart, and take up something contrary to your professed purpose.

Sect. CXXIII.—Another passage is that of Jeremiah x. 23, "I know, O Lord, that the way of man is not in himself: it is not in man that walketh to direct his steps."—This passage (says the Diatribe) rather applies "to the events of prosperity, than to the power of "Free-will."—

Here again the Diatribe, with its usual audacity, introduces a gloss according to its own pleasure, as though the Scripture were fully under its control. But in order to any one's considering the sense and intent of the prophet, what need was there for the opinion of a man of so great authority! —Erasmus says so! it is enough! it must be so! If this liberty of glossing as they lust, be permitted the adversaries, what point is there which they might not carry? Let therefore Erasmus shew us the validity of this gloss from the scope of the context, and we will believe him.

I, however, will shew from the scope of the context, that the prophet, when he saw that he taught the ungodly with so much earnestness in vain, was at once convinced, that his word could avail nothing unless God should teach them within; and that, therefore, it was not in man to hear the Word of God, and to will good. Seeing this judgment of God, he was alarmed, and asks of God that He would correct him, but with judgment, if he had need to be corrected; and that he might not be given up to His divine wrath with the ungodly, whom he suffered to be hardened and to remain in unbelief.

But let us suppose that the passage is to be understood concerning the events of adversity and prosperity, what will you say, if this gloss should go most directly to overthrow "Free-will? " This new evasion is invented, indeed, that ignorant and lazy deceivers may consider it satisfactory. The same which they also had in view who invented that evasion, 'the necessity of the consequence.' And so drawn away are they by these newly-invented terms, that they do not see that they are, by these evasions, ten-fold more effectually entangled and caught than they would have been without them.—As in the present instance: if the event of these things which are temporal, and over which man, Gen. i. 26-30, was constituted lord, be not in our own power, how, I pray you, can that heavenly thing, the grace of God, which depends on the will of God alone, be in our own power? Can that endeavour of "Free-will" attain unto eternal salvation, which is not able to retain a farthing or a hair of the head? When we have no power to obtain the creature, shall it be said that we have power to obtain the Creator? What madness is this! The endeavouring of man, therefore, unto good or unto evil, when applied to events, is a thousand-fold more enormous; because, he is in both much more deceived, and has much less liberty, than he has in striving after money, or glory, or pleasure. What an excellent evasion is this gloss, then, which denies the liberty of man in trifling and created events, and preaches it up in the greatest and divine events? This is as if one should say, Codrus is not able to pay a groat, but he is able to pay thousands of thousands of pounds! I am astonished that the Diatribe, having all along so inveighed against that tenet of Wycliff, 'that all things take place of necessity,' should now itself grant, that events come upon us of necessity.

—"And even if you do (says the Diatribe) forcedly twist this to apply to "Free-will," all confess that no one can hold on a right course of life without the grace of God. Nevertheless, we still strive ourselves with all our powers: for we pray daily, 'O Lord my God, direct my goings in Thy sight.' He, therefore, who implores aid, does not lay aside his own endeavours."—

The Diatribe thinks, that it matters not what it answers, so that it does not remain silent with nothing to say; and then, it would have what it does say to appear satisfactory; such a vain confidence has it in its own authority. It ought here to have proved, whether or not we *strive* by our *own powers*; whereas, it proved, that he who prays *attempts something*. But, I pray, is it here laughing at us, or mocking the papists? For he who prays, prays by the Spirit; nay, it is the Spirit Himself that prays in us (Rom. viii. 26-27). How then is the power of "Free-will" proved by the strivings of the Holy Spirit? Are "Free-will" and the Holy Spirit, with the Diatribe, one and the same thing? Or, are we disputing now about what the Holy Spirit can do? The Diatribe, therefore, leaves me this passage of Jeremiah uninjured and invincible; and only produces the gloss out of its own brain. I also can 'strive by my own powers:' and Luther, *will be compelled* to believe this gloss,—*if he will*!

Sect. CXXIV.—There is that passage of Prov. xvi. 1, 9, also, "It is of man to prepare the heart, but of the Lord to govern the tongue," which the Diatribe says—'refers to events of things.'—

As though this the Diatribe's own saying would satisfy us, without any farther authority. But however, it is quite sufficient, that, allowing the sense of these passages to be concerning the events of things, we have evidently come off victorious by the arguments which we have just advanced: 'that, if we have no such thing as Freedom of Will in our own things and works, much less have we any such thing in divine things and works.'

But mark the great acuteness of the Diatribe—"How can it be of man to prepare the heart, when Luther affirms that all things are carried on by necessity? "—

I answer: If the *events* of things be not in our power, as you say, how can it be in man to perform the *causing acts*? The same answer which you gave me, the same receive yourself! Nay, we are commanded to work the more for this very reason, because all things future are to us uncertain: as saith Ecclesiastes, "In the morning sow thy seed, and in the evening hold not thine hand: for thou knowest not which shall prosper, either this or that" (Eccles. xi. 6). All things future, I say, are to us uncertain in knowledge, but necessary in event. The necessity strikes into us a fear of God that we presume not, or become secure, while the uncertainty works in us a trusting, that we sink not in despair.

Sect. CXXV.—But the Diatribe returns to harping upon its old string—'that in the book of Proverbs, many things are said in confirmation of "Free-will": as this, "Commit thy works unto the Lord." Do you hear this (says the Diatribe,) *thy works*? '—

Many things in confirmation! What because there are, in that book, many imperative and conditional verbs, and pronouns of the second person! For it is upon these foundations that you build your proof of the Freedom of the Will. Thus,

"Commit"—therefore thou canst commit thy works: therefore thou doest them. So also this passage, "I am thy God," (Isa. xli. 10), you will understand thus:—that is, Thou makest Me thy God. "Thy faith hath saved thee" (Luke vii. 50): do you hear this word "thy? " therefore, expound it thus: Thou makest thy faith: and then you have proved "Free-will." Nor am I here merely game-making; but I am shewing the Diatribe, that there is nothing serious on its side of the subject.

This passage also in the same chapter, "The Lord hath made all things for Himself; yea, even the wicked for the day of evil," (Prov. xvi. 4), it modifies by its own words, and excuses God as—'having never created a creature evil.'—

As though I had spoken concerning the *creation*, and not rather concerning that *continual operation of God upon the things created*; in which operation, God acts upon the wicked; as we have before shewn in the case of Pharaoh. But He creates the wicked, not by creating wickedness or a wicked creature; (which is impossible) but, from the operation of God, a wicked man is made, or created, from a corrupt seed; not from the fault of the Maker, but from that of the material.

Nor does that of "The heart of the king is in the Lord's hand: He inclineth it whithersoever He will," (Prov. xxi. 1), seem to the Diatribe to imply force.—"He who *inclines* (it observes) does not immediately *compel*."—

As though we were speaking of *compulsion*, and not rather concerning the *necessity of Immutability*. And that is implied in the *inclining* of God: which inclining, is not so snoring and lazy a thing, as the Diatribe imagines, but is that most active operation of God, which a man cannot avoid or alter, but under which he has, of necessity, such a will as God has given him, and such as he carries along by his motion: as I have before shewn.

Moreover, where Solomon is speaking of "the king's heart," the Diatribe thinks—'that the passage cannot rightly be strained to apply in a general sense: but that the meaning is the same as that of Job, where he says, in another place, "He maketh the hypocrite to reign, because of the sins of the people." At last, however, it concedes, that the king is inclined unto evil by God: but so, that He permits the king to be carried away by his inclination, in order to chastise the people.'—

I answer: Whether God permit, or whether He incline, that permitting or inclining does not take place without the will and operation of God: because, the will of the king cannot avoid the action of the omnipotent God: seeing that, the will of all is carried along just as He wills and acts, whether that will be good or evil.

And as to my having made out of the particular will of the king, a general application; I did it, I presume, neither vainly nor unskilfully. For if the heart of the king, which seems to be of all the most free, and to rule over others, cannot will good but where God inclines it, how much less can any other among men will good! And this conclusion will stand valid, drawn, not from the will of the king only, but from that of any other man. For if any one man, how private soever he be, cannot will before God but where God inclines, the same must be said of all men. Thus in the instance of Balaam, his not being able to speak what he wished, is an evident argument from the Scriptures, that man is not in his own power, nor a free chooser and doer of what he does: were it not so, no examples of it could subsist in the Scriptures.

Sect. CXXVI.—The Diatribe after this, having said that many such testimonies, as Luther collects, may be collected out of the book of Proverbs; but which, by a convenient interpretation, may stand both for and against "Free-will"; adduces at last that Achillean and invincible weapon of Luther, "Without me ye can do nothing," &c. (John xv. 5).

I too, must laud that notable champion-disputant for "Free-will," who teaches us, to modify the testimonies of Scripture just as it serves our turn, by convenient interpretations, in order to make them appear to stand truly in confirmation of "Free-will"; that is, that they might be made to prove, not what they ought, but what we please; and who merely pretends a fear of one Achillean Scripture, that the silly reader, seeing this one overthrown, might hold all the rest in utter contempt. But I will just look on and see, by what force the full-mouthed and heroic Diatribe will conquer my Achilles; which hitherto, has never wounded a common soldier, nor even a Thersites, but has ever miserably dispatched itself with its own weapons.

Catching hold of this one word "nothing," it stabs it with many words and many examples; and, by means of a convenient interpretation, brings it to this; that "nothing," may signify that which is *in degree* and *imperfect*. That is, it means to say, in other words, that the Sophists have hitherto explained this passage thus.—"Without me ye can do nothing;" that is, perfectly. This gloss, which has been long worn out and obsolete, the Diatribe, by its power of rhetoric, renders new; and so presses it forward, as though it had first invented it, and it had never been heard of before, thus making it appear to be a sort of miracle. In the mean time, however, it is quite self-secure, thinking nothing about the text itself, nor what precedes or follows it, whence alone the knowledge of the passage is to be obtained.

But (to say no more about its having attempted to prove by so many words and examples, that the term "nothing" may, in this passage, be understood as meaning 'that which is in a certain degree, or imperfect,' as though we were disputing whether or not it *may be*, whereas, what was to be proved is whether or not it *ought to be*, so understood;) the whole of this grand interpretation effects nothing, if it affect any thing, but this:—the rendering of this passage of John uncertain and obscure. And no wonder, for all that the Diatribe aims at, is to make the Scriptures of God in every place obscure, to the intent that it might not be compelled to use them; and the authorities of the Ancients certain, to the intent that it might abuse them;—a wonderful kind of religion truly, making the words of God to be useless, and the words of man useful!

Sect. CXXVII.—But it is most excellent to observe how well this gloss, "nothing" may be understood to signify 'that which is *in degree*,' consists with itself: yet the Diatribe says,—'that in this sense of the passage, it is most true that we can do nothing without Christ: because, He is speaking of evangelical fruits, which cannot be produced but by those who remain in the vine, which is Christ.'—

Here the Diatribe itself confesses, that fruit cannot be produced but by those who remain in the vine: and it does the same in that 'convenient interpretation,' by which it proves, that "nothing" is the same as in degree, and imperfect. But perhaps, its own adverb 'can*not*,' ought also to be conveniently interpreted, so as to signify, that evangelical fruits *can* be produced without Christ *in degree* and *imperfectly*. So that we may preach, that the ungodly who are without Christ can, while Satan reigns in them, and wars against Christ, produce some of the fruits of life: that is, that the enemies of Christ may do something for the glory of Christ.—But away with these things.

Here however, I should like to be taught, how we are to resist heretics, who, using this rule throughout the Scriptures, may contend that *nothing* and *not* are to be understood as signifying that which is imperfect. Thus—Without Him "nothing" can be done; that is *a little*.—"The fool hath said in his heart there is not a God;" that is, there is an imperfect God.—"He hath made us, and not we ourselves;" that is, we did a little towards making ourselves. And who can number all the passages in the Scripture where 'nothing' and 'not' are found?

Shall we then here say that a 'convenient interpretation' is to be attended to? And is this clearing up difficulties—to open such a door of liberty to corrupt minds and deceiving spirits? Such a licence of interpretation is, I grant, convenient to you who care nothing whatever about the certainty of the Scripture; but as for me who labour to establish consciences, this is an inconvenience; than which, nothing can be more inconvenient, nothing more injurious, nothing more pestilential. Hear me, therefore, thou great conqueress of the Lutheran Achilles! Unless you shall prove, that 'nothing' not only *may be*, but *ought to be* understood as signifying a 'little,' you have done nothing by all this profusion of words or examples, but fight against fire with dry straw. What have I to do with your *may be*, which only demands of you to prove your *ought to be*? And if you do not prove that, I stand by the natural and grammatical signification of the term, laughing both at your armies and at your triumphs.

Where is now that 'probable opinion' which determined, 'that "Free-will" can will nothing good? ' But perhaps, the 'convenient interpretation' comes in here, to say, that 'nothing good' signifies, something good—a kind of grammar and logic never before heard of; that nothing, is the same as something: which, with logicians, is an impossibility, because they are contradictions. Where now then remains that article of our faith, that Satan is the prince of the world, and, according to the testimonies of Christ and Paul, rules in the wills and minds of those men who are his captives and servants? Shall that roaring lion, that implacable and ever-restless enemy of the grace of God and the salvation of man, suffer it to be, that man, his slave and a part of his kingdom, should attempt good by any motion in any degree, whereby he might escape from his tyranny, and that he should not rather spur and urge him on to will and do the contrary to grace with all his powers? especially, when the just, and those who are led by the Spirit of God, and who will and do good, can hardly resist him, so great is his rage against them?

You who make it out, that the human will is a something placed in a *free medium*, and left to itself, certainly make it out, at the same time, that there is an endeavour which can exert itself either way; because, you make both God and the devil to be at a distance, spectators only, as it were, of this mutable and "Free-will"; though you do not believe, that they are impellers and agitators of that bondage will, the most hostilely opposed to each other. Admitting, therefore, this part of your faith only, my sentiment stands firmly established, and "Free-will" lies prostrate; as I have shewn already.—For, it must either be, that the kingdom of Satan in man is nothing at all, and thus Christ will be made to lie; or, if his kingdom be such as Christ describes, "Free-will" must be nothing but a beast of burden, the captive of Satan, which cannot be liberated, unless the devil be first cast out by the finger of God.

From what has been advanced I presume, friend Diatribe, thou fully understandest what that is, and what it amounts to, where thy Author, detesting the obstinate way of assertion in Luther, is accustomed to say—'Luther indeed pushes his cause with plenty of Scriptures; but they may all, by one word, be brought to nothing.' Who does not know, that all Scriptures may, by one word, be brought to nothing? I knew this full well before I ever heard the name of Erasmus. But the question is, whether it be *sufficient* to bring a Scripture, by one word, to nothing. The point in dispute is, whether it be *rightly* brought to nothing, and whether it *ought to be* brought to nothing. Let a man consider these points, and he will then see, whether or not it be easy to bring Scriptures to nothing, and whether or not the obstinacy of Luther be detestable. He will then see, that not one word only is ineffective, but all the gates of hell cannot bring them to nothing!

Sect. CXXVIII.—What, therefore, the Diatribe cannot do in its affirmative, I will do in the negative; and though I am not called upon to prove the negative, yet I will do it here, and will make it by the force of argument undeniably appear, that "nothing," in this passage, not only *may be* but *ought to be* understood as meaning, not a certain small degree, but that which the term naturally signifies. And this I will do, in addition to that invincible argument by which I am already victorious, viz. 'that all terms are to be preserved in their natural signification and use, unless the contrary shall be proved:' which the Diatribe neither has done, nor can do.—First of all then I will make that evidently manifest, which is plainly proved by Scriptures neither ambiguous nor obscure,—that Satan, is by far the most powerful and crafty prince of this world; (as I said before,) under the reigning power of whom, the human will, being no longer free nor in its own power, but the servant of sin and of Satan, can will nothing but that which its prince wills. And he will not permit it to will any thing good: though, even if Satan did not reign over it, sin itself, of which man is the slave, would sufficiently harden it to prevent it from willing good.

Moreover, the following part of the context itself evidently proves the same: which the Diatribe proudly sneers at, although I have commented upon it very copiously in my Assertions. For Christ proceeds thus, John xv. 6, "Whoso abideth not in me, is cast forth as a branch and is withered; and men gather them and cast them into the fire, and they are burned." This, I say, the Diatribe, in a most excellent rhetorical way, passed by; hoping that the intent of this evasion would not be comprehended by the shallow-brained Lutherans. But here you see that Christ, who is the interpreter of His own similitude of the vine and the branch, plainly declares what He would have understood by the term "nothing"—that man who is without Christ, "is cast forth and is withered."

And what can the being "cast forth and withered" signify but the being delivered up to the devil, and becoming continually worse and worse; and surely, becoming worse and worse, is not doing or attempting any thing good. The withering branch is more and more prepared for the fire the more it withers. And had not Christ Himself thus amplified and applied this similitude, no one would have dared so to amplify and apply it. It stands manifest, therefore, that "nothing," ought, in this place, to be understood in its proper signification, according to the nature of the term.

Sect. CXXIX.—Let us now consider the examples also, by which it proves, that "nothing" signifies, in some places, 'a certain small degree:' in order that we may make it evident, that the Diatribe is nothing, and effects nothing in this part of it: in which, though it should do much, yet it would effect nothing:—such a nothing is the Diatribe in all things, and in every way.

It says—"Generally, he is said to do nothing, who does not achieve that, at which he aims; and yet, for the most part, he who attempts it, makes some certain degree of progress in the attempt."—

I answer: I never heard this general usage of the term: you have invented it by your own license. The words are to be considered according to the subject-matter, (as they say,) and according to the intention of the speaker.—No one calls that 'nothing' which he does in attempting, nor does he then speak of the *attempt* but of the *effect*: it is to this the person refers when he says, he *does nothing*, or he *effects nothing*; that is, achieves and accomplishes nothing. But supposing your example to stand good, (which however it does not) it makes more for me than for yourself. For this is what I maintain and would invincibly establish, that "Free-will" does many things, which, nevertheless, are "nothing" before God. What does it profit, therefore, to attempt, if it effect nothing at which it aims? So that, let the Diatribe turn which way it will, it only runs against, and confutes itself: which generally happens to those, who undertake to support a bad cause.

With the same unhappy effect does it adduce that example out of Paul, "Neither is he that planteth any thing, neither he that watereth; but God who giveth the increase." (1 Cor. iii. 7).—"That (says the Diatribe,) which is of the least moment, and useless of itself, he calls nothing."—

Who? —Do you, pretend to say, that the ministry of the word is of itself useless, and of the least moment, when Paul everywhere, and especially 2 Cor. iii. 6-9, highly exalts it, and calls it the ministration "of life," and "of glory? " Here again you neither consider the subject matter, nor the intention of the speaker. As to the gift of the increase, the planter and waterer are certainly 'nothing;' but as to the planting and sowing, they are not 'nothing;' seeing that, to teach and to exhort, are the greatest work of the Spirit in the Church of God. This is the intended meaning of Paul, and this his words convey with satisfactory plainness. But be it so, that this ridiculous example stands good; again, it stands in favour of me. For what I maintain is this: that "Free-will" is 'nothing,' that is, is useless of itself (as you expound it) before God; and it is concerning its being nothing as to what it *can do of itself* that we are now speaking: for as to what it *essentially is in itself*, we know, that an impious will must be a something, and cannot be a mere nothing.

Sect. CXXX.—There is also that of 1 Cor. xiii. 2. "If I have not charity I am nothing:"

Why the Diatribe adduces this as an example I cannot see, unless it seeks only numbers and forces, or thinks that we have no arms at all, by which we can effectually wound it. For he who is without charity, is, truly and properly, 'nothing' before God. The same also we say of "Free-will." Wherefore, this example also stands for us against the Diatribe. Or, can it be that the Diatribe does not yet know the argument ground upon which I am contending? —I am not speaking about the *essence of nature*, but the *essence of grace* (as they term it.) I know, that "Free-will" can by nature do something; it can eat, drink, beget, rule, &c. Nor need the Diatribe laugh at me as having prating frenzy enough to imply, when I press home so closely the term 'nothing,' that "Free-will" cannot even sin without Christ: whereas Luther, nevertheless says, 'that "Free-will" can do nothing but sin'—but so it pleases the wise Diatribe to play the fool in a matter so serious. For I say, that man without the grace of God, remains, nevertheless, under the general Omnipotence of an acting God, who moves and carries along all things, of necessity, in the course of His infallible motion; but that the man's being thus carried along, is nothing; that is, avails nothing in the sight of God, nor is considered any thing else but sin. Thus in grace, he that is without love, is nothing. Why then does the Diatribe, when it confesses itself, that we are here speaking of evangelical fruits, as that which cannot be produced without Christ, turn aside immediately from the subject point, harp upon another string, and cavil about nothing but natural works and human fruits? Except it be to evince, that he who is devoid of the truth, is never consistent with himself.

So also that of John iii. 27, "A man can receive nothing except it were given him from above."

John is here speaking of man, who is now a something, and denies that this man can receive any thing; that is, the Spirit with His gifts; for it is in reference to that he is speaking, not in reference to nature. For he did not want the Diatribe as an instructor to teach him, that man has already eyes, nose, ears, mouth, hands, mind, will, reason, and all things that belong to man.—Unless the Diatribe believes, that the Baptist, when he made mention of man, was thinking of the 'chaos' of Plato, the 'vacuum' of Leucippus, or the 'infinity' of Aristotle, or some other nothing, which, by a gift from heaven, should at last be made a something.—Is this producing examples out of the Scripture, thus to trifle designedly in a matter so important!

And to what purpose is all that profusion of words, where it teaches us, 'that fire, the escape from evil, the endeavour after good, and other things are from heaven,' as though there were any one who did not know, or who denied those things? We are now talking about grace, and, as the Diatribe itself said, concerning Christ and evangelical fruits; whereas, it is itself, making out its time in fabling about nature; thus dragging out the cause, and covering the witless reader with a cloud. In the mean time, it does not produce one single example as it professed to do, wherein 'nothing,' is to be understood as signifying some small degree. Nay, it openly exposes itself as neither understanding nor caring what Christ or grace is, nor how it is, that grace is one thing and nature another, when even the Sophists of the meanest rank know, and have continually taught this difference in their schools, in the most common way. Nor does it all the while see, that every one of its examples make for me, and against itself. For the word of the Baptist goes to establish this:—that man can receive nothing unless it be given him from above; and that, therefore, "Free-will" is nothing at all.

Thus it is, then, that my Achilles is conquered—the Diatribe puts weapons into his hand, by which it is itself dispatched, naked and weapon-less. And thus it is also that the Scriptures, by which that obstinate assertor Luther urges his cause, are, 'by one word, brought to nothing.'

Sect. CXXXI.—After this, it enumerates a multitude of similitudes: by which, it effects nothing but the drawing aside the witless reader to irrelevant things, according to its custom, and at the same time leaves the subject point entirely out of the question. Thus,—"God indeed preserves the ship, but the mariner conducts it into harbour:

wherefore, the mariner does not do nothing."–This similitude makes a difference of work: that is, it attributes that of preserving to God, and that of conducting to the mariner. And thus, if it prove any thing, it proves this:–that the whole work of preserving is of God, and the whole work of conducting of the mariner. And yet, it is a beautiful and apt similitude.

Thus again–"the husbandman gathers in the increase, but it was God that gave it."–Here again, it attributes different operations to God and to man: unless it mean to make the husbandman the creator also, who gave the increase. But even supposing the same works be attributed to God and to man–what do these similitudes prove? Nothing more, than that the *creature co-operates* with the *operating God*! But are we now disputing about co-operation, and not rather concerning the power and operation of "Free-will," as of itself! Whither therefore has the renowned rhetorician betaken himself? He set out with the professed design to dispute concerning a palm; whereas all his discourse has been about a gourd! 'A noble vase was designed by the potter; why then is a pitcher produced at last? '

I also know very well, that Paul co-operates with God in teaching the Corinthians, while he preaches without, and God teaches within; and that, where their works are different. And that, in like manner, he co-operates with God while he speaks by the Spirit of God; and that, where the work is the same. For what I assert and contend for is this:–that God, where He operates without the grace of His Spirit, works all in all, even in the ungodly; while He alone moves, acts on, and carries along by the motion of His omnipotence, all those things which He alone has created, which motion those things can neither avoid nor change, but of necessity follow and obey, each one according to the measure of power given of God:–thus all things, even the ungodly, co-operate with God! On the other hand, when He acts by the Spirit of His grace on those whom He has justified, that is, in His own kingdom, He moves and carries them along in the same manner; and they, as they are the new creatures, follow and co-operate with Him; or rather, as Paul saith, are led by Him. (Rom. viii. 14, 30.)

But the present is not the place for discussing these points. We are not now considering, what we can do in co-operation with God, but what we can do of ourselves: that is, whether, created as we are out of nothing, we can do or attempt any thing of ourselves, under the general motion of God's omnipotence, whereby to prepare ourselves unto the new Creation of the Spirit.–This is the point to which Erasmus ought to have answered, and not to have turned aside to a something else!

What I have to say upon this point is this:–As man, before he is created man, does nothing and endeavours nothing towards his being made a creature; and as, after he is made and created, he does nothing and endeavours nothing towards his preservation, or towards his continuing in his creature-existence, but each takes place alone by the will of the omnipotent power and goodness of God, creating us and preserving us, without ourselves; but as God, nevertheless, does not work *in* us *without* us, seeing we are for that purpose created and preserved, that He might work in us and that we might co-operate with Him, whether it be out of His kingdom under His general omnipotence, or in His kingdom under the peculiar power of His Spirit;–so, man, before he is regenerated into the new creation of the kingdom of the Spirit, does nothing and endeavours nothing towards his new creation into that kingdom, and after he is re-created does nothing and endeavours nothing towards his perseverance in that kingdom; but the Spirit alone effects both in us, regenerating us and preserving us when regenerated, without ourselves; as James saith, "Of His own will begat He us by the word of His power, that we should be a kind of first-fruits of His creatures,"–(Jas. i. 18) (where he speaks of the renewed creation:) nevertheless, He does not work *in* us *without* us, seeing that He has for this purpose created and preserved us, that He might operate in us, and that we might co-operate with Him: thus, by us He preaches, shews mercy to the poor, and comforts the afflicted.–But what is hereby attributed to "Free-will? " Nay, what is there left it but nothing at all? And in truth it is nothing at all!

Sect. CXXXII.—Read therefore the Diatribe in this part through five or six pages, and you will find, that by similitudes of this kind, and by some of the most beautiful passages and parables selected from the Gospel and from Paul, it does nothing else but shew us, that innumerable passages (as it observes) are to be found in the Scriptures which speak of the co-operation and assistance of God: from which, if I should draw this conclusion—Man can do nothing without the assisting grace of God: therefore, no works of man are good—it would on the contrary conclude, as it has done by a rhetorical inversion—"Nay, there is nothing that man cannot do by the assisting grace of God: therefore, all the works of man can be good. For as many passages as there are in the Holy Scriptures which make mention of assistance, so many are there which confirm "Free-will;" and they are innumerable. Therefore, if we go by the number of testimonies, the victory is mine."—

Do you think the Diatribe could be sober or in its right senses when it wrote this? For I cannot attribute it to malice or iniquity: unless it be that it designed to effectually wear me out by perpetually wearying me, while thus, ever like itself, it is continually turning aside to something contrary to its professed design. But if it is pleased thus to play the fool in a matter so important, then I will be pleased to expose its voluntary fooleries publicly.

In the first place, I do not dispute, nor am I ignorant, that all the works of man *may be* good, if they be done by the assisting grace of God. And moreover that there is nothing which a man might not do by the assisting grace of God. But I cannot feel enough surprise at your negligence, who, having set out with the professed design to write upon the power of "Free-will," go on writing upon the power of grace. And moreover, dare to assert publicly, as if all men were posts or stones, that "Free-will" is established by those passages of Scripture which exalt the grace of God. And not only dare to do that, but even to sound forth encomiums on yourself as a victor most gloriously triumphant! From this very word and act of yours, I truly perceive what "Free-will" is, and what the effect of it is—it makes men mad! For what, I ask, can it be in you that talks at this rate, but "Free-will!"

But just listen to your own conclusions.—The Scripture commends the grace of God: therefore, it proves "Free-will."—It exalts the assistance of the grace of God: therefore, it establishes "Free-will." By what kind of logic did you learn such conclusions as these? On the contrary, why not conclude thus? —Grace is preached: therefore "Free-will" has no existence. The assistance of grace is exalted: therefore, "Free-will" is abolished. For, to what intent is grace given? Is it for this: that "Free-will," as being of sufficient power itself, might proudly display and sport grace on fair-days, as a superfluous ornament!

Wherefore, I will invert your order of reasoning, and though no rhetorician, will establish a conclusion more firm than yours.—As many places as there are in the Holy Scriptures which make mention of assistance, so many are there which abolish "Free-will:" and they are innumerable. Therefore, if we are to go by the number of testimonies, the victory is mine. For grace is therefore needed, and the assistance of grace is therefore given, because "Free-will" can of itself do nothing; as Erasmus himself has asserted according to that 'probable opinion' that "Free-will" 'cannot will any thing good.' Therefore, when grace is commended, and the assistance of grace declared, the impotency of "Free-will" is declared at the same time.—This is a sound inference—a firm conclusion—against which, not even the gates of hell will ever prevail!

Sect. CXXXIII.—Here, I bring to a conclusion, THE DEFENCE OF MY SCRIPTURES WHICH THE DIATRIBE ATTEMPTED TO REFUTE; lest my book should be swelled to too great a bulk: and if there be any thing yet remaining that is worthy of notice, it shall be taken into THE FOLLOWING PART; WHEREIN, I MAKE MY ASSERTIONS. For as to what Erasmus says in his conclusion—'that, if my sentiments stand good, the numberless precepts, the numberless threatenings, the numberless promises, are all in vain, and no place is left for merit or demerit, for rewards or punishments; that moreover, it is difficult to defend the mercy, nay, even the justice of God, if God damn sinners of necessity; and that many other difficulties follow, which have so troubled some of the greatest men, as even to utterly overthrow them,'—

To all these things I have fully replied already. Nor will I receive or bear with that *moderate medium*, which Erasmus would (with a good intention, I believe,) recommend to me;—'that we should grant *some certain little* to "Free-will;" in order that, the contradictions of the Scripture, and the difficulties before mentioned, might be the more easily remedied.'—For by this *moderate medium*, the matter is not bettered, nor is any advantage gained whatever. Because, unless you ascribe the whole and all things to "Free-will," as the Pelagians do, the contradictions in the Scriptures are not altered, merit and reward are taken entirely away, the mercy and justice of God are abolished, and all the difficulties which we try to avoid by allowing this 'certain little ineffective power' to "Free-will," remain just as they were before; as I have already fully shewn. Therefore, we must come to the plain extreme, deny "Free-will" altogether, and ascribe all unto God! Thus, there will be in the Scriptures no contradictions; and if there be any difficulties, they will be borne with, where they cannot be remedied.

Sect. CXXXIV.—This one thing, however, my friend Erasmus, I entreat of you—do not consider that I conduct this cause more according to my temper, than according to my principles. I will not suffer it to be insinuated, that I am hypocrite enough to write one thing and believe another. I have not (as you say of me) been carried so far by the heat of defensive argument, as to 'deny here "Free-will" altogether for the first time, having conceded something to it before.' Confident I am, that you can find no such concession any where in my works. There are questions and discussions of mine extant, in which I have continued to assert, down to this hour, that there is no such thing as "Free-will;" that it is *a thing formed out of an empty term*; (which are the words I have there used). And I then thus believed and thus wrote, as overpowered by the force of truth when called and compelled to the discussion. And as to my always conducting discussions with ardour, I acknowledge my fault, if it be a fault: nay, I greatly glory in this testimony which the world bears of me, in the cause of God: and may God Himself confirm the same testimony in the last day! Then, who more happy than Luther—to be honoured with the universal testimony of his age, that he did not maintain the Cause of Truth lazily, nor deceitfully, but with a real, if not too great, ardour! Then shall I be blessedly clear from that word of Jeremiah, "Cursed be he that doeth the work of the Lord deceitfully! " (Jer. xlviii. 10).

But if I seem to be somewhat more severe than usual upon your Diatribe—pardon me. I do it not from a malignant heart, but from concern; because I know, that by the weight of your name you greatly endanger this cause of Christ; though, by your learning, as to real effect, you can do nothing at all. And who can always so temper his pen as never to grow warm? For even you, who from a show of moderation grow almost cold in this book of yours, not unfrequently hurl a fiery and gall-dipped dart: so much so, that if the reader were not very liberal and kind, he could not but consider you virulent. But however, this is nothing to the subject point. We must mutually pardon each other in these things; for we are but men, and there is nothing in us that is not touched with human infirmity.

THIRD PART.

We are now arrived at the LAST PART OF THIS DISCUSSION. Wherein I am, as I proposed, to bring forward my forces against "Free-will." But I shall not produce them all, for who could do that within the limits of this small book, when the whole Scripture, in every letter and iota, stands on my side? Nor is there any necessity for so doing; seeing that, "Free-will" already lies vanquished and prostrate under a two-fold overthrow.—The one where I have proved, that all those things, which it imagined made for itself, make directly against itself.—The other, where I have made it manifest, that those Scriptures which it attempted to refute, still remain invincible.—If, therefore, it had not been vanquished by the former, it is enough if it be laid prostrate by the one weapon or the other. And now, what need is there that the enemy, already dispatched by the one weapon or the other, should have his dead body stabbed with a number of weapons more? In this part, therefore, I shall be as brief as the subject will allow: and from such numerous armies, I shall produce only two champion-generals with a few of their legions—Paul, and John the Evangelist!

Sect. CXXXV.—Paul, writing to the Romans, thus enters upon his argument, *against* Free-will, and *for* the grace of God. "The wrath of God (saith he) is revealed from heaven against all ungodliness and unrighteousness of men, who hold the truth in unrighteousness." (Rom. i. 18)—

Dost thou hear this general sentence "against all men,"—that they are all under the wrath of God? And what is this but declaring, that they all merit wrath and punishment? For he assigns the cause of the wrath against them—they do nothing but that which merits wrath; because they are all ungodly and unrighteous, and hold the truth in unrighteousness. Where is now the power of "Free-will" which can endeavour any thing good? Paul makes it to merit the wrath of God, and pronounces it ungodly and unrighteous. That, therefore, which merits wrath and is ungodly, only endeavours and avails *against* grace, not *for* grace.

But some one will here laugh at the yawning inconsiderateness of Luther, for not looking fully into the intention of Paul. Some one will say, that Paul does not here speak of all men, nor of all their doings; but of those only who are ungodly and unrighteous, and who, as the words themselves describe them, "hold the truth in unrighteousness;" but that, it does not hence follow, that *all* men are the same.

Here I observe, that in this passage of Paul, the words "against all ungodliness of men" are of the same import, as if you should say,—against the ungodliness of all men. For Paul, in almost all these instances, uses a Hebraism: so that, the sense is,—all men are ungodly and unrighteous, and hold the truth in unrighteousness; and therefore, all merit wrath. Hence, in the Greek, there is no *relative* which might be rendered 'of those who,' but an *article*, causing the sense to run thus, "The wrath of God is revealed from heaven against all ungodliness and unrighteousness of men, holding the truth in unrighteousness." So that this may be taken as an epithet, as it were, applicable to all men as "holding the truth in unrighteousness:" even as it is an epithet where it is said, "Our Father which art in heaven:" which might in other words be expressed thus: Our heavenly Father, or Our Father in heaven. For it is so expressed to distinguish those who believe and fear God.

But these things might appear frivolous and vain, did not the very train of Paul's argument require them to be so understood, and prove them to be true. For he had said just before, "The Gospel is the power of God unto salvation to every one that believeth, to the Jew first and also to the Greek." (Rom. i. 16). These words are surely neither obscure or ambiguous, "to the Jew first and also to the Greek:" that is, the Gospel of the power of God is necessary unto all men, that, believing in it, they might be saved from the wrath of God revealed. Does he not then, I pray you, who declares, that the Jews who excelled in righteousness, in the law of God, and in the power of "Free-will," are, without difference, destitute and in need of the power of God, by which they might be saved, and who makes that power necessary unto them, consider that they are all under wrath? What men then will you pretend to say are not under the wrath of God, when you are thus compelled to believe, that the most excellent men in the world, the Jews and Greeks, were so?

And further, whom among those Jews and Greeks themselves will you except, when Paul subjects all of them, included in the same word, without difference, to the same sentence? And are we to suppose that there were no men, out of these two most exalted nations, who 'aspired to what was meritoriously good?' Were there none among them who thus aspired with all the powers of their "Free-will?" Yet Paul makes no distinction on this account, he includes them all under wrath, and declares them all to be ungodly and unrighteous. And are we not to believe that all the other Apostles each one according to the work he had to do, included all other nations under this wrath, in the same way of declaration?

Sect. CXXXVI.—This passage of Paul, therefore, stands firmly and forcibly urging—that "Free-will," even in its most exalted state, in the most exalted men, who were endowed with the law, righteousness, wisdom, and all the virtues, was ungodly and unrighteous, and merited the wrath of God; or the argument of Paul amounts to nothing. And if it stand good, his division leaves no *medium*: for he makes those who believe the Gospel to be under the salvation, and all the rest to be under the wrath of God: he makes the believing to be righteous, and the unbelieving to be ungodly, unrighteous, and under wrath. For the whole that he means to say is this:—The righteousness of God is revealed in the Gospel, that it might be by faith. But God would be wanting in wisdom, if He should *reveal* righteousness unto men, when they either knew it already or had 'some seeds' of it themselves. Since, however, He is not wanting in wisdom, and yet reveals unto men the righteousness of salvation, it is manifest, that "Free-will" even in the most exalted of men, not only has wrought, and can work no righteousness, but does not even know what is righteous before God.—Unless you mean to say, that the righteousness of God is not revealed unto these most exalted of men, but to the most vile! But the boasting of Paul is quite the contrary—that he is a debtor, both to the Jews and to the Greeks, to the wise and to the unwise, to the Greeks and to the barbarians.

Wherefore Paul, comprehending, in this passage, all men together in one mass, concludes that they are all ungodly, unrighteous, and ignorant of the righteousness of faith: so far is it from possibility, that they can will or do any thing good. And this conclusion is moreover confirmed from this:—that God *reveals* the righteousness of faith to them, as being ignorant and sitting in darkness: therefore, of themselves, they know it not. And if they be ignorant of the righteousness of salvation, they are certainly under wrath and damnation: nor can they extricate themselves therefrom, nor *endeavour* to extricate themselves: for how can you endeavour, if you know neither what you are to endeavour after, nor in what way, nor to what extent, you are to endeavour?

Sect. CXXXVII.—With this conclusion both the thing itself and experience agree. For shew me one of the whole race of mankind, be he the most holy and most just of all men, into whose mind it ever came, that the way unto righteousness and salvation, was to believe in Him who is both God and man, who died for the sins of men and rose again, and sitteth at the right hand of God the Father, that He might still that wrath of God the Father which Paul here says is revealed from heaven?

Look at the most eminent philosophers! What ideas had they of God! What have they left behind them in their writings concerning the wrath to come! Look at the Jews instructed by so many wonders and so many successive Prophets! What did they think of this way of righteousness? They not only did not receive it, but so hated it, that no nation under heaven has more atrociously persecuted Christ, unto this day. And who would dare to say, that in so great a people, there was not one who cultivated "Free-will," and endeavoured with all its power? How comes it to pass, then, that they all endeavour in the directly opposite, and that that which was the most excellent in the most excellent men, not only did not follow this way of righteousness, not only did not know it, but even thrust if from them with the greatest hatred, and wished to away with it when it was published and revealed? So much so, that Paul saith, this way was "to the Jews a stumbling-block, and to the Gentiles foolishness." (I Cor. i. 23.).

Since, therefore, Paul speaks of the Jews and Gentiles without difference, and since it is certain that the Jews and Gentiles comprehend the principal nations under heaven, it is hence certain, that "Free-will" is nothing else than the greatest enemy to righteousness and the salvation of man: for it is impossible, but that there must have been some among the Jews and Gentile Greeks who wrought and endeavoured with all the powers of "Free-will;" and yet, by all that endeavouring, did nothing but carry on a war against grace.

Do you therefore now come forward and say, what "Free-will" can endeavour towards good, when goodness and righteousness themselves are a "stumbling-block" unto it, and "foolishness." Nor can you say that this applies to *some* and not to *all*. Paul speaks of all without difference where he says, "to the Jews a stumbling-block and to the Gentiles foolishness:" nor does he except any but believers. "To us, (saith he,) who are called, and saints, it is the power of God and wisdom of God." (I Cor. i. 24). He does not say to some Gentiles, to some Jews; but plainly, to the Gentiles and to the Jews, who are "not of us." Thus, by a manifest division, separating the believing from the unbelieving, and leaving no *medium* whatever. And we are now speaking of Gentiles as working without grace: to whom Paul saith, the righteousness of God is "foolishness," and they abhor it.–This is that meritorious endeavour of "Free-will" towards good!

Sect. CXXXVIII.–See, moreover, whether Paul himself does not particularize the most exalted among the Greeks, where he saith, that the wisest among them "became vain in their imaginations, and their foolish heart was darkened;" that "they became wise in their own conceits:" that is, by their subtle disputations. (Rom. i. 21).

Does he not here, I pray you, touch that, which was the most exalted and most excellent in the Greeks, when he touches their "imaginations? " For these comprehend their most sublime and exalted thoughts and opinions; which they considered as solid wisdom. But he calls that their wisdom, as well in other places "foolishness," as here "vain imagination;" which, by its endeavouring, only became worse; till at last they worshipped an idol in their own darkened hearts, and proceeded to the other enormities, which he afterwards enumerates.

If therefore, the most exalted and devoted endeavours and works in the most exalted of the nations be evil and ungodly, what shall we think of the rest, who are, as it were, the commonalty, and the vilest of the nations? Nor does Paul here make any difference between those who are the most exalted, for he condemns all the devotedness of their wisdom, without any respect of persons. And if he condemn their very works and devoted endeavours, he condemns those who exert them, even though they strive with all the powers of "Free-will." Their most exalted endeavour, I say, is declared to be evil–how much more than the persons themselves who exert it!

So also, just afterwards, he rejects the Jews, without any difference, who are Jews "in the letter" and not "in the spirit." "Thou (saith he) honourest God in the letter, and in the circumcision." Again, "He is not a Jew which is one outwardly, but he is a Jew which is one inwardly." (Rom. i. 27-29.)

What can be more manifest than the division here made? The Jew outwardly, is a transgressor of the law! And how many Jews must we suppose there were, without the faith, who were men the most wise, the most religious, and the most honourable, who aspired unto righteousness and truth with all the dev-*ion of endeavour? Of these the apostle continually bears testimony:–that they had "a zeal of God," that they "followed after righteousness," that they strove day and night to attain unto salvation, that they lived "blameless:" and yet they are transgressors of the law, because they are not Jews "in the spirit," nay they determinately resist the righteousness of faith. What conclusion then remains to be drawn, but that, "Free-will" is then the worst when it is the best; and that, the more it endeavours, the worse it becomes, and the worse it is! The words are plain—the division is certain—nothing can be said against it.

Sect. CXXXIX.—But let us hear Paul, who is his own interpreter. In the third chapter, drawing up, as it were, a conclusion, he saith, "What then? are we better than they? No, in no wise; for we have before proved both Jews and Greeks that they are all under sin." (Rom. iii.9).

Where is now "Free-will! All, saith he, both Jews and Greeks are under sin! Are there any 'tropes' or difficulties here? What would the 'invented interpretations' of the whole world do against this all-clear sentence? He who says "all," excepts none. And he who describes them all as being "under sin," that is, the servants of sin, leaves them no degree of good whatever. But where has he given this proof that "they are all, both Jews and Gentiles, under sin? " Nowhere, but where I have already shewn: viz., where he saith, "The wrath of God is revealed from heaven against all ungodliness and unrighteousness of men." This he proves to them afterwards from experience: shewing them, that being hated of God, they were given up to so many vices, in order that they might be convinced from the fruits of their ungodliness, that they willed and did nothing but evil. And then, he judges the Jews also separately; where he saith, that the Jew "in the letter," is a transgressor of the law: which he proves, in like manner, from the fruits, and from experience: saying, "Thou who declarest that a man should not steal, stealest thyself: thou who abhorrest idols, committest sacrilege." Thus excepting none whatever, but those who are Jews "in the spirit."

Sect. CXL.—But let us see how Paul proves his sentiments out of the Holy Scriptures: and whether the passages which he adduces 'are made to have more force in Paul, than they have in their own places.' "As it is written, (saith he,) There is none righteous, no not one. There is none that understandeth, there is none that seeketh after God. They are all gone out of the way, they are all together become unprofitable: there is none that doeth good, no, not one," &c. (Rom. iii. 10-23).

Here let him that can, produce his 'convenient interpretation,' invent 'tropes,' and pretend that the words 'are ambiguous and obscure!' Let him that dares, defend "Free-will" against these damnable doctrines! Then I will at once give up all and recant, and will myself become a confessor and assertor of "Free-will." It is certain, that these words apply to all men: for the prophet introduces God, as looking down from heaven upon men and pronouncing this sentence upon them. So also Psalm xiv. 2-3. "God looked down from heaven upon the children of men, to see if there were any that did understand and seek after God. But they are all gone out of the way," &c. And that the Jews might not imagine that this did not apply to them by anticipation, and asserts, that it applied to them most particularly: saying, "We know that what things soever the law saith, it saith to them that are under the law." (Rom. iii. 19). And his intention is the same, where he saith, "To the Jew first and also to the Greek."

You hence hear, that all the sons of men, all that are under the law, that is, the Gentiles as well as the Jews, are accounted before God ungodly; not understanding, not seeking after God, no, not even one of them; being all gone out of the way and become unprofitable. And surely, among all the "children of men," and those who who are "under the law," those must also be numbered who are the best and most laudable, who aspire after that which is meritorious and good, with all the powers of "Free-will;" and those also of whom the Diatribe boasts as having the sense and certain seeds of good implanted in them;—unless it means to contend that they are the "children" of angels!

How then can they endeavour toward good, who are all, without exception, ignorant of God, and neither regard nor seek after God? How can they have a power able to attain unto good, who all, without exception, decline from good and become utterly unprofitable? Are not the words most clear? And do they not declare this,—that all men are ignorant of God and despise God, and then, turn unto evil and become unprofitable unto good? For Paul is not here speaking of the ignorance of seeking food, or the contempt of money, but of the ignorance and contempt of religion and of godliness. And that ignorance and contempt, most undoubtedly, are not in the "flesh," that is, (as you interpret it,) 'the inferior and grosser affections,' but in the most exalted and most noble powers of man, in which righteousness, godliness, the knowledge and reverence of God, ought to reign; that is, in the reason and in the will; and thus, in the very power of "Free-will," in the very seed of good, in that which is the most excellent in man!

Where are you now, friend Erasmus! you who promised 'that you would freely acknowledge, that the most excellent faculty in man is "flesh," that is, ungodly, if it should be proved from the Scriptures?' Acknowledge now, then, when you hear, that the most excellent faculty in man is not only ungodly, but ignorant of God, existing in the contempt of God, turned to evil, and unable to turn towards good. For what is it to be "unrighteous," but for the will, (which is one of the most noble faculties in man,) to be unrighteous? What is it to understand nothing either of God or good, but for the reason (which is another of the most noble faculties in man) to be ignorant of God and good, that is, to be blind to the knowledge of godliness? What is it to be "gone out of the way," and to have become unprofitable, but for men to have no power in one single faculty, and the least power in their most noble faculties, to turn unto good, but only to turn unto evil! What is it not to fear God, but for men to be in all their faculties, and most of all in their noblest faculties, contemners of all the things of God, of His words, His works, His laws, His precepts, and His will! What then can reason propose, that is right, who is thus blind and ignorant? What can the will choose that is good, which is thus evil and impotent? Nay, what can the will pursue, where the reason can propose nothing, but the darkness of its own blindness and ignorance? And where the reason is thus erroneous, and the will averse, what can the man either do or attempt, that is good!

Sect. CXLI.—But perhaps some one may here sophistically observe—though the will be gone out of the way, and the reason be ignorant, as to the perfection of the act, yet the will can make some attempt, and the reason can attain to some knowledge by its own powers; seeing that, we can attempt many things which we cannot perfect; and we are here speaking, of the existence of a power, not of the perfection of the act.—

I answer: The words of the Prophet comprehend both the *act* and the *power*. For his saying, man seeks not God, is the same as if he had said, man *cannot* seek God: which you may collect from this.—If there were a power or ability in man to will good, it could not be, but that, as the motion of the Divine Omnipotence could not suffer it to remain actionless, or to keep holiday, (as I before observed) it must be moved forth into act in some men, at least, in some one man or other, and must be made manifest so as to afford an example. But this is not the case. For God looks down from heaven, and does not see even one who seeks after Him, or attempts it. Wherefore it follows, that that power is no where to be found, which attempts, or wills to attempt, to seek after Him; and that all men "are gone out of the way."

Moreover if Paul be not understood to speak at the same time of impotency, his disputation will amount to nothing. For Paul's whole design is, to make grace necessary unto all men. Whereas, if they could make some sort of beginning themselves, grace would not be necessary. But now, since they cannot make that beginning, grace is necessary. Hence you see that "Free-will" is by this passage utterly abolished, and nothing meritorious or good whatever left in man: seeing that, he is declared to be unrighteous, ignorant of God, a contemner of God, averse to God, and unprofitable in the sight of God. And the words of the prophet are sufficiently forcible both in their own place, and in Paul who adduces them.

Nor is it an inconsiderable assertion, when man is said to be ignorant of, and to despise God: for these are the fountain springs of all iniquities, the sink of all sins, and the hell of all evils. What evil is there not, where there are ignorance and contempt of God? In a word, the whole kingdom of Satan in men, could not be defined in fewer or more expressive words than by saying—they are ignorant of and despise God! For there is unbelief, there is disobedience, there is sacrilege, there is blasphemy against God, there is cruelty and a want of mercy towards our neighbour, there is the love of self in all the things of God and man! —Here you have a description of the glory and power of "Free-will! "

Sect. CXLII.—Paul however proceeds, and testifies, that he now expressly speaks with reference to all men, and to those more especially who are the greatest and most exalted: saying, "that every mouth may be stopped, and all the world become guilty before God: for by the works of the law shall no flesh be justified in His sight." (Rom. iii. 19-20).

How, I pray you, shall every mouth be stopped, if there be still a power remaining by which we can do something? For one might then say to God—That which is here in the world is not altogether nothing. There is that here which you cannot damn: even that, to which you yourself gave the power of doing something. The mouth of this at least will not be stopped, for it cannot be obnoxious to you.—For if there be any sound power in "Free-will", and it be able to do something, to say that the whole world is obnoxious to, or guilty before God, is false; for that power, whose mouth is not to be stopped, cannot be an inconsiderable thing, or a something in one small part of the world only, but a thing most conspicuous, and most general throughout the whole world. Or, if its mouth is to be stopped, then it must be obnoxious to, and guilty before God, together with the whole world. But how can it rightly be called guilty, if it be not unrighteous and ungodly; that is, meriting punishment and vengeance?

Let your friends, I pray you, find out, by what 'convenient interpretation' that power of man is to be cleared from this charge of guilt, by which the whole world is declared guilty before God; or by what contrivance it is to be excepted from being comprehended in the expression "all the world." These words—"They are all gone out of the way, there is none righteous, no not one," are mighty thunderclaps and riving thunder-bolts; they are in reality that hammer breaking the rock in pieces mentioned by Jeremiah; by which, is broken in pieces every thing that is, not in one man only, nor in some men, nor in a part of men, but in the whole world, no one man being excepted: so that the whole world ought, at those words, to tremble, to fear, and to flee away. For what words more awful or fearful could be uttered than these—The whole world is guilty; all the sons of men are turned out of the way, and become unprofitable; there is no one that fears God; there is no one that is not unrighteous; there is no one that understandeth; there is no one that seeketh after God!

Nevertheless, such ever has been, and still is, the hardness and insensible obstinacy of our hearts, that we never should of ourselves hear or feel the force of these thunder-claps or thunder-bolts, but should, even while they were sounding in our ears, exalt and establish "Free-will" with all its powers in defiance of them, and thus in reality fulfil that of Malachi i. 4, "They build, but I will throw down! "

With the same power of words also is this said—"By the deeds of the law shall no flesh be justified in His sight."—"By the deeds of the law" is a forcible expression; as is also this, "The whole world;" and this, "All the children of men." For it is to be observed, that Paul abstains from the mention of persons, and mentions their *ways* only: that is, that he might comprehend all persons, and whatever in them is most excellent. Whereas, if he had said the commonalty of the Jews, or the Pharisees, or certain of the ungodly, are not justified, he might have seemed to leave some excepted, who, from the power of "Free-will" in them, and by a certain aid from the law, were not altogether unprofitable. But now, when he condemns the works of the law themselves, and makes them unrighteous in the sight of God, it becomes manifest, that he condemns all who were mighty in a devoted observance of the law and of works. And none devotely observed the law and works but the best and most excellent among them, nor did they thus observe them but with their best and most exalted faculties; that is, their reason and their will.

If therefore, those, who exercised themselves in the observance of the law and of works with all the devoted striving and endeavouring both of reason and of will, that is, with all the power of "Free-will," and who were assisted by the law as a divine aid, and were instructed out of it, and roused to exertion by it; if, I say, these are condemned of impiety because they are not justified, and are declared to be flesh in the sight of God, what then will there be left in the whole race of mankind which is not flesh, and which is not ungodly? For all are condemned alike who are of the works of the law: and whether they exercise themselves in the law with the utmost devotion, or moderate devotion, or with no devotion at all, it matters nothing. None of them could do any thing but work the works of the law, and the works of the law do not justify: and if they do not justify, they prove their workmen to be ungodly, and leave them so: and if they be ungodly, they are guilty, and merit the wrath of God! These things are so clear, that no one can open his mouth against them.

Sect. CXLIII.—But many elude and evade Paul, by saying, that he here calls the ceremonial works, works of the law; which works, after the death of Christ, were dead.

I answer: This is that notable error and ignorance of Jerome which, although Augustine strenuously resisted it, yet, by the withdrawing of God and the prevailing of Satan, has found its way throughout the world, and has continued down to this day. By means of which, it has come to pass, that it has been impossible to understand Paul, and the knowledge of Christ has, consequently, been obscured. Therefore, if there had been no other error in the church, this one might have been sufficiently pestilent and powerful to destroy the Gospel: for which, Jerome, if peculiar grace did not interpose, has deserved hell rather than heaven: so far am I from daring to canonize him, or call him a saint! But however, it is not truth that Paul is here speaking of the ceremonial works only: for if that be the case, how will his argument stand good, whereby he concludes, that all unrighteous and need grace? But perhaps you will say—Be it so, that we are not justified by the ceremonial works, yet one might be justified by the moral works of the decalogue. By this syllogism of yours then, you have proved, that to such, grace is not necessary. If this be the case, how very useful must that grace be, which delivers us from the ceremonial works only, the easiest of all works, which may be extorted from us through mere fear or self-love!

And this, moreover, is erroneous—that ceremonial works are dead and unlawful, since the death of Christ. Paul never said any such thing. He says, that they do not justify, and that they profit the man nothing in the sight of God, so as to make him free from unrighteousness. Holding this truth, any one may do them, and yet do nothing that is unlawful. Thus, to eat and to drink are works, which do not justify or recommend us to God; and yet, he who eats and drinks does not, therefore, do that which is unlawful.

These men err also in this.—The ceremonial works, were as much commanded and exacted in the old law, and in the decalogue, as the moral works: and therefore, the latter had neither more nor less force than the former. For Paul is here speaking, principally, to the Jews, as he saith, Rom. i.: wherefore, let no one doubt, that by the works of the law here, all the works of the whole law are to be understood. For if the law be abrogated and dead, they cannot be called the works of the law; for an abrogated or dead law, is no longer a law; and that Paul knew full well. Therefore, he does not speak of the law abrogated, when he speaks of the works of the law, but of the law in force and authority: otherwise, how easy would it have been for him to say, The law is now abrogated? And then, he would have spoken openly and clearly.

But let us bring forward Paul himself, who is the best interpreter of himself. He saith, Gal. iii. 10, "As many as are of the works of the law, are under the curse: for it is written, Cursed is every one that continueth not in all things, which are written in the book of the law, to do them." You see that Paul here, where he is urging the same point as he is in his epistle to the Romans, and in the same words, speaks, wherever he makes mention of the works of the law, of all the laws that are written in the Book of the Law.

And what is still more worthy of remark, Paul himself cites Moses, who curses those that *continue not in* the law; whereas, he himself curses those who *are of* of the works of the law; thus adducing a testimony of a different scope from that of his own sentiment; the former being in the negative, the latter in the affirmative. But this he does, because the real state of the case is such in the sight of God, that those who are the most devoted to the works of the law, are the farthest from fulfilling the law, as being without the Spirit, who only is the fulfiller of the law; which such may attempt to fulfil by their own powers, but they will effect nothing after all. Wherefore, both declarations are truth—that of Moses, that they are accursed who *continue not in* the works of the law; and that of Paul, that they are accursed who *are of* the works of the law. For both characters of persons require the Spirit, without which, the works of the law, how many and excellent soever they may be, justify not, as Paul saith; wherefore neither character of persons *continue in* all things that are written, as Moses saith.

Sect. CXLIV.—In a word: Paul by this division of his, fully confirms that which I maintain. For he divides law-working men into two classes, those who work after the spirit, and those who work after the flesh, leaving no *medium* whatever. He speaks thus: "By the deeds of the law shall no flesh be justified." (Rom. iii. 20). What is this but saying, that those whose works, profit them not, work the works of the law without the Spirit, as being themselves flesh; that is, unrighteous and ignorant of God. So Gal. iii. 2, making the same division, he saith, "received ye the Spirit by the works of the law, or by the hearing of faith? " Again Rom. iii. 21, "but now, the righteousness of God is manifest without the law." And again Rom. iii. 28, "We conclude, therefore, that a man is justified by faith without the works of the law."

From all which it is manifest and clear, that in Paul, the Spirit is set in opposition to the works of the law, as well as to all other things which are not spiritual, including all the powers of, and every thing pertaining to the flesh. So that, the meaning of Paul, is evidently the same as that of Christ, John iii. 6, that every thing which is not of the Spirit is flesh, be it never so specious, holy and great, nay, be they works of the divine law the most excellent, and wrought by all the powers imaginable; for the Spirit of Christ is wanting; without which, all things are nothing short of being damnable.

Let it then be a settled point, that Paul, by the works of the law, means not the ceremonial works, but the works of the whole law; then, this will be a settled point also, that in the works of the law, every thing is condemned that is without the Spirit. And without the Spirit, is that power of "Free-will," (for that is the point in dispute),—that most exalted faculty in man! For, to be "of the works of the law," is the most exalted state in which man can be. The apostle, therefore, does not say, who are of sins, and of ungodliness against the law, but who are "of the works of the law;" that is, who are the best of men, and the most devoted to the law: and who are, in addition to the power of "Free-will," even assisted, that is, instructed and roused into action, by the law itself.

If therefore "Free-will" assisted by the law and exercising all its powers in the law, profit nothing and justify not, but be left in sin and in the flesh, what must we suppose it able to do, when left to itself without the law!

"By the law (saith Paul) is the knowledge of sin." (Rom. iii. 20). Here he shews how much, and how far the law profits:—that "Free-will" is of itself so blind, that it does not even know what is sin, but has need of the law for its teacher. And what can that man do towards taking away sin, who does not even know what is sin? All that he can do, is, to mistake that which is sin for that which is no sin, and that which is no sin for that which is sin. And this, experience sufficiently proves. How does the world, by the medium of those whom it accounts the most excellent and the most devoted to righteousness and piety, hate and persecute the righteousness of God preached in the Gospel, and brand it with the name of heresy, error, and every opprobrious appellation, while it boasts of and sets forth its own works and devices, which are really sin and error, as righteousness and wisdom? By this Scripture, therefore, Paul stops the mouth of "Free-will" where he teaches, that by the law its sin is discovered unto it, of which sin it was before ignorant; so far is he from conceding to it any power whatever to attempt that which is good.

Sect. CXLV.—And here is solved that question of the Diatribe so often repeated throughout its book—"if we can do nothing, to what purpose are so many laws, so many precepts, so many threatenings, and so many promises? "—

Paul here gives an answer: "By the law is the knowledge of sin." His answer is far different from that which would enter the thoughts of man, or of "Free-will." He does not say, by the law is proved "Free-will," because it co-operates with it unto righteousness. For righteousness is not by the law, but, "by the law is the knowledge of sin:" seeing that, the effect, the work, and the office of the law, is to be a light to the ignorant and the blind; such a light, as discovered to them disease, sin, evil, death, hell, and the wrath of God; though it does not deliver from these, but shews them only. And when a man is thus brought to a knowledge of the disease of sin, he is cast down, is afflicted, nay despairs: the law does not help him, much less can he help himself. Another light is necessary, which might discover to him the remedy. This is the voice of the Gospel, revealing Christ as the Deliverer from all these evils. Neither "Free-will" nor reason can discover Him. And how should it discover Him, when it is itself dark and devoid even of the light of the law, which might discover to it its disease, which disease, in its own light it seeth not, but believes it to be sound health.

So also in Galatians iii., treating on the same point, he saith, "Wherefore then serveth the law? " To which he answers, not as the Diatribe does, in a way that proves the existence of "Free-will," but he saith, "it was added because of transgressions, until the Seed should come, to whom the promise was made." (Gal. iii. 19). He saith, "because of transgressions;" not, however, to restrain them, as Jerome dreams; (for Paul shews, that to take away and to restrain sins, by the gift of righteousness, was that which was promised to the Seed to come;) but to cause transgressions to abound, as he saith Rom. v. 20, "The law entered that sin might abound." Not that sins were not committed and did not abound without the law, but they were not known to be transgressions and sins of such magnitude; for the most and greatest of them, were considered to be righteousnesses. And while sins are thus unknown, there is no place for remedy, or for hope; because, they will not submit to the hand of the healer, considering themselves to be whole, and not to want a physician. Therefore, the law is necessary, which might give the knowledge of sin; in order that, he who is proud and whole in his own eyes, being humbled down into the knowledge of the iniquity and greatness of his sin, might groan and breathe after the grace that is laid up in Christ.

Only observe, therefore, the simplicity of the words—"By the law is the knowledge of sin;" and yet, these alone are of force sufficient to confound and overthrow "Free-will" altogether. For if it be true, that of itself, it knows not what is sin, and what is evil, as the apostle saith here, and Rom. vii. 7-8, "I should not have known that concupiscence was sin, except the law had said, Thou shalt not covet," how can it ever know what is righteousness and good? And if it know not what righteousness is, how can it endeavour to attain unto it? We know not the sin in which we were born, in which we live, in which we move and exist, and which lives, moves, and reigns in us; how then should we know that righteousness which is without us, and which reigns in heaven? These works bring that miserable thing "Free-will" to nothing—nothing at all!

Sect. CXLVI.—The state of the case, therefore, being thus, Paul speaks openly with full confidence and authority, saying, "But now the righteousness of God is manifest without the law, being witnessed by the law and the prophets; even the righteousness of God which is by faith of Jesus Christ unto all and upon all them that believe in Him: (for there is no difference, for all have sinned and are without the glory of God:) being justified freely by His grace through the redemption that is in Christ Jesus: Whom God hath set forth to be a propitiation for sin, through faith in His blood, &c." (Rom. iii. 22-26).

Here Paul speaks forth very thunder-bolts against "Free-will." First, he saith, "The righteousness of God without the law is manifested." Here he marks the distinction between the righteousness of God, and the righteousness of the law: because, the righteousness of faith comes by grace, without the law. His saying, "without the law," can mean nothing else, but that Christian righteousness exists, without the works of the law: inasmuch as the works of the law avail nothing, and can do nothing, toward the attainment unto it. As he afterwards saith, "Therefore we conclude that a man is justified by faith without the deeds of the law." (Rom. iii. 28). The same also he had said before, "By the deeds of the law shall no flesh be justified in His sight." (Rom. iii. 20).

From all which it is most clearly manifest, that the endeavour and desire of "Free-will" are a nothing at all. For if the righteousness of God exist without the law, and without the works of the law, how shall it not much rather exist without "Free-will"! especially, since the most devoted effort of "Free-will" is, to exercise itself in moral righteousness, or the works of that law, from which its blindness and impotency derive their 'assistance! ' This word "without," therefore abolishes all moral works, abolishes all moral righteousness, abolishes all preparations unto grace. In a word, scrape together every thing you can as that which pertains to the ability of "Free-will," and Paul will still stand invincible saying,—the righteousness of God is "without" it!

But, to grant that "Free-will" can, by its endeavour, move itself in some direction, we will say, unto good works, or unto the righteousness of the civil or moral law; yet, it is not moved toward the righteousness of God, nor does God in any respect allow its devoted efforts to be worthy unto the attainment of this righteousness: for He saith, that His righteousness availeth without the works of the law. If therefore, it cannot move itself unto the attainment of the righteousness of God, what will it be profited, if it move itself by its own works and endeavours, unto the attainment of (if it were possible) the righteousness of angels! Here, I presume, the words are not 'obscure or ambiguous,' nor is any place left for 'tropes' of any kind. Here Paul distinguishes most manifestly the two righteousnesses; assigning the one to the law, the other to grace; and declares that the latter is given without the former, and without its works; and that the former justifies not, nor avails any thing, without the latter. I should like to see, therefore, how "Free-will" can stand, or be defended, against these Scriptures!

Sect. CXLVII.—Another thunder-bolt is this—The apostle saith, that the righteousness of God is manifested and avails, "unto all and upon all them that believe" in Christ: and that, "there is no difference." (Rom. iii. 21-22).—

Here again, he divides in the clearest words, the whole race of men into two distinct divisions. To the believing he gives the righteousness of God, but takes it from the unbelieving. Now, no one, I suppose, will be madman enough to doubt, whether or not the power or endeavour of "Free-will" be a something that is not faith in Christ Jesus. Paul then denies that any thing which is not this faith, is righteous before God. And if it be not righteous before God, it must be sin. For there is with God no *medium* between righteousness and sin, which can be as it were *a neuter*—neither righteousness nor sin. Otherwise the whole argument of Paul would amount to nothing: for it proceeds wholly upon this distinct division—that whatever is done and carried on by men, must be in the sight of God, either righteousness or sin: righteousness, if done in faith; sin, if faith be wanting. With men, indeed, things pass thus.—All cases in which men, in their intercourse with each other, neither owe any thing as a due, nor do any thing as a free benefit, are called *medium* and *neuter*. But here the ungodly man sins against God, whether he eat, or whether he drink, or whatever he do; because, he abuses the creature of God by his ungodliness and perpetual ingratitude, and does not, at any one moment, give glory to God from his heart.

Sect. CXLVIII.—This also, is no powerless thunder-bolt where the apostle says. "All have sinned and are without the glory of God: for there is no difference." (Rom. iii. 23).

What, I pray you, could be spoken more clearly? Produce one of your "Free-will" workmen, and say to me—does this man, sin in this his endeavour? If he does not sin, why does not Paul except him? Why does he include him also without difference? Surely he that saith "all," excepts no one in any place, at any time, in any work or endeavour. If therefore you except any man, for any kind of devoted desire or work, you make Paul a liar; because he includes that "Free-will"-workman or striver, among all the rest, and in all that he saith concerning them; whereas, Paul should have had some respect for this person, and not have numbered him among the general herd of sinners!

There is also that part, where he saith, that they are "without the glory of God."

You may understand "the glory of God" here two ways, *actively* and *passively*. For Paul writes thus from his frequent use of Hebraisms. "The glory of God," understood actively, is that glory by which God glories in us; understood passively, it is that glory by which we glory in God. But it seems to me proper, to understand it now, passively. So, "the faith of Christ," is, according to the Latin, the faith which Christ has; but, according to the Hebrew, "the faith of Christ," is the faith which we have in Christ. So, also, "the righteousness of God," signifies, according to the Latin, the righteousness which God has; but according to the Hebrews, it signifies the righteousness which we have from God and before God. Thus also "the glory of God," we understand according to the Latin, not according to the Hebrew; and receive it as signifying, the glory which we have from God and before God; which may be called, our glory in God. And that man glories in God who knows, to a certainty, that God has a favour unto him, and deigns to look upon him with kind regard; and that, whatever he does pleases God, and what does not please him, is borne with by Him and pardoned.

If therefore, the endeavour or desire of "Free-will" be not sin, but good before God, it can certainly glory; and in that glorying, say with confidence,—This pleases God, God favours this, God looks upon and accepts this, or at least, bears with it and pardons it. For this is the glorying of the faithful in God: and they that have not this, are rather confounded before God. But Paul here denies that these men have this; saying, that they are all entirely without this glory.

This also experience itself proves.—Put the question to all the exercisers of "Free-will" to a man, and see if you can shew me one, who can honestly, and from his heart, say of any one of his devoted efforts and endeavours,—This pleases God! If you can bring forward a single one, I am ready to acknowledge myself overthrown, and to cede to you the palm. But I know there is not one to be found. And if this glory be wanting, so that the conscience dares not say, to a certainty, and with confidence,—this pleases God, it is certain that it does not please God. For as a man believes, so it is unto him: because, he does not, to a certainty, believe that he pleases God; which, nevertheless, it is necessary to believe; for to doubt of the favour of God, is the very sin itself of unbelief; because, He will have it believed with the most assuring faith that He is favourable. Therefore, I have convinced them upon the testimony of their own conscience, that "Free-will," being "without the glory of God," is, with all its powers, its devoted strivings and endeavours, perpetually under the guilt of the sin of unbelief.

And what will the advocates of "Free-will" say to that which follows, "being justified freely by His grace? " (Rom. iii. 24). What is the meaning of the word "freely? " What is the meaning of "by His grace? " How will merit, and endeavour, accord with freely-given righteousness? But, perhaps, they will here say—that they attribute to "Free-will" *a very little indeed*, and that which is by no means the 'merit of worthiness' (*meritum condignum*!) These, however, are mere empty words: for all that is sought for in the defence of "Free-will," is to make place for *merit*. This is manifest: for the Diatribe has, throughout, argued and expostulated thus,

—"If there be no freedom of will, how can there be place for merit? And if there be no place for merit, how can there be place for reward? To whom will the reward be assigned, if justification be without merit? "–

Paul here gives you an answer.–That there is no such thing as merit at all; but that all who are justified are justified "freely;" that this is ascribed to no one but to the grace of God.–And when this righteousness is given, the kingdom and life eternal are given with it! Where is your endeavouring now? Where is your devoted effort? Where are your works? Where are your merits of "Free-will?" Where is the profit of them all put together? You cannot here make, as a pretence, 'obscurity and ambiguity:' the facts and the works are most clear and most plain. But be it so, that they attribute to "Free-will" a very little indeed, yet they teach us that by that very little we can attain unto righteousness and grace. Nor do they solve that question, *Why does God justify one and leave another*? in any other way, than by asserting the freedom of the will, and saying, *Because, the one endeavours and the other does not: and God regards the one for his endeavouring, and despises the other for his not endeavouring; lest, if he did otherwise, He should appear to be unjust.*

And notwithstanding all their pretence, both by their tongue and pen, that they do not profess to attain unto grace by the 'merit of worthiness' (*meritum condignum*) nor call it the merit of worthiness, yet they only mock us with a term, and hold fast their tenet all the while. For what is the amount of their pretence that they do not call it 'the merit of worthiness,' if nevertheless they assign unto it all that belongs to the merit of worthiness? –saying, that he in the sight of God attains unto grace who endeavours, and he who does not endeavour, does not attain unto it? Is this not plainly making it to be the merit of worthiness? Is it not making God a respecter of works, of merits, and of persons, to say that one man is devoid of grace from his own fault, because he did not endeavour after it, but that another, because he did endeavour after it, has attained unto grace, unto which he would not have attained, if he had not endeavoured after it? If this be not, 'the merit of worthiness,' then I should like to be informed what it is that is called 'the merit of worthiness.'

In this way you may play a game of mockery upon all words; and say, it is not indeed the merit of worthiness, but is in effect the same as the 'merit of worthiness.'–The thorn is not a bad tree, but is in effect the same as a bad tree! –The fig is not a good tree, but is in effect the same as a good tree! –The Diatribe is not, indeed, impious, but says and does nothing but what is impious!

Sect. CXLIX.–It has happened to these assertors of "Free-will" according to the old proverb, 'Striving dire Scylla's rock to shun, they 'gainst Charybdis headlong run.' For devotedly striving to dissent from the Pelagians, they begin to deny the 'merit of worthiness;' whereas, by the very way in which they deny it, they establish it more firmly than ever. They deny it by their word and pen, but establish it in reality, and in heart-sentiment: and thus, they are worse than the Pelagians themselves: and that, on two accounts. First, the Pelagians plainly, candidly, and ingenuously, assert the 'merit of worthiness;' thus calling a boat a boat, and a fig a fig; and teaching what they really think. Whereas, our "Free-will" friends, while they think and teach the same thing, yet mock us with lying words and false appearances, as though they dissented from the Pelagians; when the fact is quite the contrary. So that, with respect to their hypocrisy, they seem to be the Pelagians' strongest opposers, but with respect to the reality of the matter, and their heart-tenet, they are twice-dipped Pelagians. And next, under this hypocrisy, they estimate and purchase the grace of God at a much lower rate than the Pelagians themselves. For these assert, that it is not a certain little something in us by which we attain unto grace, but whole, full, perfect, great, and many, devoted efforts and works. Whereas, our friends declare, that it is a certain little something, almost a nothing, by which we deserve grace.

If therefore there must be error, they err with more honesty and less pride, who say, that the grace of God is purchased at a great price, and who account it dear and precious, that those who teach, that it may be purchased at that which is very little, and inconsiderable, and who account it cheap and contemptible. But however, Paul pounds both in pieces in one mortar, by one word, where he saith, that all are "justified freely;" and again that they are justified "without the law" and "without the works of the law." And he who asserts that the justification must be free in all who are justified, leaves none excepted who work, deserve, or prepare themselves; he leaves no work which can be called 'merit of congruity' or 'merit of worthiness;' and by the one hurling of this thunder-bolt, he dashes in pieces both the Pelagians with their 'whole merit,' and the Sophists with their 'very little merit.' For a free justification allows of no workmen: because, a free gift, and a work-preparation, are manifestly in opposition to each other.

Moreover, the being justified through grace, will not allow of respect unto the worthiness of any person: as the apostle saith also afterwards, chap. xi., "If by grace then it is no more of works: otherwise, grace is no more grace." (Rom. xi. 6). He saith the same also, "Now to him that worketh, is the reward not reckoned of grace, but of debt." (Rom. iv. 4). Wherefore, my Paul stands an invincible destroyer of "Free-will," and lays prostrate two armies by one word. For if we be justified "without works," all works are condemned, whether they be very little, or very great. He excepts none, but thunders alike against all.

Sect. CL.—Here you may see the yawning inconsiderateness of all our friends, and what it profits a man to rely upon the ancient fathers, who have been approved through the series of so many ages. Were they not also all alike blind to, nay rather, did they not disregard, the most clear and most manifest words of Paul? Pray what is there that can be spoken clearly and plainly in defence of grace, against "Free-will," if the argument of Paul be not clear and plain? He proceeds with a glow of argument, and exalts grace against works; and that, in words the most clear and most plain; saying, that we are "justified freely," and that grace is no more grace, if it be sought by works. Thus most manifestly excluding all works in the matter of justification, to the intent that, he might establish grace only and free justification. And yet we, in all this light, still seek after darkness; and when we cannot ascribe unto ourselves great things, and all things, we endeavour to ascribe unto ourselves a something 'in degree,' 'a very little;' merely that, we might maintain our tenet, that justification through the grace of God is not "free" and "without works."—As though he who declares, that greater things, and all things profit us nothing unto justification, does not much more deny that things 'in degree,' and things 'very little,' profit us nothing also: particularly when he has settled the point, that we are justified by grace alone without any works whatever, and therefore, without the law itself, in which are comprehended all works, great and little, works of 'congruity' and works of 'worthiness.'

Go now then and boast of the authorities of the ancients, and depend on what they say; all of whom you see, to a man, disregarded Paul, that most plain and most clear teacher; and, as it were, purposely shunned this morning star, yea, this sun rather, because, being wrapped up in their own carnal reason, they thought it absurd that no place should be left to merit.

Sect. CLI.—Let us now bring forward that example of Abraham which Paul afterwards adduces. "If (saith he) Abraham were justified by works, he hath whereof to glory, but not before God. For what saith the Scripture? Abraham believed God, and it was counted unto him for righteousness." (Rom. iv. 2-3).

Mark here again, I pray you, the distinction of Paul, where he is shewing the two-fold righteousness of Abraham.—The one, is of works; that is, moral and civil; but he denies that he was justified by this before God, even though he were justified by it before men. Moreover, by that righteousness, "he hath whereof to glory" before men, but is all the while himself without the glory of God. Nor can any one here say, that they are the works of the law, or of ceremonies, which are here condemned; seeing that, Abraham existed so many years before the law. Paul plainly speaks of the works of Abraham, and those his *best works*. For it would be ridiculous to dispute, whether or not any one were justified by *evil works*.

If therefore, Abraham be righteous by no works whatever, and if both he himself and all his works be left under sin, unless he be clothed with another righteousness, even with the righteousness of faith, it is quite manifest, that no man can do any thing by works towards his becoming righteous: and moreover, that no works, no devoted efforts, no endeavours of "Free-will," avail any thing in the sight of God, but are all judged to be ungodly, unrighteous, and evil. For if the man himself be not righteous, neither will his works or endeavours be righteous: and if they be not righteous, they are damnable, and merit wrath.

The other righteousness is that of faith; which consists, not in any works, but in the favour and imputation of God through grace. And mark how Paul dwells upon the word "imputed;" how he urges it, repeats it, and inculcates it.—"Now (saith he) to him that worketh, is the reward not reckoned of grace, but of debt. But to him that worketh not, but believeth in Him that justifieth the ungodly, his faith is counted for righteousness," (Rom. iv. 4-5), according to the purpose of the grace of God. Then he adduces David, saying the same thing concerning the imputation through grace. "Blessed is the man to whom the Lord will not impute sin," &c. (Rom. iv. 6-8).

In this chapter, he repeats the word "impute" above ten times. In a word, he distinctively sets forth "him that worketh," and "him that worketh not," leaving no *medium* between them. He declares, that righteousness is not imputed "to him that worketh," but asserts that righteousness is imputed "to him that worketh not," if he believe! Here is no way by which "Free-will," with its devoted efforts and endeavours, can escape or get off: it must be numbered with "him that worketh," or with "him that worketh not." If it be numbered with "him that worketh," you hear that righteousness is not imputed unto it; if it be numbered with "him that worketh not, but believeth" in God, righteousness is imputed unto it. And then, it will not be the power of "Free-will," but the new creature by faith. But if righteousness be not imputed unto it, being "him that worketh," then, it becomes manifest, that all its works are nothing but sins, evils, and impieties before God.

Nor can any Sophist here snarl, and say, that, although *man* be evil, yet his *work* may not be evil. For Paul speaks not of the man simply, but of "him that worketh," to the very intent that, he might declare in the plainest words, that the works and devoted efforts themselves of man are condemned, whatever they may be, by what name soever they may be called, or under what form soever they may be done. He here also speaks of good works; because, the points of his argument are, justification, and merits. And when he speaks of "him that worketh," he speaks of all workers and of all their works; but more especially of their good and meritorious works. Otherwise, his distinction between "him that worketh," and "him that worketh not," will amount to nothing.

Sect. CLII.—I here omit to bring forward those all-powerful arguments drawn from the purpose of grace, from the promise, from the force of the law, from original sin, and from the election of God; of which, there is no one that would not of itself utterly overthrow "Free-will." For if grace come by the purpose of God, or by election, it comes of necessity, and not by any devoted effort or endeavour of our own; as I have already shewn. Moreover, if God promised grace before the law, as Paul argues here, and in his epistle to the Galatians also, then it does not come by works or by the law; otherwise, it would be no longer a *promise*. And so also faith, if works were of any avail, would come to nothing: by which, nevertheless, Abraham was justified before the law was given. Again, as the law is the strength of sin, and only discovers sin, but does not take it away, it brings the conscience in guilty before God. This is what Paul means when he saith, "the law worketh wrath." (Rom. iv. 15). How then can it be possible, that righteousness should be obtained by the law? And if we derive no help from the law, how can we derive any help from the power of "Free-will" alone?

Moreover, since we all lie under the same sin and damnation of the one man Adam, how can we attempt any thing which is not sin and damnable? For when he saith "all," he excepts no one; neither the power of "Free-will," nor any workman; whether he work or work not, attempt or attempt not, he must of necessity be included among the rest in the "all." Nor should we sin or be damned by that one sin of Adam, if the sin were not our own: for who could be damned for the sin of another, especially in the sight of God? Nor is the sin ours by imitation, or by working; for this would not be the one sin of Adam; because, then, it would not be the sin which he committed, but which we committed ourselves;—it becomes our sin by generations.—But of this in some other place.—Original sin itself, therefore, will not allow of any other power in "Free-will," but that of sinning and going on unto damnation.

These arguments, I say, I omit to bring forward, both because they are most manifest and most forcible, and because I have touched upon them already. For if I wished to produce all those parts of Paul which overthrow "Free-will," I could not do better, than go through with a continued commentary on the whole of his epistle, as I have done on the third and fourth chapters. On which, I have dwelt thus particularly, that I might shew all our "Free-will" friends their yawning inconsiderateness, who so read Paul in these all-clear parts, as to see any thing in them but these most powerful arguments against "Free-will;" and that I might expose the folly of that confidence which they place in the authority and writings of the ancient teachers, and leave them to consider with what force the remaining most clear arguments must make against them, if they should be handled with care and judgment.

Sect. CLIII.—As to myself, I must confess, I am more than astonished, that, when Paul so often uses those universally applying words "all," "none," "not," "not one," "without," thus, "they are all gone out of the way, there is none that doeth good, no not one;" all are sinners and condemned by the one sin of Adam; we are justified by faith "without" the law; "without" the works of the law; so that, if any one wished to speak otherwise so as to be more intelligible, he could not speak in words more clear and more plain;—I am more than astonished, I say, how it is, that words and sentences, contrary and contradictory to these universally applying words and sentences, have gained so much ground; which say,—Some are not gone out of the way, are not unrighteous, are not evil, are not sinners, are not condemned: there is something in man which is good and which endeavours after good: as though that man, whoever he be, who endeavours after good, were not comprehended in this one word "all," or "none," or "not."

I could find nothing, even if I wished it, to advance against Paul, or to reply in contradiction to him: but should be compelled to acknowledge that the power of my "Free-will," together with its endeavours, is comprehended in those "alls," and "nones," of whom Paul here speaks; if, that is, no new kind of grammar or new manner of speech were introduced.

Moreover, if Paul had used this mode of expression once, or in one place only, there might have been room for imagining a trope, or for taking hold of and twisting some detached terms. Whereas, he uses it perpetually both in the affirmative and in the negative: and so expresses his sentiments by his argument and by his distinctive division, in every place and in all parts, that not the nature of his words only and the current of his language, but that which follows and that which precedes, the circumstances, the scope, and the very body of the whole disputation, all compel us to conclude, according to common sense, that the meaning of Paul is,—that out of the faith of Christ there is nothing but sin and damnation.

It was thus that we promised we would refute "Free-will," so that all our adversaries should not be able to resist: which, I presume, I have effected, even though they shall not so far acknowledge themselves vanquished, as to come over to my opinion, or to be silent: for that is not in my power: that is the gift of the Spirit of God!

Sect. CLIV.—But however, before we hear the Evangelist John, I will just add the crowning testimony from Paul: and I am prepared, if this be not sufficient, to oppose Paul to "Free-will" by commenting upon him throughout. Where he divides the human race into two distinctive divisions, "flesh" and "spirit," he speaks thus—"They that are after the flesh, do mind the things of the flesh; but they that are after the Spirit, do mind the things of the Spirit," (Rom. viii. 5). As Christ also does, "That which is born of the flesh is flesh; and that which is born of the Spirit is spirit," (John iii. 6).

That Paul here calls all carnal who are not spiritual, is manifest, both from the division itself and the opposition of spirit to flesh, and from the very words of Paul himself, where he adds, "But ye are not in the flesh but in the Spirit, if so be that the Spirit of God dwell in you. Now if any man have not the Spirit of Christ he is none of His" (Rom. viii. 9). What else is the meaning of "But ye are not in the flesh, but in the Spirit, if so be that the Spirit of Christ dwell in you," but, that those who have not the "Spirit," are, necessarily, in the "flesh?" And if any man be not of Christ, what else is he but of Satan? It is manifest, therefore, that those who are devoid of the Spirit, are "in the flesh," and under Satan.

Now let us see what his opinion is concerning the endeavour and the power of "Free-will" in the carnal, who are in the flesh. "They cannot please God." Again, "The carnal mind is death." Again, "The carnal mind is enmity against God." And again, "It is not subject to the law of God neither indeed can be." (Rom. viii. 5-8). Here let the advocate for "Free-will" answer me—How can that endeavour toward good "which is death," which "cannot please God," which "is enmity against God," which "is not subject to God," and "cannot" be subject to him? Nor does Paul mean to say, that the carnal mind is dead and inimical to God; but that, it is death itself, enmity itself which cannot possibly be subject to the law of God or please God; as he had said just before, "For what the law could not do, in that it was weak through the flesh, God did," &c. (Rom. viii. 3).

But I am very well acquainted with that fable of Origen concerning the *three-fold affection*; the one of which he calls 'flesh,' the other 'soul,' and the other 'spirit,' making the soul that *medium* affection, *vertible* either way, towards the flesh or towards the spirit. But these are merely his own dreams; he speaks them forth only, but does not prove them. Paul here calls every thing "flesh" that is without the "Spirit," as I have already shewn. Therefore, those most exalted virtues of the best men are in the flesh; that is, they are dead, and at enmity against God; they are not subject to the law of God, nor indeed can be; and they please not God. For Paul does not only say that such men *are not* subject, but that they *cannot be* subject. So also Christ saith, "An evil tree cannot bring forth good fruit." (Matt. vii. 17). And again, "How can ye being evil speak that which is good," (Matt. xii. 34). Here you see, we not only speak that which is evil, but cannot speak that which is good.

And though He saith in another place, that we who are evil know how to give good gifts unto our children, (Matt. vi. 11), yet He denies that we do good, even when we give good gifts; because those good gifts which we give are the creatures of God; but we ourselves not being good, cannot give those good gifts well. For He is speaking unto all men; nay, even unto His own disciples. So that these two sentiments of Paul, that the just man liveth "by faith," (Rom. i. 17), and that "whatsoever is not of faith is sin," (Rom. xiv. 23), stand confirmed: the latter of which follows from the former. For if there be nothing by which we are justified by faith only, it is evident that those who are not of faith, are not justified. And if they be not justified, they are sinners. And if they be sinners, they are evil trees and can do nothing but sin and bring forth evil fruit—Wherefore, "Free-will" is nothing but the servant of sin, of death, and of Satan, doing nothing, and being able to do or attempt nothing, but evil!

Sect. CLV.—Add to this that example, Rom. x. 24, taken out of Isaiah, "I was found of them that sought Me not, I was made manifest unto them that asked not for Me." He speaks this with reference to the Gentiles:—that it was given unto them to hear and know Christ, when before, they could not even think of Him, much less seek Him, or prepare themselves for Him by the power of "Free-will." From this example it is sufficiently evident, that grace comes so free, that no thought concerning it, or attempt or desire after it, precedes. So also Paul—when he was Saul, what did he do by that exalted power of "Free-will? " Certainly, in respect of reason, he intended that which was best and most meritoriously good. But by what endeavours did he come unto grace? He did not only not seek after it, but received it even when he was furiously maddened against it!

On the other hand, he saith of the Jews—"The Gentiles which followed not after righteousness have attained unto the righteousness which is of faith. But Israel which followed after the law of righteousness hath not attained unto the law of righteousness" (Rom. ix. 30-31). What has any advocate for "Free-will" to mutter against this? The Gentiles when filled with ungodliness and every vice, receive righteousness freely from a mercy-shewing God: while the Jews, who follow after righteousness with all their devoted effort and endeavour, are frustrated. Is this not plainly saying, that the endeavour of "Free-will" is all in vain, even when it strives to do the best; and that "Free-will," of itself, can only fall back and grow worse and worse?

Nor can any one say, that the Jews did not follow after righteousness with all the power of "Free-will." For Paul himself bears this testimony of them, "That they had a zeal of God, but not according to knowledge," (Rom. x. 2). Therefore, nothing which is attributed to "Free-will" was wanting to the Jews; and yet, it attained unto nothing, nay unto the contrary of that after which they strove. Whereas, there was nothing in the Gentiles which is attributed to "Free-will," and they attained unto the righteousness of God. And what is this but a most manifest example from each nation, and a most clear testimony of Paul, proving that grace is given freely to the most undeserving and unworthy, and is not attained unto by any devoted efforts, endeavours, or works, either small or great, of any men, be they the best and most meritorious, or even of those who have sought and followed after righteousness with all the ardour of zeal?

Sect. CLVI.—Now let us come to JOHN, who is also a most copious and powerful subverter of "Free-will."

He, at the very first outset, attributes to "Free-will" such blindness, that it cannot even see the light of the truth: so far is it from possibility, that it should endeavour after it. He speaks thus, "The light shineth in darkness, and the darkness comprehended it not." (John i. 5). And directly afterwards, "He was in the world, and the world knew Him not; He came unto His own, and His own knew Him not." (Verses 10-11).

What do you imagine he means by "world? " Will you attempt to separate any man from being included in this term, but him who is born again of the Holy Spirit? The term "world" is very particularly used by this apostle; by which he means, the whole race of men. Whatever, therefore, he says of the "world," is to be understood of the whole race of men. And hence, whatever he says of the "world," is to be understood also of "Free-will," as that which is most excellent in man. According to this apostle, then, the "world" does not know the light of truth; the "world" hates Christ and His; the "world" neither knows nor sees the Holy Spirit; the whole "world" is settled in enmity; all that is in the "world," is "the lust of the flesh, the lust of the eyes, and the pride of life." "Love not the world." "Ye (saith He) are not of the world." "The world cannot hate you; but Me it hateth, because I testify of it that the works thereof are evil."

All these and many other like passages are proclamations of what "Free-will" is—'the principal part' of the world, ruling the empire of Satan! For John also himself speaks of the world by antithesis; making the "world" to be, every thing in the world which is not translated into the kingdom of the Spirit. So also Christ saith to the apostles, "I have chosen you out of the world, and ordained you," &c. (John xv. 16). If therefore, there were any in the world, who, by the powers of "Free-will," endeavoured so as to attain unto good, (which would be the case if "Free-will" could do any thing) John certainly ought, in reverence for these persons, to have softened down the term, lest, by a word of such general application, he should involve them in all those evils of which he condemns the world. But as he does not this, it is evident that he makes "Free-will" guilty of all that is laid to the charge of the world: because, whatever the world does, it does by the power of "Free-will": that is, by its will and by its reason, which are its most exalted faculties.—He then goes on,

"But as many as received Him, to them gave He power to become the sons of God; even to them that believe on His Name. Which were born, not of blood, nor of the will of the flesh, nor of the will of man, but of God." (John i. 12-13).

Having finished this distinctive division, he rejects from the kingdom of Christ, all that is "of blood," "of the will of the flesh," and "of the will of man." By "blood," I believe, he means the Jews; that is, those who wished to be the children of the kingdom, because they were the children of Abraham and of the Fathers; and hence, gloried in their "blood." By "the will of the flesh," I understand the devoted efforts of the people, which they exercised in the law and in works: for "flesh" here signifies the carnal without the Spirit, who had indeed a will, and an endeavour, but who, because the Spirit was not in them, were carnal. By "the will of man," I understand the devoted efforts of all generally, that is, of the nations, or of any men whatever, whether exercised in the law, or without the law. So that the sense is—they become the sons of God, neither by the birth of the flesh, nor by a devoted observance of the law, nor by any devoted human effort whatever, but by a Divine birth only.

If therefore, they be neither born of the flesh, nor brought up by the law, nor prepared by any human discipline, but are born again of God, it is manifest, that "Free-will" here profits nothing. For I understand "man," to signify here, according to the Hebrew manner of speech, *any man*, or *all men*; even as "flesh," is understood to signify, by antithesis, the people without the Spirit: and "the will of man," I understand to signify the greatest power in men, that is, that 'principal part,' "Free-will."

But be it so, that we do not dwell thus upon the signification of the words, singly; yet, the sum and substance of the meaning is most clear;—that John, by this distinctive division, rejects every thing that is not of Divine generation; since he says, that men are made the sons of God none otherwise than by being born of God; which takes place, according to his own interpretation—*by believing on His name*! In this rejection therefore, "the will of man," or "Free-will," as it is not of divine generation, nor faith, is necessarily included. But if "Free-will" avail any thing, "the will of man" ought not to be rejected by John, nor ought men to be drawn away from it, and sent to faith and to the new birth only; lest that of Isaiah should be pronounced against him, "Woe unto you that call good evil." Whereas now, since he rejects alike all "blood," "the will of the flesh," and "the will of man," it is evident, that "the will of man" avails nothing more towards making men the sons of God, than "blood" does, or the carnal birth. And no one doubts whether or not the carnal birth makes men the sons of God; for as Paul saith, "They which are the children of the flesh, these are not the children of God;" (Rom. ix. 8), which he proves by the examples of Ishmael and Esau.

Sect. CLVII.—The same John, introduces the Baptist speaking thus of Christ, "And of His fulness have all we received, and grace for grace." (John i. 16).

He says, that grace is received by us out of the fulness of Christ—but for what merit or devoted effort? "For grace," saith He; that is, of Christ; as Paul also saith, "The grace of God, and the gift by grace, which is by one man Jesus Christ, hath abounded unto many." (Rom. v. 15).—Where is now the endeavour of "Free-will" by which grace is obtained! John and Paul here saith, that grace is not only not received for any devoted effort of our own, but even for the grace of another, or the merit of another, that is "of one Man Jesus Christ." Therefore, it is either false, that we receive our grace for the grace of another, or else it is evident, that "Free-will" is nothing at all; for both cannot consist—that the grace of God, is both so cheap, that it may be obtained in common and every where by the 'little endeavour' of any man; and at the same time so dear, that it is given unto us only in and through the grace of one Man, and He so great!

And I would also, that the advocates for "Free-will" be admonished in this place, that when they assert "Free-will," they are deniers of Christ. For if I obtain grace by my own endeavours, what need have I of the grace of Christ for the receiving of my grace? Or, what do I want when I have gotten the grace of God? For the Diatribe has said, and all the Sophists say, that we obtain grace, and are prepared for the reception of it, by our own endeavours; not however according to 'worthiness,' but according to 'congruity.' This is plainly denying Christ: for whose grace, the Baptist here testifies, that we receive grace. For as to that fetch about 'worthiness' and 'congruity,' I have refuted that already, and proved it to be a mere play upon empty words, while the 'merit of worthiness' is really intended; and that, to a more impious length than ever the Pelagians themselves went, as I have already shewn. And hence, the ungodly Sophists, together with the Diatribe, have more awfully denied the Lord Christ who bought us, than ever the Pelagians, or any heretics have denied Him. So far is it from possibility, that grace should allow of any particle or power of "Free-will! "

But however, that the advocates for "Free-will" deny Christ, is proved, not by this Scripture only, but by their own very way of life. For by their "Free-will," they have made Christ to be unto them no longer a sweet Mediator, but a dreaded Judge, whom they strive to please by the intercessions of the Virgin Mother, and of the Saints; and also, by variously invented works, by rites, ordinances, and vows; by all which, they aim at appeasing Christ, in order that He might give them grace. But they do not believe, that He intercedes before God and obtains grace for them by His blood and grace; as it is here said, "for grace." And as they believe, so it is unto them! For Christ is in truth, an inexorable judge to them, and justly so; for they leave Him, who is a Mediator and most merciful Saviour, and account His blood and grace of less value than the devoted efforts and endeavours of their "Free-will! "

Sect. CLVIII.—Now let us hear an example of "Free-will."—Nicodemus is a man in whom there is every thing that you can desire, which "Free-will" is able to do. For what does that man omit either of devoted effort, or endeavour? He confesses Christ to be true, and to have come from God; he declares His miracles; he comes by night to hear Him, and to converse with Him. Does he not appear to have sought after, by the power of "Free-will," those things which pertain unto piety and salvation? But mark what shipwreck he makes. When he hears the true way of salvation by a new-birth to be taught by Christ, does he acknowledge it, or confess that he had ever sought after it? Nay, he revolts from it, and is confounded; so much so, that he does not only say he does not understand it, but heaves against it as impossible—"How (says he) can these things be? " (John iii. 9).

And no wonder: for who ever heard, that man must be born again unto salvation "of water and of the Spirit? " (5). Who ever thought, that the Son of God must be exalted, "that whosoever should believe in Him, should not perish, but have everlasting life? " (15). Did the greatest and most acute philosophers ever made mention of this? Did the princes of this world ever possess this knowledge? Did the "Free-will" of any man ever attain unto this, by endeavours? Does not Paul confess it to be "wisdom hidden in a mystery," foretold indeed by the Prophets, but revealed by the Gospel? So that, it was secret and hidden from the world.

In a word: Ask experience: and the whole world, human reason itself, and in, consequence, "Free-will" itself is compelled to confess, that it never knew Christ, nor heard of Him, before the Gospel came into the world. And if it did not know Him, much less could it seek after Him, search for Him, or endeavour to come unto Him. But Christ is "the way" of truth, life, and salvation. It must confess, therefore, whether it will or no, that, of its own powers, it neither knew nor could seek after those things which pertain unto the way of truth and salvation. And yet, contrary to this our own very confession and experience, like madmen we dispute in empty words, that there is in us that power remaining, which can both know and apply itself unto those things which pertain unto salvation! This is nothing more or less than saying, that Christ the Son of God was exalted for us, when no one could ever have known it or thought of it; but that, nevertheless, this very ignorance is not an ignorance, but a knowledge of Christ; that is, of those things which pertain unto salvation.

Do you not yet then see and palpably feel out, that the assertors of "Free-will" are plainly mad, while they call that knowledge, which they themselves confess to be ignorance? Is this not to "put darkness for light? " (Isaiah v. 20). But so it is, though God so powerfully stop the mouth of "Free-will" by its own confession and experience, yet even then, it cannot keep silence and give God the glory.

Sect. CLIX.—And now farther, as Christ is said to be "the way, the truth, and the life," (John xiv. 6), and that, by positive assertion, so that whatever is not Christ is not the way but error, is not the truth but a lie, is not the life but death, it of necessity follows, that "Free-will," as it is neither Christ nor in Christ, must be bound in error, in a lie, and in death. Where now will be found that medium and neuter—that the power of "Free-will," which is not in Christ, that is, in the way, the truth, and the life, is yet not, of necessity, either error, or a lie, or death?

For if all things which are said concerning Christ and grace were not said by positive assertion, that they might be opposed to their contraries; that is, that out of Christ there is nothing but Satan, out of grace nothing but wrath, out of the light nothing but darkness, out of the life nothing but death—what, I ask you, would be the use of all the Writings of the Apostles, nay, of the whole Scripture? The whole would be written in vain; because, they would not fix the point, that Christ is necessary (which, nevertheless, is their especial design) and for this reason,—because a medium would be found out, which of itself, would be neither evil nor good, neither of Christ nor of Satan, neither true nor false, neither alive nor dead, and perhaps, neither any thing nor nothing; and that would be called, 'that which is most excellent and most exalted' in the whole race of men!

Take it therefore which way you will.—If you grant that the Scriptures speak in positive assertion, you can say nothing for "Free-will," but that which is contrary to Christ: that is, you will say, that error, death, Satan, and all evils, reign in Him. If you do not grant that they speak in positive assertion, you weaken the Scriptures, make them to establish nothing, not even to prove that Christ is necessary. And thus, while you establish "Free-will," you make Christ void, and bring the whole Scripture to destruction. And though you may pretend, verbally, that you confess Christ; yet, in reality and in heart, you deny Him. For if the power of "Free-will" be not a thing erroneous altogether, and damnable, but sees and wills those things which are good and meritorious, and which pertain unto salvation, it is whole, it wants not the physician Christ, nor does Christ redeem that part of man.—For what need is there for light and life, where there is light and life already?

Moreover, if that power be not redeemed, the best part in man is not redeemed, but is of itself good and whole. And then also, God is unjust if He damn any man; because, He damns that which is the most excellent in man, and whole; that is, He damns him when innocent. For there is no man who has not "Free-will." And although the evil man abuse this, yet this power itself, (according to what you teach) is not so destroyed, but that it can, and does endeavour towards good. And if it be such, it is without doubt good, holy, and just: wherefore, it ought not to be damned, but to be distinctly separated from the man who is to be damned. But this cannot be done, and even if it could be done, man would then be without "Free-will," nay, he would not be man at all, he would neither have merit nor demerit, he could neither be damned nor saved, but would be completely a brute, and no longer immortal. It follows therefore, that God is unjust who damns that good, just, and holy power, which, though it be in an evil man, does not need Christ as the evil man does.

Sect. CLX.—But let us proceed with John. "He that believeth on Him, (saith he) is not condemned; but he that believeth not is condemned already, because he hath not believed on the Name of the only begotten Son of God." (John iii. 18).

Tell me! —Is "Free-will" included in the number of those that believe, or not? If it be, then again, it has no need of grace; because, of itself, it believes on Christ—whom, of itself it never knew nor thought of! If it be not, then it is judged already: and what is this but saying, that it is damned in the sight of God? But God damns none but the ungodly: therefore, it is ungodly. And what godliness can that which is ungodly endeavour after? For I do not think that the power of "Free-will" can be excepted; seeing that, he speaks of the whole man as being condemned.

Moreover, unbelief is not one of the grosser affections, but is that chief affection seated and ruling on the throne of the will and reason; just the same as its contrary, faith. For to be unbelieving, is to deny God, and to make him a liar; "If we believe not we make God a liar," (1 John v. 10). How then can that power, which is contrary to God, and which makes Him a liar, endeavour after that which is good? And if that power be not unbelieving and ungodly, John ought not to say of the *whole man* that he is condemned already, but to speak thus,—Man, according to his 'grosser affections,' is condemned already; but according to that which is best and 'most excellent,' he is not condemned; because, that endeavours after faith, or rather, is already believing.

Hence, where the Scripture so often saith, "All men are liars," we must, upon the authority of "Free-will," on the contrary say—the Scripture rather, lies; because, man is not a liar as to his *best part*, that is, his reason and will, but as to his *flesh* only, that is, his blood and his grosser part: so that that *whole*, according to which he is called man, that is, his reason and his will, is sound and holy. Again, there is that of the Baptist, "He that believeth on the Son hath everlasting life; he that believeth not the Son shall not see life, but the wrath of God abideth on him." (John iii. 36). We must understand "upon him" thus:—that is, the wrath of God abideth upon the 'grosser affections' of the man: but upon that power of "Free-will," that is, upon his will and his reason, abide grace and everlasting life.

Hence, according to this, in order that "Free-will" might stand, whatever is in the Scriptures said against the ungodly, you are, by the figure synecdoche, to twist round to apply to that brutal part of man, that the truly rational and human part might remain safe. I have therefore, to render thanks to the assertors of "Free-will;" because, I may sin with all confidence; knowing that, my reason and will, or my "Free-will," cannot be damned, because it cannot be destroyed by my sinning, but for ever remains sound, righteous, and holy. And thus, happy in my will and reason, I shall rejoice that my filthy and brutal flesh is distinctly separated from me, and damned; so far shall I be from wishing Christ to become its Redeemer! —You see, here, to what the doctrine of "Free-will" brings us—it denies all things, divine and human, temporal and eternal; and with all these enormities, makes a laughing-stock of itself!

Sect. CLXI—Again, the Baptist saith, "A man can receive nothing, except it were given him from above." (John iii. 27).

Let not the Diatribe here produce its forces, where it enumerates all those things which we have from heaven. We are now disputing, not about nature, but about grace: we are inquiring, not what we are upon earth, but what we are in heaven before God. We know that man was constituted lord over those things which are beneath himself; over which, he has a right and a Free-will, that those things might do, and obey as he wills and thinks. But we are now inquiring whether he has a "Free-will" over God, that He should do and obey in those things which man wills: or rather, whether God has not a Free-will over man, that he should will and do what God wills, and should be able to do nothing but what He wills and does. The Baptist here says, that he "can receive nothing, except it be given him from above."—Wherefore, "Free-will" must be a nothing at all!

Again, "He that is of the earth, is earthly and speaketh of the earth, He that cometh from heaven is above all." (John iii. 31).

Here again, he makes all those earthly, who are not of Christ, and says that they savour and speak of earthly things only, nor does he leave any medium characters. But surely, "Free-will" is not "He that cometh from heaven." Wherefore it must of necessity, be "he that is of the earth," and that speaks of the earth and savours of the earth. But if there were any power in man, which at any time, in any place, or by any work, did not savour of the earth, the Baptist ought to have excepted this person, and not to have said in a general way concerning all those who are out of Christ, that they are of the earth, and speak of the earth.

So also afterwards, Christ saith, "Ye are of the world, I am not of the world. Ye are from beneath, I am from above." (John viii. 23).

And yet, those to whom He spoke had "Free-will," that is, reason and will; but still He says, that they are "of the world." But what news would He have told, if He had merely said, that they were of the world, as to their 'grosser affections?' Did not the whole world know this before? Moreover, what need was there for His saying that men were of the world, as to that part in which they are brutal? For according to that, beasts are also of the world.

Sect. CLXII.—And now what do those words of Christ, where He saith, "No one can come unto Me except My Father which hath sent Me draw him," (John vi. 44), leave to "Free-will?" For He says it is necessary, that every one should hear and learn of the Father Himself, and that all must be "taught of God." Here, indeed, He not only declares that the works and devoted efforts of "Free-will" are of no avail, but that even the word of the Gospel itself, (of which He is here speaking,) is heard in vain, unless the Father Himself speak within, and teach and draw. "No one can," "No one can (saith He) come:" by which, that power, whereby man can endeavour something towards Christ, that is, towards those things which pertain unto salvation, is declared to be a nothing at all.

Nor does that at all profit "Free-will," which the Diatribe brings forward out of Augustine, by way of casting a slur upon this all-clear and all-powerful Scripture—'that God draws us, in the same way as we draw a sheep, by holding out to it a green bough.' By this similitude he would prove, that there is in us *a power to follow the drawing of God*. But this similitude avails nothing in the present passage. For God holds out, not one of His good things, only, but many, nay, even His Son, Christ Himself; and yet no man follows Him, unless the Father hold Him forth otherwise within, and draw otherwise! —Nay, the whole world follows the Son whom He holds forth!

But this similitude harmonises sweetly with the experience of the godly, who are now made sheep, and know God their Shepherd. These, living in, and being moved by, the Spirit, follow wherever God wills, and whatever He holds out to them. But the ungodly man comes not unto Him, even when he hears the word, unless the Father draw and teach within: which He does by shedding abroad His Spirit. And where that is done, there is a different kind of drawing from that which is without: there, Christ is held forth in the illumination of the Spirit, whereby the man is drawn unto Christ with the sweetest of all drawing: under which, he is passive while God speaks, teaches, and draws, rather than seeks or runs of himself.

Sect. CLXIII.—I will produce yet one more passage from John, where, he saith, "The Spirit shall reprove the world of sin, because they believe not in me." (John xvi. 9).

You here see, that it is sin, not to believe in Christ: And this sin is seated, not in the skin, nor in the hairs of the head, but in the very reason and will. Moreover, as Christ makes the whole world guilty from this sin, and as it is known by experience that the world is ignorant of this sin, as much so as it is ignorant of Christ, seeing that, it must be *revealed* by the *reproof* of the Spirit; it is manifest, that "Free-will," together with its will and reason, is accounted a captive of this sin, and condemned before God. Wherefore, as long as it is ignorant of Christ and believes not in Him, it can will or attempt nothing good, but necessarily serves that sin of which it is ignorant.

In a word: Since the Scripture declares Christ everywhere by positive assertion and by antithesis, (as I said before), in order that, it might subject every thing that is without the Spirit of Christ, to Satan, to ungodliness, to error, to darkness, to sin, to death, and to the wrath of God, all the testimonies concerning Christ must make directly against "Free-will;" and they are innumerable, nay, the whole of the Scripture. If therefore our subject of discussion is to be decided by the judgment of the Scripture, the victory, in every respect, is mine; for there is not one jot or tittle of the Scripture remaining, which does not condemn the doctrine of "Free-will" altogether!

But if the great theologians and defenders of "Free-will" know not, or pretend not to know, that the Scripture every where declares Christ by positive assertion and by antithesis, yet all Christians know it, and in common confess it. They know, I say, that there are two kingdoms in the world mutually militating against each other.—That Satan reigns in the one, who, on that account is by Christ called "the prince of this world," (John xii. 31), and by Paul "the god of this world;" (2 Cor. iv. 4), who, according to the testimony of the same Paul, holds all captive according to his will, who are not rescued from him by the Spirit of Christ: nor does he suffer any to be rescued by any other power but that of the Spirit of God: as Christ testifies in the parable of "the strong man armed" keeping his palace in peace.—In the other kingdom Christ reigns: which kingdom, continually resists and wars against that of Satan: into which we are translated, not by any power of our own, but by the grace of God, whereby we are delivered from this present evil world, and are snatched from the power of darkness. The knowledge and confession of these two kingdoms, which thus ever mutually war against each other with so much power and force, would alone be sufficient to confute the doctrine of "Free-will:" seeing that, we are compelled to serve in the kingdom of Satan, until we be liberated by a Divine Power. All this, I say, is known in common among Christians, and fully confessed in their proverbs, by their prayers, by their pursuits, and by their whole lives.

Sect. CLXIV.—I omit to bring forward that truly Achillean Scripture of mine, which the Diatribe proudly passes by untouched—I mean, that which Paul teaches, Rom. vii. and Gal. v., that there is in the saints, and in the godly, so powerful a warfare between the spirit and the flesh, that they cannot do what they would. From this warfare I argue thus:—If the nature of man be so evil, even in those who are born again of the Spirit, that it does not only not endeavour after good, but is even averse to, and militates against good, how should it endeavour after good in those who are not born again of the Spirit, and who are still in the "old man," and serve under Satan? Nor does Paul there speak of the 'grosser affections' only, (by means of which, as a common scape-gap, the Diatribe is accustomed to get out of the way of all the Scriptures,) but he enumerates among the works of the flesh heresy, idolatry, contentions, divisions, &c.; which he describes as reigning in those most exalted faculties; that is, in the reason and the will. If therefore, flesh with these affections war against the Spirit in the saints, much more will it war against God in the ungodly, and in "Free-will. Hence, Rom. viii. 7, he calls it "enmity against God."—I should like, I say, to see this argument of mine overturned, and "Free-will" defended against it.

As to myself, I openly confess, that I should not wish "Free-will" to be granted me, even if it could be so, nor anything else to be left in my own hands, whereby I might endeavour something towards my own salvation. And that, not merely because in so many opposing dangers, and so many assaulting devils, I could not stand and hold it fast, (in which state no man could be saved, seeing that one devil is stronger than all men;) but because, even though there were no dangers, no conflicts, no devils, I should be compelled to labour under a continual uncertainty, and to beat the air only. Nor would my conscience, even if I should live and work to all eternity, ever come to a settled certainty, how much it ought to do in order to satisfy God. For whatever work should be done, there would still remain a scrupling, whether or not it pleased God, or whether He required any thing more; as is proved in the experience of all justiciaries, and as I myself learned to my bitter cost, through so many years of my own experience.

But now, since God has put my salvation out of the way of *my* will, and has taken it under *His own*, and has promised to save me, not according to my working or manner of life, but according to His own grace and mercy, I rest fully assured and persuaded that He is faithful, and will not lie, and moreover great and powerful, so that no devils, no adversities can destroy Him, or pluck me out of His hand. "No one (saith He) shall pluck them out of My hand, because My Father which gave them Me is greater than all." (John x. 27-28). Hence it is certain, that in this way, if all are not saved, yet some, yea, many shall be saved; whereas by the power of "Free-will," no one whatever could be saved, but all must perish together. And moreover, we are certain and persuaded, that in this way, we please God, not from the merit of our own works, but from the favour of His mercy promised unto us; and that, if we work less, or work badly, He does not impute it unto us, but, as a Father, pardons us and makes us better.—This is the glorying which all the saints have in their God!

Sect. CLXV.—And if you are concerned about this,—that it is difficult to defend the mercy and justice of God, seeing that, He damns the undeserving, that is, those who are for that reason ungodly, because, being born in iniquity, they cannot by any means prevent themselves from being ungodly, and from remaining so, and being damned, but are compelled from the necessity of nature to sin and perish, as Paul saith, "We all were the children of wrath, even as others," (Eph. ii. 3.), when at the same time, they were created such by God Himself from a corrupt seed, by means of the sin of Adam,—

Here God is to be honoured and revered, as being most merciful towards those, whom He justifies and saves under all their unworthiness: and it is to be in no small degree ascribed unto His wisdom, that He causes us to believe Him to be just, even where He appears to be unjust. For if His righteousness were such, that it was considered to be righteousness according to human judgment, it would be no longer divine, nor would it in any thing differ from human righteousness. But as He is the one and true God, and moreover incomprehensible and inaccessible by human reason, it is right, nay, it is necessary, that His righteousness should be incomprehensible: even as Paul exclaims, saying, "Oh the depth of the riches, both of the wisdom and knowledge of God, how unsearchable are His judgments, and His ways past finding out! " (Rom. xi. 33). But they would be no longer "past finding out" if we were in all things able to see how they were righteous. What is man, compared with God! What can our power do, when compared with His power! What is our strength, compared with His strength! What is our knowledge compared with His wisdom! What is our substance, compared with His substance! In a word, what is all that we are, compared with all that He is!

If then we confess, even according to the teaching of nature, that human power, strength, wisdom, knowledge, substance, and all human things together, are nothing when compared with the divine power, strength, wisdom, knowledge, and substance, what perverseness must it be in us to attack the righteousness and judgments of God only, and to arrogate so much to our own judgment, as to wish to comprehend, judge, and rate, the divine judgments! Why do we not, here in like manner say at once—What! is our judgment nothing, when compared with the divine judgments! —But ask reason herself if she is not, from conviction, compelled to confess, that she is foolish and rash for not allowing the judgments of God to be incomprehensible, when she confesses that all the other divine things are incomprehensible? In every thing else we concede to God a Divine Majesty; and yet, are ready to deny it to His judgments! Nor can we for a little while believe, that He is just, even when He promises that it shall come to pass, that when He shall reveal His glory, we shall all see, and palpably feel, that He ever was, and is,—just!

Sect. CLXVI.—But I will produce an example that may go to confirm this faith, and to console that "evil eye" which suspects God of injustice.—Behold! God so governs this corporal world in external things, that, according to human reason and judgment, you must be compelled to say, either that there is no God, or that God is unjust: as a certain one saith, 'I am often tempted to think there is no God.' For see the great prosperity of the wicked, and on the contrary the great adversity of the good; according to the testimony of the proverbs, and of experience the parent of all proverbs. The more abandoned men are, the more successful! "The tabernacles of robbers (saith Job) prosper." And Psalm lxxiii. complains, that the sinners of the world abound in riches. Is it not, I pray you, in the judgment of all, most unjust, that the evil should be prosperous, and the good afflicted? Yet so it is in the events of the world. And here it is, that the most exalted minds have so fallen, as to deny that there is any God at all; and to fable, that fortune disposes of all things at random: such were Epicurus and Pliny. And Aristotle, in order that he might make his 'First-cause Being' free from every kind of misery, is of opinion, that he thinks of nothing whatever but himself; because he considers, that it must be most irksome to him, to see so many evils and so many injuries.

But the Prophets themselves, who believed there is a God, were tempted still more concerning the injustice of God, as Jeremiah, Job, David, Asaph, and others. And what do you suppose Demosthenes and Cicero thought, who, after they had done all they could, received no other reward than a miserable death? And yet all this, which is so very much like injustice in God, when set forth in those arguments which no reason or light of nature can resist, is most easily cleared up by the light of the Gospel, and the knowledge of grace: by which, we are taught, that the wicked flourish *in their bodies*, but lose *their souls*! And the whole of this insolvable question is solved in one word—There is a life after this life: in which will be punished and repaid, every thing that is not punished and repaid here: for this life is nothing more than an entrance on, and a beginning of, the life which is to come!

If then even the light of the Gospel, which stands in the word and in the faith only, is able to effect so much as with ease to do away with, and settle, this question which has been agitated through so many ages and never solved; how do you suppose matters will appear, when the light of the word and of faith shall cease, and the essential Truth itself shall be revealed in the Divine Majesty? Do you not suppose that the light of glory will then most easily solve that question, which is now insolvable by the light of the word and of grace, even as the light of grace now easily solves that question, which is insolvable by the light of nature?

Let us therefore hold in consideration the three lights—the light *of nature*, the light *of grace*, and the light *of glory*; which is the common, and a very good distinction. By the light of nature, it is insolvable *how* it can be just, that the good man should be afflicted and the wicked should prosper: but this is solved by the light of grace. By the light of grace it is insolvable, *how* God can damn him, who, by his own powers, can do nothing but sin and become guilty. Both the light of nature and the light of grace here say, that the fault is not in the miserable man, but in the unjust God: nor can they judge otherwise of that God, who crowns the wicked man freely without any merit, and yet crowns not, but damns another, who is perhaps less, or at least not more wicked. But the light of glory speaks otherwise.—That will shew, that God, to whom alone belongeth the judgment of incomprehensible righteousness, is of righteousness most perfect and most manifest; in order that we may, in the meantime, believe it, being admonished and confirmed by that example of the light of grace, which solves that, which is as great a miracle to the light of nature!

CONCLUSION

Sect. CLXVII.—I shall here draw this book to a conclusion: prepared if it were necessary to pursue this Discussion still farther. Though I consider that I have now abundantly satisfied the godly man, who wishes to believe the truth without making resistance. For if we believe it to be true, that God fore-knows and fore-ordains all things; that He can be neither deceived nor hindered in His Prescience and Predestination; and that nothing can take place but according to His Will, (which reason herself is compelled to confess;) then, even according to the testimony of reason herself, there can be no "Free-will"—in man,—in angel,—or in any creature!

Hence:—If we believe that Satan is the prince of this world, ever ensnaring and fighting against the kingdom of Christ with all his powers; and that he does not let go his captives without being forced by the Divine Power of the Spirit; it is manifest, that there can be no such thing as—"Free-will! "

Again:—If we believe that original sin has so destroyed us, that even in the godly who are led by the Spirit, it causes the utmost molestation by striving against that which is good; it is manifest, that there can be nothing left in a man devoid of the Spirit, which can turn itself towards good, but which must turn towards evil!

Again:—If the Jews, who followed after righteousness with all their powers, ran rather into unrighteousness, while the Gentiles who followed after unrighteousness attained unto a free righteousness which they never hoped for; it is equally manifest, from their very works, and from experience, that man, without grace, can do nothing but will evil!

Finally:—If we believe that Christ redeemed men by His blood, we are compelled to confess, that the whole man was lost: otherwise, we shall make Christ superfluous, or a Redeemer of the grossest part of man only,—which is blasphemy and sacrilege!

Sect. CLXVIII.—And now, my friend Erasmus, I entreat you for Christ's sake to perform what you promised. You promised 'that you would willingly yield to him, who should teach you better than you knew.' Lay aside all respect of persons. You, I confess, are great and adorned with many, and those the most noble, gifts of God; (to say nothing of the rest,) with talent, with erudition, and with eloquence to a miracle. Whereas I, have nothing and am nothing, excepting that, I glory in being almost a Christian!

In this, moreover, I give you great praise, and proclaim it—you alone in pre-eminent distinction from all others, have entered upon the thing itself; that is, the grand turning point of the cause; and, have not wearied me with those irrelevant points about popery, purgatory, indulgences, and other like *baubles*, rather than *causes*, with which all have hitherto tried to hunt me down,—though in vain! You, and you alone saw, what was the grand hinge upon which the whole turned, and therefore you attacked the vital part at once; for which, from my heart, I thank you. For in this kind of discussion I willingly engage, as far as time and leisure permit me. Had those who have heretofore attacked me done the same, and would those still do the same, who are now boasting of new spirits, and new revelations, we should have less sedition and sectarianism, and more peace and concord.—But thus has God, by the instrumentality of Satan, avenged our ingratitude!

But however, if you cannot manage this cause otherwise than you have managed it in this Diatribe, do, I pray you, remain content with your own proper gift. Study, adorn, and promote literature and languages, as you have hitherto done, to great advantage, and with much credit. In which capacity, you have rendered me also a certain service: so much so, that I confess myself to be much indebted to you: and in that character, I certainly venerate, and honestly respect you. But as to this our cause:—to this, God has neither willed, nor given it you, to be equal: though I entreat you not to consider this as spoken in arrogance. No! I pray that the Lord may, day by day, make you as much superior to me in these matters, as you are superior to me in all others. And it is no new thing for God to instruct a Moses by a Jethro, or to teach a Paul by an Ananias. And as to what you say,—"You have greatly missed the mark after all, if you are ignorant of Christ."—You yourself, if I mistake not, know what that is. But all will not therefore err, because you or I may err. God is glorified in His saints in a wonderful way! So that, we may consider those saints who are the farthest from sanctity. Nor is it an unlikely thing, that you, as being man, should not rightly understand, nor with sufficient diligence weigh, the Scriptures, or the sayings of the Fathers: under which guides, you imagine you cannot miss the mark. And that such is the case, is quite manifest from this:—your saying that you do not *assert*, but *collect*. No man would write thus, who was fully acquainted with, and well understood his subject. On the contrary I, in this book of mine, have *collected* nothing, but have *asserted*, and still *do assert*: and I wish none to become judges, but all to yield assent.—And may the Lord, whose cause this is, illuminate you, and make you a vessel to honour and to glory.—Amen!

FINIS.

1525.

MARTIN LUTHER'S JUDGMENT

OF

ERASMUS OF ROTTERDAM.

TO A CERTAIN FRIEND.

Grace and peace in Christ,

I received your last letter gladly, my excellent friend, because I believe you wish well to, and are concerned for, the state of the Christian cause. And I wish and pray, that the Lord would perfect that which he hath begun in you.

I am grieved at hearing, that among you also this cruel persecution is carried on against Christ. But it will come to this:—either that cruel tyrant will change his fury of his own accord, or you will change it for him, and that shortly.

Concerning Predestination, I knew long ago, that Mosellanus agrees with Erasmus: for he is an Erasmian altogether. My fixed opinion is, however, that Erasmus knows less about Predestination, (or rather pretends to know) than even the schools of the Sophists have known. Nor have I any need to fear a fall, while I maintain my sentiments unchanged. Erasmus is not to be dreaded on this point, nor indeed on any essential point of Christianity. Truth is more powerful than eloquence; the Spirit is far above human talent; faith is beyond all erudition; and, as Paul saith, "the foolishness of God is wiser than men! " (1 Cor. i. 25). The eloquence of Cicero, was often overthrown by inferior eloquence, in the discussion of public causes. Julian, was more eloquent than Augustine. In a word, the victory is in the hands of child-speaking truth, not in the hands of lying eloquence! —As it is written, "Out of the mouth of babes and sucklings has thou ordained strength, that thou mightest still the enemy and avenger." (Ps. viii. 2; Matt. xxi. 16).

I will not provoke Erasmus, nor will I even when provoked once or twice, return the blow. And yet I do not think he shews his wisdom, in directing the powers of his eloquence against me. For I fear he will not find in Luther a Faber of Picardy, nor be able to exult over me, as he does over him, where he says, 'All congratulate me upon my victory over the Gaul.' But however, if he will enter the lists with me, he shall find, that Christ fears neither the powers of the air, nor the gates of hell. And I, a most weak-tongued babe, will meet the all-eloquent Erasmus with confidence, caring nothing for his authority, his name, or his reputation. I know well what is in the man; seeing that, I am well acquainted with the thoughts of Satan; though I expect he will daily manifest more and more that disposition towards me which he fosters in his heart.

I express myself thus plainly, that you might have no fear or concern on my account, nor be frightened at the great and swelling words of others. I wish you to salute Mosellanus in my name: for I am not therefore ill-affected towards him, because he leans to the side of Erasmus rather than to mine. Nay tell him to stand by Erasmus firmly: for the time will come, when he will think otherwise. In the meantime, the weakness of an excellent heart is to be borne with. And may you also prosper in the Lord.

Wirtemberg, 1522.

MARTIN LUTHER TO NICHOLAS ARMSDOFF

CONCERNING

ERASMUS OF ROTTERDAM.

Grace and peace in Christ.

I thank you, my excellent friend, that you give me so candidly your opinion on my book. I care not at all that the Papists are offended: I did not write on their account, for they are not worth my writing or speaking in consideration of them any more. God has given them up to a reprobate mind; so that they even fight against that, which they know to be the truth.

My cause was heard at Augsberg, before the emperor Charles, and the whole world, and found to be irreprehensible, and to contain sound doctrine. Moreover, my Confession and Apology are made public, and set in the open light throughout the world. By these, I have answered an infinity of my adversaries' books, and all the lies of the Papists past, present and to come!

I have confessed Christ before this wicked and adulterous generation, and I doubt not but that He will also confess me before His Father, and the holy angels. My light is set on a candlestick! —Let him that seeth it, see it more clearly still; let him that is blind, be blinder still; let him that is just, be juster still; let him that is filthy, be filthier still;—their blood be upon themselves;—I am clean from their blood! I have declared to the unrighteous his unrighteousness, and he will not be converted;—let him therefore die in his sins;—I have saved my own soul! There is no need, therefore, that I should write, or care to write on their account, any farther.

And as to your advice, that that grammarian or vocabularian whom you call the Erasmian plagiary should be held in contempt, and that Erasmus himself should rather be answered: know, that I have held him in sufficient contempt already: for I have not read one page of his writings. Jonas answered him once, although I was much against his doing it; and advised him, according to your opinion, to hold him in contempt. For I know the man well, from his skin to his heart, that he is not worthy of being spoken to, or dealt with, by any good man; such a hypocrite is he, and so full of reprobate envy and malevolence.

Moreover, you know my usual way of overthrowing writers of this stamp—by holding them in silent contempt. For how many books of Eccius, Faber, Emser, Cochles, and many others, who seemed to be as mountains in labour, and about to bring forth I know not what wonders, have I myself, by my silence only, so utterly brought to nothing that no memory of them is left. Cato calls such pettifoggers, and allows all their pratings to pass by unnoticed: whereas, if he had at all considered them worthy of being noticed and answered, they might have procured to themselves a lasting fame. And there is a trite, but true proverb,—

Full well I know, that if with dung embroiled,
Conqu'or or conquer'd, still I am besoiled.

But here is my glorying.—Whatever could be brought against me from the Scriptures and from the fathers, has been produced and published: and now, all the glorying they have left, is in slanders, lies, and calumnies. And why should I envy them that, when they have no power or desire whatever to be renowned for any other virtues!

Your judgment of Erasmus I much admire: wherein you say plainly, that he has no other basis wherein to build his doctrine but the favour of men; and attribute to him, moreover, ignorance and malice. And if you could but convey this judgment of yours with conviction to the minds of men in general, you would in truth, like another stripling David, by this one blow, lay our boasting Goliath prostrate, and at the same time, eradicate the whole of his sect. For what is more vain, more fallacious, in all things, than the applause of men, especially in things spiritual! For, as the Psalms testify, "There is no help in them:" again, "All men are liars." If therefore Erasmus be nothing but vanity, and rest alone on vanity and a lie, what need is there to reply to him at all? He himself, together with all his vanity, will at length vanish like smoke, if we but treat him as I have treated those former scare-crows and pettifoggers, whom, by my silence only, I have committed to utter oblivion.

I at one time attributed to him a singular kind of inconsistency and vain-talking, for he seemed to treat on sacred and serious things with the greatest unconcern; and on the contrary, to pursue baubles, vanities, and things laughable and ridiculous with the utmost avidity; though an old man, and a theologian; and that, in an age, the most industrious and laborious. So that I really thought, that what I had heard many men of wisdom and gravity say, was true—that Erasmus was actually mad.

When I first wrote against his Diatribe, and was compelled to weigh his words, (as John says "try the Spirits,") being disgusted at his inconsiderateness in a subject of so much importance; in order that I might rouse up the cold and doltish disputer, I goaded him as if in a snoring sleep; calling him a disciple, at one time, of Epicurus, at another, of Lucian, and then again, declaring him to be of the opinion of the sceptics; supposing, that by these means he might, perhaps, be roused up to enter upon the subject with more feeling. But all was in vain. I only irritated the viper, so as to cause him at last to give birth to his VIPERASPIS, an off-spring worthy of, and exactly like, its parent. But however, he proudly omitted to say one single word to the subject point. So that, from that time, I have despaired of his theology altogether.

Now, however, I am quite of your opinion, that it was not inconsiderateness in him, but as you say, real ignorance and malice. For he was unacquainted with our doctrines, or the doctrines of Christianity; he knew them, but from policy would not know them. And though he may not understand, nor indeed can understand, those doctrines which are peculiar to our fraternity, and which we maintain against the synagogue of the Pope, yet he cannot be ignorant of those which are held in common by us and the church under the Pope; because, he writes on these very largely, or rather, laughs at them.—Such as, the Trinity of the Divine Persons, the Divinity and humanity of Christ, sin, the redemption of the human race, the resurrection of the dead, eternal life, and the like: he knows, I say, that these things are taught and believed even by many ungodly and false Christians. But the truth is, he hates all the doctrines together. Nay, there can be no doubt in the mind of a true believer, who has the Spirit in his nostrils, that his mind is alienated from, and utterly hates, all religion together; and especially, the religion of Christ. Many proofs of this are scattered here and there. And it will come to pass by and by, that alike the mole, he will throw up some dirt, that will shew where and what he is, and prove his own destruction.

He published lately, among his other works, his CATECHISM, a production evidently of Satanic subtlety. For, with a purpose full of craft, he designs to take children and youths at the outset, and to infect them with his poisons, that they might not afterwards be eradicated from them; just as he himself, in Italy and at Rome, so sucked in his doctrines of sorcerers and of devils, that now all remedy is too late. But who would bear with this method of bringing up children, or the weak in faith, which Erasmus proposes to us? The tender and unexperienced mind is to be formed at first by certain, plain, and necessary principles, which it may firmly believe. Because, it is necessary that every one who would learn, should believe: for what will he ever learn, who either doubts himself, or is taught to doubt?

But this new chatechist of ours, aims only at rendering his catechumens, and the doctrines of faith, suspicious. For at the very outset, laying aside all solid foundation, he does nothing but set before them those heresies and offences of opinions, by which the Church has been troubled from the beginning. So that in fact, he would make it appear, that there has been nothing certain in the Christian religion. And if an unexperienced mind be from the very beginning poisoned by principles and questions of this kind, what else can it be expected to think of or do, but, either to withdraw itself secretly from, or, if it dare, to hold the Christian religion in utter detestation, as a pest to mankind?

He imagines however, all the while, that no one will discover the craft of this design. As though we had not in the Scriptures numberless examples of these bug-bears of the devil. It was thus the serpent dealt with Eve. He first entangled her in doubts, and brought her to suspect the reality of the precept of God concerning the tree of knowledge of good and evil, and when he had brought her to a stand-still of doubt, overthrew and destroyed her.—Unless Erasmus considers this to be a mere fable also!

It is with the same serpent-like attack that he creeps upon, and deceives, simple souls; saying—'How is it, that there have been so many sects and errors in this one true religion, (as it is believed to be?) How is it, that there have been so many creeds? Why, in the Apostles' Creed, is the Father called God, the Son not God, but Lord, and the Spirit neither God nor Lord, but Holy?' And so on.—Who I would ask troubles unexperienced souls, whom he undertakes to instruct, with questions like these, but the devil himself? Who would dare to speak thus upon a creed of faith, but the very mouth and instrument of the devil? —Here you have the Plot, the Execution, and the catastrophic End, of a soul-murdering tragedy!

But behold, I am here almost carried into a refutation of his catechism; whereas, I merely intended to shew you, why I thought it better not to answer this viper at all:—because, he will most effectually refute himself in the minds of all godly and good men.

The like game also he played on the apostle Paul, in his preface to the Romans; (to say nothing about his paraphrases, or his mad vagaries (*paraphroneses*,) to use his own term;) where he speaks of the praises of Paul in that way, that no simple reader whatever who is unacquainted with rhetoric, could be more effectually drawn away, and beaten off, from reading and studying Paul: so confused, intricate, self-contradictory, diverse, and disgusting, does he represent him to be: so that, the reader must of necessity believe the epistle to be the production of some mad man: so far is it from possibility, that he should consider it to be profitable.

And among the rest of his sharp-razor cuts, he could not receive, without venting his spleen, even this:—'that Peter should call Christ Man, and say nothing of His Godhead.'—A notable annotation truly! And most appropriately applicable to the passage!

And then as to his METHOD, with all its twistings and windings, what is it but a holding up Christ, and every thing done by Him, to derision? Who could gather any thing from this Method but a disgust at, nay a hatred of, attending to a religion so confused and perplexed, and perhaps after all, merely fabulous?

Who, moreover, ever spoke in so much disdain and contempt (not to say enmity) of the apostle and evangelist John, who, among Christians is held to be of the highest authority after Christ? —'He merely scolds little children; except it be when he considers a man to be a dolt or a logger-head.'—Christians ever speak of the Apostles with reverence and fear: whereas, this fellow would teach us to speak of them with profane pride and contempt. And this is the first step towards speaking profanely of God Himself, whose the Apostles are. Nay, it is the same as saying in contempt of the Holy Spirit, (whose the words of the Apostles are,) that *He* merely scolds little children!

Numberless things of this kind are to be found in Erasmus; or rather, this is his whole character in theology. And this many others have observed before me, and still do observe daily more and more: nor does he cease to go on and to publish daily his annotations more and more grossly, for his "judgment now for a long time lingereth not," and his "damnation slumbereth not."

This is also a notable instance of the piety of Erasmus! —In his letter upon 'Christian philosophy,' which is published with his New Testament, and used in common throughout all the churches, when he had propounded the question,—'Why Christ, so great a teacher, descended from heaven, when there are many things taught even among the heathens which are precisely the same, if not more perfect,'—he answers, 'Christ came (which I doubt not but he believed most Erasmianly) from heaven, that He might exemplify those things more perfectly and more fully than any of the saints before Him! '

Thus, this miserable renewer of all things, Christ, (for so He reproaches the Lord of glory) has lost the glory of a Redeemer, and becomes only one more holy than others.—This sentiment could not be expressed in ignorance, but must have been designed and wilful; because, even those who do not truly believe, know, and every where confess, that Christ descended from heaven to redeem us men from sin and death.

This was the sentiment that first alienated my mind from Erasmus. From that moment, I began to suspect him of being a plain Democritus or Epicurus, and a crafty derider of Christ: for he every where intimates to his fellow Epicureans, his hatred against Christ: though he does it in words so figurative and insidious, that he leaves himself a clue for raging most furiously against those Christians, who, from being offended at his suspicious and double meaning words, will not interpret them as standing in favour of their Christ.—As though Erasmus himself had an all-free prerogative through out the world, of speaking on divine things with obliquity and craft, and had all men so under his thumb, that they must interpret all his obliquities and crafty manoeuvres, as having an upright and honest intent!

Why does he not rather speak openly and plainly? Why does he always deal in these crafty and ensnaring figures of speech? So great a rhetorician and theologian ought not only to know, but to act according to, that which Fabius says, 'An ambiguous word should be avoided as a rock.' Where it happens now and then inadvertently, it may be pardoned: but where it is sought for designedly and purposely, it deserves no pardon whatever, but justly merits the abhorrence of every one. For to what does this hateful double-tongued way of speaking tend? It only furnishes an opportunity of disseminating and fostering in safety the seeds of every heresy, under the cover of words and letters that have a shew of Christian faith. And thus, while religion is believed to be taught and defended, it is, in reality, utterly destroyed, and subverted from its foundation before it is understood.

Wherefore, all are perfectly in the right who interpret his suspicions and insidious words against himself. Nor is any notice to be taken of him when he cries out calumny! calumny! because his words are not fairly and candidly interpreted. Why does he himself ever avoid fair words, and designedly express himself in those which are unfair? For it is an unheard-of kind of tyranny to wish to have the whole human race so under his thumb, that they should be compelled to understand fairly what he says insidiously and dangerously, and thus cede to him the prerogative of expressing himself insidiously. No! Let him rather be reduced to order, and commanded to bow to the whole human race; that is, by abstaining from that profane and double-tongued vertibility of speech and vain-talking, and by avoiding, as Paul saith, "profane and vain babblings."

For this it was, that even the public laws of the Roman empire condemned this manner of speaking, and punished it thus.—They commanded, 'that the words of him who should speak obscurely, when he could speak more plainly, should be interpreted against himself.' And Christ also, condemned that wicked servant who excused himself by an evasion; and interpreting his own words against himself, said, "Out of thine own mouth will I judge thee, thou wicked servant." For if in religion, in laws, and in all weighty matters, we should be allowed to express ourselves ambiguously and insidiously, what could follow but that utter confusion of Babel, where no one could understand another! This would be, to learn the language of eloquence, and in so doing, to lose the language of nature!

Moreover, if this licence should prevail, I might 'conveniently' interpret all that the whole herd of heretics ever said, nay all that the devil himself ever did or said, or could say or do, to all eternity. Where then would be the power of refuting the heretics and the devil? Where would be that wisdom of the Lord Christ, which all the adversaries shall not be able to resist? What would become of logic, the instructor of teaching rightly? What would become of rhetoric, the faculty of persuading? Nothing would be taught, nothing would be learned, no persuasion could be carried home, no consolation would be given, no fear would be wrought: because, nothing would be spoken or heard that was certain.

When, therefore, Erasmus lightly and ridiculously says of John the Evangelist, 'that he merely scolds babes,' he is to be adjudged immediately a disciple of Epicurus or Democritus, and to be addressed thus—Learn to speak of Majesty with more reverence. Some noted jesters have, indeed, sometimes spoken of princes thus irreverently, and fool-like, but not always with impunity. But if any one else of a sound mind and judgment had done the same, he might, perhaps, have lost his head, for the crime of insulted majesty.

Thus, when Erasmus says, 'Peter addresses Christ as Man, and says nothing of His Divinity,' he is to be condemned of Arianism and heresy: because, he could have omitted this insidious observation altogether, in a matter where the divine Majesty is eminently concerned, or have spoken more reverently: for the words plainly imply, that the Arians do not like that Christ should be called God, but consider it better that He should be called man only. And how conveniently soever they may be interpreted in favour of the Divinity of Christ; yet, as they stand and are read according to their plain meaning, especially since their author is suspicious, they offend Christian minds: because, they have not one plain meaning, and may be more easily understood to favour the Arians, than the orthodox.

Hence Jerome, writing of the Arians of his time who taught in the same artful way, says, 'Their priests say one thing, and their people understand another.' In like manner, there was no necessity for observing to Christians on that passage, that Peter did not call Christ, God; though in truth he did not omit to call Christ, God. Nor is it enough to pretend, 'that he called Him man only, on account of the common multitude:' for though he did call Him Man, yet, he did not therefore omit to call Him God, except that he did not pronounce these three letters, GOD: but this Erasmus rigidly deems was necessary: by so doing, however, he does nothing here, as well as in every other place, but lay snares, without any cause whatever, to entrap the inexperienced, and to render our religion suspicious.

That Carpisian, whoever he was, justly condemns him as a favourer of the Arians in his preface to Hilary, where he has said, 'We dare to call the Holy Spirit, God, which the ancients did not dare to do.' And when, having been faithfully admonished, he ought to have acknowledged his high-flown figures of speech, and his Arianisms, and to have corrected them, he not only did not do that, but even inveighed against the admonition, as a calumny proceeding from Satan, and laughed at the Divinity two-fold more than ever:—such a confidence has he in his pliability of speech, and his circumlocutive evasions. Nevertheless, he very seriously confesses the Trinity, and would not by any means whatever be thought to deny the Trinity of the God-head, but only wishes to say, that the *curiosity* (which he afterwards requests will be 'conveniently interpreted' *diligence*) of the moderns, has received and dared many things from the Scriptures which the ancients dared not.—As though the Christian religion rested on the authority of men: (for this is what he would persuade us to.) And what is this, but considering all religion together to be a mere fable!

Here, although the Carpisian be in many things of no weight whatever, and ever an enemy to Luther, yet Erasmus, from an unheard-of pride, thinks all men together to be mere stocks and stones; who neither understand any subject, nor see through the meaning of any words. Read that observation of his, and say, if you do not discover the incarnate devil! This observation fixes in me a determination (let others do as they please) not to believe Erasmus, even if he should openly confess in plain words,—that Christ is God. But I would address to him that sophistical saying of Chrysippus, 'If you lie, you lie even when you speak the truth.' For what need was there, if he in verity believed that the Holy Spirit is God, to say, 'We dare to call the Holy Spirit, God, which the ancients did not dare to do?' What need was there to use this vertible word 'dare,' that it might apply both to the praise and dispraise of these same moderns, when we received this doctrine from the ancients, and did not 'dare' to receive it first?

But however, it is a stark lie, to say, that the ancients did not first 'dare' to call the Holy Spirit, God:—unless by ancients, according to one of his very beautiful figures of speech, he means Democritus and Epicurus: or unless, he means God, materially, that is, these three letters, GOD! But to what purpose is all this hateful manoeuvering, but to make of a gnat an elephant, as a stumbling-block to the unexperienced, and to intimate, that the Christian religion is a nothing at all! and that, for no other reason, than because these three Letters, GOD, are not written in every place, where he considers they ought to have been written!

In the same manner his fathers, the Arians, made numberless quibbles, because these letters HOMOUSIOS, and INNASCIBILIS, were not found in the Sacred Writings: considering it nothing to the purpose, that the same thing could be solidly proved in substance. And where the name God *was* written, they were ready with their gloss to elude the truth, by contending, that it did not mean God *in reality*, but God *by appellation*. So that, you can do nothing with these vipers, whether you speak to them by the Scriptures, or without the Scriptures.

This is the way of the malice of Satan. When he cannot deny the fact, he turns to demanding certain particular terms, which he himself prescribes. And thus the devil himself may say, even to Christ—Although Thou speakest the truth, yet since Thou dost not speak it in the terms which I think requisite, Thou sayest nothing at all: and I wish the truth to be spoken in no words whatever.—This is like Marcolfus, who wished to be hung upon a tree chosen by himself, and yet wished to choose no tree at all. But of this elsewhere, if the Lord shall give me leisure, and length of life. For it is my determination to leave behind me my true and faithful testimony concerning Erasmus: and thus, to expose Luther to be bitten and stung by these vipers, but not to be utterly torn in pieces and destroyed! —

I now return to my observation upon my liberty which I have asserted; giving it as my sentiments, that the tyranny of Erasmus which he would exercise by means of circumlocutive evasions, is not to be borne, but that he is to be judged openly, out of his own mouth. Where he speaks as an Arian, let him be judged an Arian; where he speaks as a Lucian, let him be judged a Lucian; where he speaks as a Gentile, let him be judged a Gentile; unless he repent and cease to defend such ways of expressing himself.

For instance. In one of his epistles on the Incarnation of the Son of God, he uses a most abominable term, calling it 'the intercourse of God with the Virgin'—here he is to be judged, a horrible blasphemer of God and the Virgin! Nor does it make him at all better, his afterwards expounding 'intercourse' as applying to the form of the Christian doctrine. Why did he not speak of the form of Christian doctrine? For he well knew, that by this word, 'intercourse,' Christians could not but be greatly offended—and let him be judged ungodly who would not be offended at a term so abominably obscene, in a matter so sacred: knowing that, an ambiguous expression of such a nature, is always taken in its worst sense, even though we be not ignorant, that the term may have another meaning. If it take place from inadvertency, it may be pardoned: if from design and wilfulness, it is to be condemned, as I said, without mercy. For to hold a doctrine of faith is arduous, and a divine work, even when delivered in proper, evident, and certain words. How then shall it be held, if it be delivered in ambiguous, doubtful, and oblique words!

St. Augustine says, 'philosophers ought to speak freely on difficult points, fearing no offence: but we (says he) must speak according to a certain rule.' And therefore, he blames the use of the term *fortune*, or *fate*, both in himself and others. For even though the person may by fortune mean the divine mind, the agent of all things, from which nature is known to be distinctly different, and thus may not think impiously, yet, says he, 'Let him hold his sentiment, but correct his expression.'

And even to suppose that Augustine did not say this, and never had any certain rule according to which he expressed himself, yet nature will tell us, that every profession, sacred as well as profane, uses certain terms of its own, and avoids all ambiguities. For even common tradesmen, either reprove or condemn, or hold up to ridicule, the man who speaks of his own trade in the technical terms (as they are called) peculiar to the trade of another. With how much greater force will this apply to things sacred, where certain salvation, or eternal perdition is the consequence, and where all must be taught in certain and proper terms! Let us, if we must do it, trifle with ambiguities in other things that are of no moment, as nuts, apples, pence, and other things which are the toys of children and of fools: but in religion, and weighty matters of state, let us shun, with all possible care, an ambiguity, as we would shun death or the devil!

Our king of ambiguity, however, sits upon his ambiguous throne in security, and destroys us stupid Christians with a double destruction. First, it is his will, and it is a great pleasure to him, to offend us by his ambiguous words: and indeed he would not like it, if we stupid blocks were not offended. And next, when he sees that we are offended, and have run against his insidious figures of speech, and begin to exclaim against him, he then begins to triumph and rejoice that the desired prey has been caught in his snares. For now, having found an opportunity of displaying his rhetoric, he rushes upon us with all his powers and all his noise, tearing us, flogging us, crucifying us, and sending us farther than hell itself; saying, that we have understood his words calumniously, virulently, satanically; (using the worst terms he can find;) whereas, he never meant them to be so understood.

In the exercise of this wonderful tyranny, (and who would think that this Madam ambiguity could make so much ado, or who could suppose that any one would be so great a madman as to have so much confidence in a vain figure of speech?) he not only compels us to put up with his all-free prerogative of using ambiguities, but binds us down to the necessity of keeping silence. He plainly designs all the while, and wishes us to be offended, that he, and his herd of Epicureans with him, may have a laugh at us as fools: but on the other hand, he does not like to hear that we are offended, lest it should appear that we are true Christians. Thus must we suffer wounds without number, and yet, not utter a groan or a sigh!

We Christians, however, who are to judge, not meats and drinks only, but angels and the whole world, and who actually judge, even now, not only do not bear with this tyranny of ambiguities, but on the contrary, oppose to it our liberty of pronouncing a two-fold condemnation. The first is, as I have already observed, we condemn all the ambiguous expressions of Erasmus, and interpret them against himself: as Christ saith, "Out of thine own mouth will I judge thee, thou wicked servant." Again, "By thine own words shalt thou be condemned: for wherefore hast thou spoken against thine own soul? " "Thy blood be upon thine own head." The second condemnation is, we condemn and curse again and again his glosses and 'convenient interpretations,' by which, he not only does not correct his ungodly expressions, but even defends them: that is, he laughs at us twice as much in his after interpretations, as he does in his first expressions.

For example: He says, that by 'the intercourse of God with the Virgin' he does not mean a common intercourse, but another kind of marriage between God and the Virgin, where the angel Gabriel is the bridegroom, and the Holy Spirit performs the act of consummation. Only observe what this fellow, by his interpretation, would have us to hear and understand Christ to be. And he says these things, that he might defend the filthiness and obscenity of his expression in the face of offended Christians, and laugh at them all the while; and thus, he forces upon us this offensive term, when he knows very well, that this mystery of the most holy Incarnation, cannot be explained to the mind of man by all the obscene and ambiguous words of the whole world: but how it is understood by the Epicureans, I dare not, for horror, imagine. Why do we not call the conversation of God with Moses and the other prophets, 'intercourse' also, and make the angels bridegrooms, and the Holy Spirit the consummator of the act, or make of it something still more obscene? Moreover, here is the impious idea of *sex* introduced, to perfect this monstrous derision of saying, that God had 'intercourse with the Virgin;'—in order that, the whole might be made a fable, like that wherein Mars is said to have had intercourse with Rhea, and Jupiter with Semele; and that Christianity might be reduced to a level with one of the fabulous stories of old, and men represented as fools and pitiable madmen for believing such a story to be serious and true, not considering what turpitudes and obscenities were the objects of their faith and worship! And therefore, Christians, that stupid set of creatures, were to be admonished by means of figures like these, to begin to doubt, and then, from doubting to depart from the faith; that thus, religion might be utterly destroyed before any one could be aware of it.

This is the verification of that parable, Matt. xiii. where the enemy is represented as sowing tares in the night, and going his way. Thus, we Christians are sleeping in security: and even if we were not sleeping, those bewitching Syrens, by their honey of speech, would soon lull us to sleep, and bring a cloud of night over our eyes. In the meantime, are sown those tares of figurative and insidious words: and yet when Sacramentarians, Donatists, Arians, Anabaptists, Epicureans, &c. are sprung up, we ask—How is it that our Lord's field hath tares? They, however, who have sown them, are gone away; that is, they so paint and set themselves off by their 'convenient interpretations,' and withdraw themselves from sight, that they seem as if they had sown nothing but wheat. Thus the enemy slides away, and is off in safety, and crowned with honour and applause, and appears to be a friend, when he is in truth the greatest of enemies. This is the way with the strange woman, Prov. xxx. who, "when she has eaten, wipeth her mouth, and saith, I have done no wickedness! "

Thus have I replied to your letter, my friend Armsdorff, though perhaps I have been too long and tedious. But I wished to shew you, why I judged it best not to answer Erasmus any farther. I am moreover abundantly engaged in teaching, confirming, correcting, and governing my flock. And my work of translating the Bible, alone requires the devotion of my whole time: from which work, Satan with all his might endeavours to withdraw me, as he has done upon former occasions; that he might get me to leave the best things, to follow after those which are nothing but vain and empty vapours. For my Bondage of the Will proves to you how difficult a task it is to cope with that proteus Erasmus, on account of his vertibility and slipperiness of speech; in which alone is all his confidence. He never remains in one position, but, with the deepest craft, evades every blow, and is like an irritated hornet.

Whereas, miserable I, am compelled to stand my ground in one position, and that upon unequal ground, as "a sign to be spoken against." For whatever Luther writes, is condemned before ten years are at an end. Luther is the only one who writes from envy, from pride, from bitterness, and in a word, at the instigation of Satan himself; but all who write against him, write under the influence of the Holy Spirit!

Before my time, it required a great to-do, and an enormous expense, to canonize a dead monk. But now, there is no easier way for canonizing even living Neroes and Caligulas, than the declaration of hatred against Luther. Only let a man hate and bravely curse Luther, and that, immediately, makes him a saint, equal almost to our holy Lord, the servant of the servants of God. But who could ever believe that hatred against Luther would be attended with so much power and advantage? It fills the coffers of very beggars; nay, it introduces obscure moles and bats to the favour of princes and of kings; it procures prebendaries and dignities; it procures bishoprics; it procures the reputation of wisdom and of learning to the most consummate asses; it procures to petty teachers of grammar, the authority of writing books; nay, it procures the crown of victory and of glory, eternal in the heavens! Nay, happy are all who hate Luther, for they obtain, by that one vile and easy service, those great and mighty things, which none of the most excellent of men could ever obtain with all their wisdom and their virtues; no, not even Christ himself, with all His own miracles, and the miracles of His apostles and all His saints!

Thus are the Scriptures fulfilled.—Blessed are ye who persecute Luther, for yours in the kingdom of heaven! Blessed are ye who curse and say all manner of evil against Luther; rejoice and be exceeding glad in that day, for great is your reward in heaven; for so persecuted they the apostles, the holy bishops, John Huss, and others who were before Luther! —Wherefore, I feel more and more persuaded, that I shall act rightly by answering Erasmus no farther: but I will leave my testimony concerning him, even for his own sake, that he might hereafter be unburdened from that concern which, as he complains, is completely death to him: viz., that he is commonly called a Lutheran. But, as Christ liveth, they do him a great injury who call him a Lutheran, and I will defend him against his enemies: for I can bear a true and faithful testimony, that he is no Lutheran, but Erasmus himself!

And if I could have my will, Erasmus should be exploded from our schools altogether: for if he be not pernicious, he is certainly useless: because he, in truth, discusses and teaches nothing. Nor is it at all advisable to accustom Christian youth to the diction of Erasmus: for they will learn to speak and think of nothing with gravity and seriousness, but only to laugh at all men as babblers and vain-talkers. In a word, they will learn nothing, but to play the fool! And from this levity and vanity they will, by degrees, grow tired of religion, till at last they will abhor and profane it! Let him be left to the Papists only, who are worthy of such an apostle, and whose lips relish his dainties!

May our Lord Jesus Christ, whom, according to *my* faith, Peter did not omit to call GOD; by whose power I know, and am persuaded, that I have often been delivered from death, and by faith in whom I have undertaken and hitherto accomplished all these things which excite the wonder even of my enemies; may this same Jesus guard and deliver us unto the end—for He is the Lord our God! —To whom alone, with the Father and the Holy Spirit, be glory for ever and ever! Amen!

Printed in the United States
50227LVS00005B/37-45